BURDEN O

By

WILLIAM S. HAYES

PUNK HOSTAGE PRESS

BURDEN OF CONCRETE

Editor
Jack Grisham

Assistant Editor
Nadia Bruce Rawlings

Interior Layout
Iris Berry

Cover Design
Michelle Don Vito

Cover Layout
Scott Aicher

Back Cover Photo
Jack Grisham

Cover Photos
Courtesy of King County Jail

PUNK HOSTAGE PRESS
Hollywood, USA
www.punkhostagepress.com

"Now, you're lookin' at a man that's gettin' kinda mad. I had a lot of luck but it's all been bad. No matter how I struggle and strive…I'll never get out of this world alive."

Hank Williams

CON AIR

By the amount of time we'd been on the plane, my guess was we were over Kansas or Nebraska, and I knew it wouldn't be long until the farmlands abruptly faded and were replaced by the mountainous terrain of the Rockies. The view of seemingly endless fields from 35,000 feet was mesmerizing in a sense, lending an elusive tranquility…one I knew I should appreciate because there wasn't going to be much of it when I got to L.A.

A flight attendant walked down the aisle toward the back of the plane and I asked her for a cup of coffee as she moved past, breaking two rules by doing so. First, I leaned a little too close to the guard sitting next to me, and second, I had spoken to a civilian. I was nudged back in my seat with his elbow and told to shut the fuck up, but was rewarded a few minutes later with a hot cup of coffee and a smile. She made a move as if to pass it to me directly but thought better of it after observing the shackles on my wrists, and instead gave it to the officer in the aisle seat. I took the coffee knowing I'd won a small victory, then sat back and continued watching the earth pass below me.

It would've been a fair assessment to label me a small-time criminal, one without the balls or vision necessary for the big heist. While certainly lacking magnetism, the label hit the mark and personified my existence. To counter with a claim stating otherwise would've been absurd—my criminal record reflected a life of doing time for property crimes and minor drug offenses. Was I a victim of circumstance? To a certain extent but not really. The choices were mine and I had to live with the consequences.

I had heard stories from guys I'd done time with over the years who actually aspired to do time. With them, prison was a proving ground; a place where a man could earn a notch on his belt in his quest for the ultimate validation—making a name for himself on the streets and the respect that came with it. That was not the case with me. Going to prison was the price I paid in a high-stakes game of life on the hustle. If I won, I'd make enough money to support a debilitating drug habit; and if I lost, the desolation of living in a concrete hell.

When I was a kid, I spent a lot of time with my family camping along the Skykomish River in Washington State. Driving there and back, we'd pass a prison outside of the small city of Monroe and my young eyes would stay glued to its razor wire fences and guard towers, wondering what went on behind its walls. It was an ominous setting and one that left an imprint in my mind.

My perception had been shaped by the nightly news and movies like *Escape from Alcatraz*. I'd heard stories of prisoners getting raped, jailbreaks, executions, riots and murders. The tales were legion and believable, even though most came from sources who had, at best, only driven by a penitentiary a time or two. The violent reputation of the prison system preceding the firsthand knowledge I'd later discover shook me to the core, enough that when I was finally sentenced to do state time, I was scared to death. That fear might have been enough to set me straight, but a curious thing happened...I adapted.

I wasn't one who got comfortable doing time, but I also never found comfort in the "real world". There was a missing element in the way I thought, separating me from the vast majority of society. Having and keeping a job was foreign to me, as was paying bills, shopping for groceries and even something as basic as brushing my teeth. I used to attribute my lack of adherence to society's rules as being dedicated to a code of recklessness, labeling anyone who thought different as fools, worthy of my ridicule. When my drug use progressed to the point of using every day, I discovered a lifestyle that offered me a semblance of purpose, however misguided it turned out to be. The bitter irony was that the freedom I found through drugs would ultimately put me in chains.

I asked the guard if I could have another cup of coffee, then sat back in my seat after he shook his head no. Looking out the window, I could see the jagged peaks of the Rockies rising from below, creating a natural barrier and effectively separating the East from the West. It wouldn't be long until the sprawling city of Los Angeles was in my sights. And then it was off to the L.A. County Jail.

SOME KIDS PLAYED BASEBALL

As I approached the exit to the store, a man lunged at me from the magazine rack, grabbing me by the arm and telling me I was busted. My first thought was to run and he must've sensed it because his grip simultaneously became that of a vice around my scrawny thirteen-year-old arm. The Reese's Peanut Butter Cups I'd attempted to liberate were now weights in my pocket, filling me with a nascent regret over my decision to steal them.

He escorted me on a long walk to a nondescript office in the back of the store and called the police. They showed up a short time later, stuck me in the backseat of their car, put my bike in the trunk and drove me to the King County Youth Services Center in the Central District, east of downtown Seattle. Nobody tried employing any absurd scare tactics; they just put me in a cell, called my dad and dropped me off in North Seattle after the process had run its course.

Getting arrested never evoked a fear sufficient enough to stop me from stealing, and it was about a year later that I had my next run-in with the law. After getting out of school, I walked into a Safeway by my house and helped myself to candy from a bulk bin. As I was walking toward the exit a store detective apprehended me. I'd only taken a handful of saltwater taffy but that didn't stop him from calling the cops, and this time I was handcuffed. I wouldn't go so far as to say the metal bracelets were comfortable, but they were a good fit in the sense that I already aspired to be a criminal. As I jockeyed for comfort in the backseat of the cruiser, two girls from my school walked by and stared at me. I knew the word would spread I'd been arrested—bolstering the reputation I was shooting for.

I was again brought to the juvenile detention center but held this time until my father picked me up. He was not thrilled, and the ride home was filled with silence. His calm demeanor was surprising; I'd expected him to be angry and explode as soon as I got in the car with him. Love was strong in our household, as was the anger he'd unleash when he got home from work to find the house was a mess or that I'd skipped school again. Toward the end of that long ride, he broke the silence by telling me about his experiences going to jail due to his drinking when he was young. He seemed to know reprimanding me wouldn't have done any good and that I'd have to learn from my own mistakes.

That summer I moved in with my mom to an area of Seattle called the University District. She rented a room in a boarding house from a slumlord and was willing to take me in. Living with her was a sharp contrast from living with my dad. He demanded order and discipline within the household, while she, most definitely, did not. I'd spend much of my time on a street called "the Ave", hanging out with other punk rockers, skateboarding, drinking beer, dropping acid and smoking pot. Consequently, I started having more encounters with the police.

My run-ins with the cops were usually brief—some citations for drinking in parks and alleys, and a couple of "cite and release" shoplifting tickets—but there were two separate instances in which I was arrested and brought to a precinct. The first was on Broadway on Capitol Hill. The city decided to remove the benches from the street because they enabled loitering, a strong pastime among the punks. To counter their action, my friend Janos and I brought a couch we'd found sitting in an alley to Broadway and set it out on the sidewalk where a bench had just been removed. A protest was organized that day over their removal, with a group of punks present to voice their opinions over the matter. The city couldn't remove the couch with a group of kids hanging around, so the police were called, and they ended up taking an older punk named Cutter and myself to East Precinct. They took Cutter because he was the oldest and they took me because I was an obnoxious little shit. I don't know what happened to him, I never saw him again after that day, but they held me for a few hours and upon release, they let me know I was lucky they didn't beat my ass.

The second was with some friends, skating high on acid in a parking garage on the University of Washington campus. We'd been there for hours, watching the walls breathe and "being at one" with our boards when the cops showed up. They swooped on us when we were on the bottom level, taking a breather and enjoying the psychedelic effects of the LSD. They searched us and found a sheet of acid on my friend Ron, then brought us down to the UW precinct. The holding cells were painted in bright repulsive colors, and after sitting in one for five long hours, I was unceremoniously dropped off at my mom's to a new dawn and the sounds of birds chirping.

—

I managed to stay away from any type of holding facility over the next two years, ending my lengthy run in '89. Some friends and I had just finished smoking a bowl on a stretch of lawn at the edge of UW campus, when a university cop came out of nowhere wanting to know where our drugs were. He didn't find anything when he searched us, but he did find a pipe on me. The pipe was still warm, and he correctly presumed we'd used it to smoke out of. He then wrote me a ticket for possession of marijuana, took my pipe and sent us on our way. Fortunately for me, the cop didn't feel the fat sack I had stuffed down the front of my jeans, so I took the ticket knowing I'd dodged a bullet.

About six months later, in the fall of '89, I had to make a court appearance for some community service I neglected to do. I wasn't eighteen yet, which meant a trip to King County Youth Services Center to plead my case. I only owed the city twenty-four hours of service but knowing twenty-four hours was the equivalent to three days in juvie, I went in knowing it was possible I'd be detained. I didn't really believe they'd lock me up but gave my girlfriend the weed I had just in case, thinking it was better to be safe than sorry. It turned out to be a good thing I did because the judge didn't appreciate the fact that I didn't follow through with my obligation and decided to teach me a lesson.

I knew I was fucked the minute I walked into the courtroom. The hearing wasn't anything like the ones I'd seen in the movies or on TV; it was more like a gathering of people wanting nothing more than to bury me. My public defender didn't show any interest in representing me nor would he look me in the eye, a fat bailiff stood in a corner eyeing me with contempt, and then there was the prosecutor...she was the worst. She glared at me with what I perceived to be hatred, exacerbated by a tic in her eye that seemed to jump out at me. I pictured her carving me up and feeding my corpse to her dogs.

Courtrooms are loaded with tradition and absurd etiquette. First comes an "all rise" commanded by the bailiff, followed by the judge entering the room, carrying an unspoken announcement that you're in the presence of a deity. Then there's the solemn oath to God, and the subtleties such as removing your hat and dressing respectfully, which I certainly didn't do. My courtroom attire was checkered Van's, ripped up Levi's, a black T-shirt and a leather jacket, so it shouldn't come as a surprise the court wasn't sympathetic to my

—

5

plight. But truth be told, I wasn't overly concerned, either. I was only looking at three days in jail and wouldn't have to cut blackberry bushes, or some other bullshit, if I ended up doing the time.

Considering the sadistic-like appearance of the court, I think they wanted me to grovel and beg for forgiveness, and when that didn't happen, the judge ordered that I be taken into custody. After the order was made, I conjured the demeanor of a convict walking the prison yard. I was more than a little nervous, but certainly not enough to give them satisfaction regarding my misfortune. The bailiff put me in cuffs and then escorted me to the booking area of the juvenile lockup, located below the court building. I was placed in the same cell I'd been in when I was thirteen, then stripped naked and given the standard issue for juveniles: pants with an elastic waistband, a white T-shirt, a sweatshirt and some slippers. A lady asked me information regarding emergency contacts and then let me call my girlfriend. I told her I'd be gone for a while, doing my best to sound hard, but likely coming across flat.

I was put in a large unit holding eight cells, with six juveniles in each one. There were only two other white kids in my unit, feeding me the impression that doing time was an inner-city phenomenon. The racial disparity surprised me—as did being confined with people of color. I'd been raised in North Seattle, an area that was primarily white. It scared the shit out of me at first, and I thought for sure they'd jump me or somehow conspire against me. Neither of those things happened, though, and I got along with almost everyone, offering a clear glimpse in how fear of the unknown had shaped my perception.

Most of the other kids were in gangs, a lifestyle that was foreign to me. I'd heard of Crips and Bloods, but only from what I'd seen on the nightly news. I had always thought they were exclusive to Los Angeles. They'd sit within their respective cliques when we were let out to watch TV in the dayroom, and although I could see the potential for violence, nothing kicked off while I was there.

One of the other white kids was a friend of mine named Jesse who was in for selling fake acid to a cop. He hung with the Broadway crowd and had gotten hooked on heroin. He'd already been in a few months and gave me a rundown of the place, telling me what I could and couldn't do in relation to prisoner conduct. He had a good rapport with the correctional officers and was somehow able to convince them

—

6

to let us dine together in the mess hall, giving me cause to get excited when chow was served.

The three days went by quickly and without any major incidents. They were all curious why I called myself a punk, because where they were from a punk was the same thing as a bitch. I had to explain to them on numerous occasions that I was a punk rocker and not a punk bitch, which got tiring but also brought about laughter, making the time flow. Church and gym were serious matters with them and when I voiced my displeasure over both, I could tell it pissed some of them off. I had thought going in that the biggest issue I'd encounter would have to do with me being white, but it was actually my uncleanliness—I didn't take many showers because of the time I spent fucking around on the streets. The racial tension present in jails and prisons was nonexistent in our world. We were set on doing our little bits of time and going home.

On Monday morning I was called for release. I quickly rolled up my property and said my goodbyes, then made my way to the release tank, excited to see my girlfriend and to get out. After sitting in a cold cell for an hour, a guard came in to tell me I had a warrant for possession of marijuana. The ticket I received on the UW campus six months prior had turned into a hold. I'd given the cop who wrote the ticket a fake address, thinking I could weasel my way out of the charge, but it came back to fuck me.

I was minutes from being released only to discover I was going back. They'd known about the warrant all along, as did the court when I was sentenced, and I felt the humane thing to do would've been to tell me so I could've at least tried to do something about it. I was in utter disbelief that I was going back in for a pipe and felt like the system had wronged me. I knew this situation never would've come about had I just given the cop my address, but that was irrelevant to me. I justified my deception by the pettiness of the charge, my lack of respect for the law and my own self-preservation.

I was escorted back to the detention center and given a bed in my old unit. My cellies had a laugh at my expense, but also related to my misfortune. Most of them had been around the court system enough to be somewhat knowledgeable and began telling me similar stories, either from their own experiences or from their friends and family. According to the tales I heard, this kind of shit happened a lot.

—

7

Aside from their initial laughter, they were sympathetic to my plight and assured me that I'd be released once I made it to court.

It took another two days, but a Seattle police officer came to pick me up and brought me to the King County Jail, an immense concrete structure downtown. I'd driven by it a thousand times and thought nothing of it, other than it being just another building next to the freeway, but I appraised it from a new perspective after that day. We drove in through a huge sally port after getting clearance from within the jail, then pulled up to a line of cruisers and parked. Once the massive door shut, sealing me in, he opened my door. Being inexperienced in the art of navigating my body with cuffs on my wrists, I managed to make my way out of the car.

I found myself standing in a fully enclosed area for emergency, transport and maintenance vehicles. It was essentially a parking lot within the jail, but with doors that wouldn't open until an unknown presence from within opened them. It made me think of the docking bay in the Death Star from the movie *Star Wars*—when the Millennium Falcon gets pulled in by a tractor beam—except I wasn't there to escape from the clutches of Darth Vader. I just wanted to see the judge so I could go home.

We walked to a steel door and after the officer spoke through an intercom announcing we were ready for entry, it opened with a buzz and I was brought into a holding cell and searched. Once the cop had sufficient reason to believe I wasn't concealing any drugs, weapons, bombs or whatever else, I was escorted through a maze of concrete corridors to a holding tank for criminals waiting to see the judge. I was surprised how filthy the jail was—the concrete had a dirty tint to it that was only made worse by the fluorescent lights flickering overhead, and it smelled like a combination of puke, piss and body sweat.

There were a dozen inmates in the court hold, loitering about on stainless-steel benches and sitting on the concrete. Most of them wore red uniforms and a few wore blue. I found out later red meant felony charges and blue misdemeanor. They all stared at me when I was brought in and I felt different, and more than a little nervous, right away. Not only was I wearing different attire—I was still wearing the standard-issue pants and sweatshirt of the juvenile wards—I was also much younger than all of them. One of the inmates asked what I was in for and when I told him I'd gotten busted with a pipe, he laughed and told me they'd throw it out. It took a total of ten seconds for their

—

8

interest and curiosity to be transformed into dismissiveness. It made me feel insignificant, but I'll take that over feeling like potential prey any day of the week.

A few of them had their names called to see the judge and finally, mine was also. A bailiff stood by the door to the courtroom and motioned me toward a public defender who was waiting for me. He asked me my name, told me what I was being charged with and said it was being thrown out. Before I could express my gratitude, the judge said the case was dismissed, and even made a comment reflecting the incompetence of the UW police as I was led out of the courtroom.

Not long after, the same cop drove me back to the Youth Detention Center to be placed in their custody. I signed some release papers and was asked if I'd left any property in my housing unit. I assured them I didn't have any valuables and wouldn't object to being released right then and there. With a farewell, they gave me my clothes and a bus token for the Metro, and then let me out to a sunny and warm Seattle afternoon. A cigarette never tasted so good.

KING COUNTY JAIL

Late on a Friday night in 1991, riding the tail end of a cold Seattle winter, my friend Todd and I drove on a mission to score some weed. It was dead that night and Todd had only been able to pick up an ounce, and that was only for himself. He had me driving everywhere, chasing his ideas on where we could go next and I was over it, so I decided to call it a night.

I was driving northbound toward 145th Street with the intention of jumping on the freeway when the flashing lights of a cruiser appeared in my rearview mirror. I'd missed a court appearance earlier that morning and was also driving without a license, so I thought the chances were pretty good I'd be taken in. Todd quickly stuffed the sack of weed down his pants and we began discussing warrants. He told me there was a possibility he had one and I told him I'd missed court and might have one as well. He assured me warrants never popped up that fast and because I'd called my public defender that morning to set up a new hearing, it wouldn't show up in the system.

I pulled into a small parking lot off Lake City Way, killed the motor and waited for the cop to come walking up. He sauntered alongside my car in typical police fashion and when he got to my window, told me that he pulled me over because my taillights were out. The car was a '69 VW Fastback I'd bought from a junkie and the taillights had a separate switch from the headlights—rigged so he'd have a better chance of getting away during his nightly thieving runs. In my frustration over the evening's events, I forgot to hit the switch. I told him why the lights weren't on (minus a few details, of course) and showed him that they worked. He responded by asking for my license. I didn't have one, but gave him my name and registration. The cop then walked back to his car to see if I was clean. He ran Todd's name also, and the whole time we were sitting there, Todd was sweating like a priest at a boy's camp thinking he was going to jail. Todd had convinced me so thoroughly my warrant wouldn't be in the system that I offered to hold his weed for him and it was a good thing I didn't. When he came back to my car, he told me to step out because I had a warrant for my arrest.

Somewhat surprised, I told him what happened, that I had another court date on Monday and asked for a little leniency, but he wasn't having it. He told me to tell it to the judge, then went on to tell me that if I'd told him upfront I would've had a chance, but because he had already radioed my name in, he was obligated to arrest me. I didn't believe him for a second, but he did let me give my keys to Todd, an act that made him all right in my eyes. He knew Todd didn't have a license and that my car would end up getting towed if it wasn't moved by the morning—knowing it wasn't going to be left there made being handcuffed a bit more tolerable.

I was taken to North Precinct, a block west of the I-5 corridor. He brought me in through the back and escorted me to a booking station, where my name was run again to verify my warrant. He then took my belt so I couldn't hang myself, put the rest of my belongings in a bag, fingerprinted me and then placed me in a cell.

I knew the system well enough from friends who'd been arrested that I'd be released once I got to see the judge. I certainly wasn't thrilled I was going to jail, but there was a level of excitement about it all. I thought to myself that at just nineteen, I'd made it to the big leagues. It all seemed like a game to me, one only those deemed worthy could play, and I was willing to ante up.

A transport vehicle arrived later in the evening to take me and another guy downtown—a large paddy wagon with two steel benches and a bright heat lamp that blasted down on us from the back of the cab. We climbed in, had a seat on the benches and prepared ourselves for the ride to the jail.

The transport had no windows, and because the guy sitting across from me wasn't talkative, I entertained myself by reading the graffiti etched on the walls and guessing our location as we travelled south. The sound of the vehicle's tread on the interstate and the other cars buzzing by had a curious tranquilizing effect, and by the time we got off the freeway downtown, I felt ready for the unknown. After stopping and going through a couple of lights, I heard the driver speak into a radio to be let in, the mechanical sound of a giant door opening, then the muffled echo of our vehicle driving into a garage.

The driver parked the vehicle and I heard the engine cease its rumble, followed by the sound of the officers talking to each other while their footsteps approached the back of the paddy wagon. One of them popped the door open and when he did, I looked out and saw the

---

parking garage I'd been in as a juvenile almost two years prior. It looked the same: polished concrete, dirty and smudged by countless vehicles driving in over the course of a day, with signs and statements stenciled on the walls warning prisoners that "CONTRABAND IS ILLEGAL AND NEW CHARGES WILL BE ADDED" and "PRISONERS SHALL FACE THE WALL" and "NO FIREARMS BEYOND THIS POINT". The only difference was that I was going to be booked this time.

One of our escorts hit an intercom button on the door leading to the interior of the jail, telling a voice inside that the prisoners were "non-combative", and a short moment later the door buzzed open. The cops put their pistols into a gun safe upon entry and after they were secured, another door buzzed open to a room with a podium and a county correctional officer standing behind it. He told us to take off our shoes and to leave one shirt on, then to put the clothes we'd taken off on the counter. As our clothes were being bagged, the cops who escorted us left out the door from which we came, leaving us under the care and watch of our new ward.

We were then told to proceed to a cell, one with a TV blaring and two phones mounted on one of its walls, and the first of many more cells lined up in a row. On the way there, we passed a chair with restraining straps built into it, designed to limit movement of a combative inmate's arms, legs and neck. The gothic-looking contraption was obviously placed in front of the first cell as a warning.

The cell had about a dozen guys milling about, some passed out on the concrete floor and the others sitting on benches adopting the posture of the fucked—they reminded me of Rodin's sculpture *The Thinker*, but instead of the head resting on one hand, deep in thought, these guys had their heads buried in both of their hands and they looked like they were consumed with misery and guilt. Both phones were being used, one by a guy pleading for forgiveness and the other begging for bail money.

I sat in that first cell, feeling sorry for the guys offering their pathetic pleas into the phones but glad I wasn't wearing their shoes, and waited. I was spared from hearing more of their suffering when I heard a lady call my name and was told to step out of the cell. A plain-Jane woman standing behind a counter looked me in the eye and asked what my full name was, then asked me where I lived, who I was employed with and if I'd been arrested before. When she was finished with her inquiries, she told me I was in for failure to appear on a theft charge, that I'd need to post $475 to make bail and then directed me to a redneck-looking man to get fingerprinted. He looked like Kurt Russell from the movie *Tombstone*, except he was about six inches taller, looked angrier, and had a bigger belt buckle. He inked all my fingers individually, rolling each finger's impression onto a piece of paper bearing my name. I was then instructed to walk to the next open cell and listen for my name.

This cell was much smaller and consisted of a metal bench, a stainless-steel toilet/sink combo, a filthy concrete floor and walls graffitied by inmates swearing allegiance to God, their girlfriends and their gang's set, and talking shit about God, their girlfriends and their enemies' sets. There were two guys passed out and snoring incredibly loud, making me wonder how long they'd been there and if they were still there because they hadn't heard their names called or if they'd been forgotten about. It smelled like a musky combination of butt, dick and pussy, and I hoped I'd be moved in short order.

After an immeasurable amount of time in which I started to think I'd been forgotten about, I was called up to the counter again, only this time a little further down the line. A lady asked if there were any groups I belonged to or any I thought I'd need protection from, if I'd ever attempted suicide, if I felt suicidal, if I had any medical issues, if I was a veteran and if I graduated high school. I told her a bunch of "NO's" and that I'd gotten my GED, then was sent down to yet another holding tank.

The cell was packed with men lying in various poses and sitting on benches, and it stunk from the combined odors of dirty feet, body funk and rotten milk. Empty milk cartons, bread crusts and rotten apple cores from sack lunches littered the floor, with some of the trash put into piles and used as pillows by the more down-and-out inmates. Within a few minutes of being there, an officer came by to pass more lunches out, causing everyone to jump up from their positions of discomfort and line up by the door to receive a sack. I was starving and followed suit, but couldn't muster the stomach to eat any of its contents, so I gave my lunch to a drunk who'd seen better days.

I could tell the prisoners here had been waiting a long time. The cell wasn't in direct line of sight from the staff working up front and was tucked away in a corner, giving the impression inmates were put in there to be worried about later. Everyone was dead tired, and the ones who weren't passed out on the concrete using trash for pillows and garbage bags for blankets were sitting in their commandeered stations, eyeing everyone with a tense energy.

I hadn't been there long when an officer came to the door and started calling names. Bodies which had been curled up in corners and lying under benches began to stir and rise groggily to their feet, shaking off whatever dreams of freedom they were having, then shambled toward the door as their names were called. The men who were called had been arrested hours before me.

The cop shut the door and the other inmates began staking out spots to claim as their own. Some sprawled out on the concrete and others took a seat on one of the benches and waited. I sat on the bench and watched everything. A guard would open the door to give us lunches and let more prisoners in from time to time, each one eyeing the situation carefully as he came in, acclimating themselves to whichever area of the cell they felt most comfortable in. The trash on the floor steadily grew with each prisoner brought in to the cell, offering a wealth of bedding supplies for the man brave enough or foolish enough willing to dive in. It was the land of the lost.

An unhealthy abundance of trash and jailhouse tension had accumulated by the time the officer came to the door to get another batch of prisoners. There were ten names called, mine being one of them, and we lined up by the door, ready to move on. He escorted us down a hall to a cell with a large plastic receptacle in the corner, containing a mountain of shower slippers. As we entered the cell, half of our group ran to the container and frantically searched for good matching pairs. They were the veterans and knew the importance of finding some that fit and weren't terribly beat up. It seemed silly to me because I found a suitable pair with hardly any effort, but then again, I had yet to understand the psychology behind it. It was truly a dog-eat-dog mentality within the system, a way of thinking that was carried in and reflective of the lawlessness on the streets.

The cop disappeared behind a door in another corridor and soon after I heard a motor whine and a metal window shutter slide up. He called a name and one of the inmates who'd worked so hard to get a good pair of kicks walked up to a window behind a partition, then walked out a few minutes later wearing a red jail uniform.

A few others were called after him and then my name was called to walk up to the window. The cop was standing in a room that

14

looked like one you'd see in a laundromat, with clothing hampers hanging from hooks on a track and separated from me by a grated window. He told me to strip and to put my clothes on the counter. After doing so, standing naked and cold in front of him, he gave my clothes a perfunctory search, put them in a bag and put it with the others on the track. I was then told to open my mouth and wiggle my tongue, run my hands through my hair and finally, to turn around and spread my cheeks. When he was satisfied with what he'd seen, he gave me a pair of socks, some underwear, blue trousers and a blue top. I quickly put them on and then got in line with the others who'd already been changed out.

After we'd all gone through the ceremony of baring ourselves and were dressed in our new threads, he closed the window with a clang and came out to escort us to our next destination. Most of us wore blue, which meant we were in on misdemeanor charges, but a few of the guys wore red. The ones wearing red carried themselves in a manner reflecting the severity of their charges and I knew enough not to ask them what they were in for, but I was dying to know if any of them were in for any hardcore shit like murder.

The cop came out from the clothing room and turned his key in a lock mechanism, causing the door to slowly open on its rollers. As we passed through the doorway, heading deeper into the bowels of the jail, he instructed us to grab a bedroll from a laundry cart sitting out. I took one from the top of the pile, but some of the frequent fliers rummaged through, looking for quality bedding. They were searching for good blankets because, even though they were all made of thin cloth, some were smaller, had holes in them or weren't as soft. Wrapped within the roll were a sheet and various Bob Barker hygiene products. (I'd thought for years it was that bastard from *The Price Is Right*, but it was not. The Bob Barker of jailhouse fame was actually a former North Carolina state senator who started the company in the '70s, becoming the nation's leading supplier of detention products and handsomely profiting from the lucrative business of locking people up.)

We were led to an elevator and rode it up to a floor where inmates were housed until they were classified. The officer walked us down a wide corridor with polished concrete floors to an officer's station on a landing between two floors. Paint stenciled in random places on the walls told me I was on 9 South, and I noticed there was

---

15

a total of eight housing units—four on an upper level and four below. The only lights on in the units were dimly lit fluorescents, but I could see silhouettes of people getting up to look at us as we were being brought in. The officer on the landing called out our names from deck cards in his hand, told us to pick up a mattress from underneath the stairs and to wait by the door of whichever unit we were assigned to open.

The units comprised of a large dayroom, surrounded by bunk beds and concrete slabs to put mattresses on, with a bathroom off to the side. There were a couple of inmates awake who briefly looked at me as I came in, and I quickly found an empty slab to use, putting my mattress down to stake my claim.

It was difficult to close my eyes because of the strangeness of it all and had just gotten to sleep when I was woken by the sound of a guard screaming into a PA, "Chow time! Chow time! Line up for chow!" Half of the unit, a ragtag group of mostly drunks and crackheads, lined up at the door to get fed and the rest stayed in bed. A large cart wheeled up from the kitchen was brought to our dorm and a guard gave us our trays through a slot in the door, making it so we never had to leave the unit. Most of the inmates took a seat at one of the tables but being the new guy, I decided to sit on my bunk. The food looked disgusting: cornmeal-like hot cereal congealed in the tray, two pieces of stale bread, a sausage patty and a small milk carton.

I went back to sleep after eating breakfast and slept through the blare of daytime talk shows blasting from the TV set, announcements from guards and the sounds of the cell door being opened and closed. I was more tired than nervous and had no problem sleeping through the throng of activity. Everyone was awake by the time I got out of bed and the unit was abuzz with activity—lunch was about to be served. The inmates were mostly black and white, with a few Asians and Native Americans. Most of us wore blue and a few wore felony red. Everyone seemed to be excited over the prospect of lunch and I overheard people saying they'd trade this for that, mostly regulars working some kind of jailhouse hustle.

After everyone had finished their lunch and the deck officer counted and collected the trays, the dayroom activity resumed. The TV's volume was up full blast and it seemed the only programs it showed were *COPS* and court shows. I didn't understand why anyone would want to watch *COPS* while they were locked up, but then again,

I was with a crowd who watched the show thinking they might learn something or see someone they knew. Besides the TV, the only other things to do were take showers or use the phone. Because it was an orientation unit, books and games weren't allowed on the floor, but I did see a group of men sitting around one of the tables playing dominoes made from bars of soap. They had to put the dominoes on the table gingerly or they'd end up breaking them, instead of the hard slapping that's synonymous with the game in the 'hood. Watching them play was entertainment in itself.

I watched the dayroom activities unfold with a twisted fascination. Being there didn't seem that bad; it was boring and lacked excitement, but I could see how someone without drive or aspirations might find comfort in the way the days dragged on. It was the perfect place to lose your name and identity. As I was pondering this philosophy, I heard my name called over the PA, telling me to stand by the door for night court. It had me in disbelief. I thought night court was just a comedy show on NBC with a character named Bull.

I waited by the officer's station for the others going to court and we were taken in a group. The courtroom was one floor below the main processing area of the jail and was used primarily for arraignments and other pretrial hearings. I'd been here before. This was the same courtroom I was arraigned in as a juvenile, however the fact that I was back here again was lost on me. A bailiff was waiting for us when we came out of the elevator and told us court would soon begin. Everyone in the tank was wearing blue and it didn't seem like any of us were too concerned with our cases, although it did get extremely quiet after he left. About fifteen minutes later, the door leading to the courtroom popped open and a lawyer walked in, telling us he was there to represent us if we didn't have the money to hire a personal attorney.

We were all poor apparently because everyone ended up talking to him. I didn't know what the others were being charged with, but they were all being released. They went in at least somewhat nervous and came out grinning ear to ear, so by the time my name was called I felt relatively calm. I walked into the courtroom to an area designated for defendants and stood inside a small enclosure with a Plexiglas partition that separated criminals from the rest of the court. As the judge began with the formalities, asking me my name and if I understood the charges being brought against me, I looked around to

---

17

take it all in. There were no people in the audience and only a few in the courtroom itself—the judge, the prosecutor, the public defender, the bailiff, the stenographer and me. After telling the judge I was guilty, I was told I had time served and would be out that night. It took under two minutes.

I was the last one to see the judge and it wasn't long before an officer came down and escorted us back to our unit. Because it was night court, all of us had missed dinner and were issued a round of the sack lunches given out in booking. I was content with waiting until I was released and had my mind set on a chicken-fried steak, so I gave mine to a regular, knowing it was probably the last meal he was going to eat for some time. By the way he devoured it, it was safe to say he knew it also—a steady diet of crack cocaine was calling his name when he got out.

I spent the evening lying on my bunk watching television, minding my own business, and heard my name called over the PA just after midnight to roll it up. The deck officer had me put my mattress back in the pile under the stairs and I lined up with the others being released. The cop snickered "Good luck" and sent us down in the elevator to booking. I was with the same guys who were in court earlier and we were put into a small room to wait for our clothes. On the way there, I saw a group of guys still in their street clothes, walking in a line to dig for shower shoes and then strip. I looked at them and felt a touch of gratitude I was walking out and related to their misfortune.

The room we were in was connected to where the cop dressed us out a day prior and when the window shutter came sliding up, I could see our clothes hanging from hooks on a track. A county worker showed up at the window to pass them out and told us not to smoke, then went on to say if we did, we'd have to sit in there for another six hours or some shit. When she said that, we all looked at one another with desperate eyes that pleaded to follow her orders, emphasizing our desire to make it out of the jail on time. The excitement in the air was palpable…each of us looking forward to whatever it was we were going to do when we hit the street.

We were then fingerprinted and given the money we had on our books when we came in. I had a little over $300 and was down to party. One of the others being released said he could score some heroin, but we'd have to catch a cab to an area called Ballard to do so. Heroin was still new to me in a sense; I'd been turned on to it a few

18

years prior but had only done it a handful of times. Not because it scared me or that I thought I'd end up like one of the many junkies hustling on the "Ave", but because it rarely presented itself to me. We planned right then to make it happen, giving me an excitement comparable to going on a date with a girl I secretly had a crush on.

We were left to sit on a bench, being reprimanded from time to time for being too loud, while they ran our names to see if we had any warrants or holds. I sat there nervously, remembering the warrant that popped up when I was released from juvie, but nothing happened. Thirty tension-filled minutes later a female officer walked out and told us to follow her. We went through a series of locked doors, moving on to the next one after the one behind us had closed, and when we got to the last door, she left us with a "See you next time" and a smirk on her face. We were free.

INTO THE SPOON

By the fall of '94, I had a healthy dope habit. The tarred talons of heroin had finally dug deep into my skin and my addiction to the drug was akin to being stuck in a cosmic black hole; I found there was a wretched force draining me of my light. That fall had been rough. I had been in Canada over the summer for some skateboarding events and came back to Seattle in time to get evicted. With nowhere to live, I separated from my friends and started gravitating toward the ever-increasing legions of dope fiends who were running the streets.

My tolerance was so low at first it was easy to get high. With time, however, it became evident I needed more. The thought of quitting never presented itself, but what did was the knowledge I needed money to pursue my endeavors. All junkies have a hustle, and that hustle is the deciding factor in the quantity of dope they can ingest—some sold drugs to support their habits, some sold their ass. There were a small percentage of hypes who held legitimate jobs but they were a rarity, and those gigs tended to disappear, causing the addict to venture into uncharted territory in the pursuit of the next fix. It didn't matter whether it was robbing banks, robbing old ladies for their pension checks or robbing tip jars from coffee shops, it was all game and your game was only as good as how much money you could pull—and if your hustle was weak, you'd end up sick.

Prior to that fall I'd only get high on occasion, the main reason being that I rarely had any money. I loved the drug but had no hustle. The only time I ever got loaded was when I could trade some weed for dope, score for someone else or on the rare occasions I had money to spend. All of that changed after that summer. I suddenly found myself needing it to feel normal and obsessing over how I was going to get my next fix. I'd crossed the line.

I grew up watching the junkies on the streets. I was fascinated by the shit they did to maintain their habits. They were specters hiding in doorways and alleys, their eyes forever on the prowl for an easy hit and the cops waiting to take them down. Most exuded a criminality I found intriguing.

I'd been exposed to drugs at an early age and had every reason to be wary of the lifestyle, yet I was curiously drawn to them. When I was fifteen, I'd heard Lou Reed singing about heroin and "waiting for the man", fascinated by his words. It was safe to say I was a junkie long before I stuck a needle in my arm.

* * * * *

After I felt the tug, I became a booster. With the need for money becoming more apparent, I began eyeing book and music stores from a different perspective. The University District had plenty of both and they paid cash for pretty much anything they could sell. Bookstores were easy to hit, but it took a lot of learning by trial and error to know what was sellable. Music stores were more difficult to steal from, but the product was easier to unload. There were many times when I had to run out of stores because of alarms being triggered due to my negligence in removing sensors.

I also saw how the boosters with the best hustles operated; they returned what they stole to the stores they'd stolen from. Some stores had good return policies and others were more difficult. I discovered that around Christmas, stores would return without receipts much of the time, for obvious reasons, but many of those were large department stores that specialized in clothes. I preferred smaller stores that didn't have an army of detectives working for them.

One of such being a store called Fred Meyer on Capitol Hill. I'd stolen from them as a kid and never had any problems, giving me the balls to hit them with regularity. You didn't need a receipt to return anything under $50 and they'd give you cash with no questions asked. I went in one day and grabbed a $40 Walkman, then walked down an aisle and stuck it down my pants. I didn't notice the security guards tailing me and when I approached the exit, they nabbed me and brought me to an office in the back. They called the police and instead of citing me out, the cop decided I should take a trip downtown.

Going to jail knowing I was about to get dope sick was an agonizing prospect. I'd always perceived jail as a twisted adventure land, a place to endure with eyes cautious and new, but that was an easy position to take when my release date was around the corner. Going in with a habit and an uncertainty as to when I was getting out was an entirely different scenario. I would've done just about anything at that moment to get out of the hell that was awaiting me. Fear and intense depression overtook my thoughts, and I knew the only thing that would fix me was a shot in the arm.

I was still new to the dope game at that point. I would wake up a little sick, and it might take a while to get well, but never long enough to go into full withdrawals. When I got to the jail, after the five hours it took to be transported from East Precinct, I was starting to feel it coming on. The muscle spasms, vomiting and diarrhea hadn't yet hit, but I certainly felt the unease and anxiety. All I could think about was getting out. I knew it was going to be a while before I saw the judge, and I was praying he or she would release me.

I was getting worse with each passing moment, and by the time I was able to speak to one of the intake nurses, the fear I had turned into panic. I decided to tell her I was not only kicking heroin, but that I was suicidal as well, which turned out to be a terrible decision. They put me in a cell by myself and less than ten minutes later, a guard escorted me to the area where the uniforms were given out. The good thing was I didn't have to wait for hours in the booking cells, but the flipside was that I earned a trip to suicide watch.

I was given a set of county blues but no underwear or socks, and when I was given my bedroll, they took out the sheet and towel. I understood the precautions they took regarding the sheet and towel, but there wasn't a chance in hell of me strangling myself with a pair of tighty-whities. The guard then brought me to the 7th floor, where the psych ward and infirmary were located, and housed me in an observation unit. The module was filled to capacity, with many of us having to find floor space to put our mats.

The unit was a repository for the mentally unstable. I didn't see anyone trying to kill themselves, but a few were rocking on the floor in catatonic dazes, mumbling incoherently to themselves. One man would bang his head against the wall every so often, stopping when the watch guard commanded him to, only to resume his activity a short time later. Quite a few of us were there seeking medication to help with the kick. One of the inmates told me that if I told the doctor I had a benzodiazepine habit, they'd prescribe me something to help stave it off. I gave it a shot and was rewarded with an anti-seizure medication called Tegretol that didn't do a goddamn thing.

I had court the next day and spent the night in the throes of sickness—sweating profusely but shivering uncontrollably, suffering spasms in my legs and back, puking streams of bile, topped with the agony of not being able to sleep. The night was spent rolling around on a thin bare mat, feeling the perforated shell of the plastic against my slick and damp skin. The cacophony of snoring heard throughout the unit was maddening. At one point I threw a bar of soap at one of the sources, stopping it for a minute, but only long enough to gather its strength and come back in full force.

The morning couldn't get there quick enough. After a breakfast I couldn't eat was served, the deck officer called out the names of those going to court and we shuffled out to our fate. We were brought to the municipal court holding tank and pulled in almost immediately. I was nervous yet optimistic I'd be released, but when I entered the courtroom and saw Judge Hightower sitting on the bench my optimism sank considerably. We'd established a relationship due to my indulgence in an array of petty crimes and the last time I was in her court, she told me she'd seen enough of me.

My public defender met me on the other side of the defendant's stand and said they were offering ten days. In King County Jail, you did 2/3 of your time—they called it "good time, work time"—so with two days in, it meant I'd still have four days to do. Four days seemed an eternity at the time and I was still clinging to the hope that if I pled "not guilty", the judge would release me on a personal recognizance. The thought of having to spend another dope-sick minute in there sounded hellish, so it was never even a decision. I rolled the dice.

I prepared myself to deliver a heartwarming speech condemning my actions and to beg for a chance to right myself from my evil ways, but she never gave me a chance to speak. Knowing I rejected the deal, she ordered that I stay confined, set my next court date for two weeks and told me that I had a bail of $200. I knew it was possible something like this could happen but was still devastated. The hope I'd held for getting out that night was effectively smashed.

When she said that I could get out if I posted $200, my mind immediately went on the prowl and I got on the phone as soon as I was

—

23

brought back to the housing unit. All my friends knew I'd been fucking with heroin and weren't going to help me kill myself, so I ended up concocting some bullshit story and called my friend James' dad. I laid it on him like a champ and he said he'd be able to post the bail, but it wouldn't be for a couple days. This was certainly good news, but two days to a dope fiend was another life away. I didn't have anyone else to call for the measly $200, giving me valid cause to regret my decision in not taking the deal that had been offered.

The unit I was in seemed even darker and dirtier than before, being that I now had nothing to hope for. The dinner cart came rolling up and I traded what was on my tray for a small piece of dry cake, needing the sugar to help with my kick. Shortly after the guards took the trays, my name was called over the PA system. My heart jumped thinking my bail had been posted, only to crash when I discovered I was being transferred to NERF, the minimum-security compound in North Seattle. But I did feel a subtle tug of optimism when the realization I was going to a better place began to sink in. The North End Rehabilitation Facility was next to Shorecrest High School and Hamlin Park, both places I knew well from my youth. My dad had rented a house two blocks from there when I was a kid and I remembered playing in the woods and seeing inmates through the fence.

I was brought down to a cell next to the transport garage and waited with ten other guys who were just as eager as me to get there. The ones who'd been there before told us stories about how good the food tasted, being able to breathe clean air and that smoking was permitted. An old codger who looked like he'd been working there since the Second World War called us out of the cell and after going through all the procedures clearing us, we were on our way. My recollection of the area from my youth brought forth a strong emotional tie as we pulled in. Back when I was still somewhat innocent, I'd played army and rode my BMX bike within an earshot of the property. I was swept with memories and had to hold back the tears, wishing I could go back in time to those fond remembrances of when life was carefree.

The facility bordered a vast wooded expanse and an area with buildings of all shapes and sizes used for purposes other than keeping men confined. The housing units were in old army barracks, and in each barrack were a score of two and three-man rooms. Compared to

---

24

the county jail it was heaven. I had a real bed with blankets and a pillow, was able to go outside and smoke, there was a library with music, a gym, acupuncture and even a Tai Chi class. There were also various training programs, educational services and twelve-step meetings. The program offered was one of rehabilitation and progress as opposed to a system of warehousing individuals and hoping they'd learn their lesson.

It was also much easier to escape from. Early in the morning a man crawled out his window and made a break. The barracks weren't locked nor were there fences surrounding the perimeter, so if you were ever overcome with an urge to split, it was more than possible. I found out later he'd been "hard-timing" over his lady. It was a common occurrence at NERF, apparently, because shortly after the flurry of activity from the guards died down, the lights went back out and we were told to stay in our rooms.

As I was lying on my bunk, making an escape began to enter my consciousness. I didn't have anywhere to go but that hardly mattered—all I cared about was getting well. The more I thought about it, however, the more it started sounding like a chore. After sneaking off the property, I'd have to steal some clothes from someone's backyard and hide until the busses began to run. I also knew that I'd be considered a flight risk and didn't want to do any time in maximum-security when I was inevitably caught. My mind was plagued by the prospect of a fix and the work it would take to get it, but I didn't want to take the chance, so I settled in for the ride.

My body felt like crap and I couldn't sleep but being there gave me a sense of comfort and optimism. The clean air and bite-size taste of freedom made me feel like everything was going to be okay. My serenity was ripped from me an hour before breakfast was served, however, when a trustee came into my room and said I needed to roll up my property. He told me I was going back to KCJ because I had a medical hold and probably wouldn't be brought back to NERF until it was cleared. In the blink of an eye, my disposition went from a state of burgeoning positivity to one of crushing negativity. Before grabbing my bedroll and reporting to the transfer hold, I packed some tobacco in a plastic bag and stuffed it into my sock.

Being somewhat new to doing time, I hadn't thought about the search that would occur during the transfer process. Prior to leaving the facility, the transport officer lined us up to pat us down and I was

---

certain he'd find my stash. He must not have sensed my nervousness because he only did a half-ass search. I breathed a sigh of relief and made a mental note to do a better job in the future. I wasn't sure what the consequences would've been had I been caught, but was fairly certain it would've meant a trip to the hole.

When we got downtown, we were put in a holding cell within sight of all the inmates being released. I had to watch two different groups of prisoners being escorted to the exit doors on their way out to freedom. They were dressed in their street clothes and I could feel the aura of excitement they exuded as they looked forward to getting in bed with their wife or hooker, loaded their crack pipe, filled their spoon, or whatever else it was that got their rocks off. I felt an immediate envy and longing to be free, and I ended up smoking all my tobacco in that little cell, quietly cursing them for their fortune.

I was brought back to the suicide wing on the 7th floor and told I never should've been cleared to go. Before leaving, I told the staff I wasn't suicidal and that it was just an over-exaggeration on my part, but that wasn't the issue. The Tegretol I'd been prescribed—or, more accurately, my telling the medical staff I had a benzo habit and was prone to seizures because of them—was reason to keep me downtown. The seemingly harmless advice offered by an inmate had come back to fuck me. I didn't know any better and made yet another mental note to think things through when attempting to manipulate jail staff.

Being back on that floor was agonizing. As I got off the elevator and walked to my wing, some of the guys in the other housing units pointed and laughed at me through their windows, knowing exactly what had happened. It must've been evident to all who saw me leave how happy I looked to go, and I'm sure it was just as apparent how depressed I looked coming back. It was easy to find satisfaction in another man's misery when you were stuck eating shit from the barrel, and that's exactly what they were doing. I hated them all from afar, secretly hoping they'd lose their cases and never get out.

I ended up getting the last laugh, however. I was back on the floor for maybe three hours when I heard my name called over the PA system. I walked out to the landing where the deck officer was stationed and told my bail had been posted. I made sure to look at all the fuckers who'd laughed at me on the way out, pointing to the bedroll in my hand as if to emphasize I was leaving. One of the guys, a giant black dude, looked like he would've killed me if given the opportunity, and I got on the elevator hoping I'd wouldn't run in to him any time soon.

Physically, I was starting to feel fine. I'd only been strung out a few months, so three days without using put me over the hump. When I was told I was being released though, my mind and body started doing somersaults. The runs that had started to subside came back with a vengeance and I couldn't stop thinking about how I was going to get my first fix. Being released this time seemed to take 100 times longer. But even though time always seems to stop in such situations, it never truly does, and within a few hours I found myself walking out of the jail, heading toward another shot of dope.

TIME FLIES AND JUNKIES CRASH

I managed to elude the shackles of the law for another fourteen months. Necessity dictated that I hone my skills or face the pounding of the judge's gavel, so I got good at my trade. It also helped that I had a girlfriend who worked at a strip joint downtown called the Lusty Lady. She'd turn tricks on the side, but her money wasn't always solid and we both had monster habits, so my hustle was necessary for us to maintain. Our relationship was solely based around drugs, heroin our criminal wedding band.

In January of '96, I was in a store called "Play It Again Sports" on Broadway and Pine, on a mission to steal some baseball mitts—there was a store next to East Precinct that bought sporting equipment and they didn't seem to mind that I brought them stolen merchandise. I was in the store with two gloves down my pants and happened to see a squad car pull up out of the corner of my eye. As soon as I saw the cops walk into the store, I hid behind a clothing rack, pulled out the gloves, dropped them to the floor and headed for the door.

The cops had been talking to the sales clerks and followed me out after I made my exit. They pulled me aside and searched me knowing I was up to no good, but couldn't prove anything because I didn't have any merchandise on me. Unfortunately, I'd been caught stealing three pairs of Levi's from a store directly across the street the day before and got into an altercation with an employee as I made my escape. One of the cops had heard the dispatch when the crime went down and because I matched the description, he quickly surmised I was the culprit. I was put in handcuffs and told I was being detained under suspicion. My begging and pleading to let me go didn't do a bit of good, and I was soon back at East Precinct waiting to be transported to the county jail.

When I was in the holding cell, the arresting officer came in and told me they had me on film, that the cashier was going to testify and asked if I wanted to make a statement. He then said I was being charged with strong-armed robbery and the court would perceive a confession as willingness to cooperate. I certainly wasn't the wisest criminal on the streets, but I knew enough to use my right to remain silent. He was trying to get a confession to make himself look better to his superiors, make detective or whatever other kind of shit cops shoot for.

When my charges were read to me downtown, they told me I was being booked for 3rd degree theft—shoplifting. There wasn't a chance in hell of them pinning a robbery on me. I never hit the cashier, nor did I threaten him or make a move like I was going to hit him. I just broke free of his half-ass full nelson. I never even made it out of the store with the jeans. As the cashier approached me, telling me I was under citizen's arrest, I pulled the Levi's out of my waistband and threw them on the ground. When it came down to it, because I never left the store with the merchandise, I had a plausible defense if it went to trial.

Knowing I was facing a misdemeanor as opposed to a felony was cause for rejoice but it really didn't do much toward lightening my load. My habit had grown significantly since the last time I was in and I knew I'd soon be in a world of shit. When I saw the intake nurse, I told her I was going to be kicking dope, but I made sure to avoid saying anything that could be even half-construed as suicidal. My trip to the 7th floor had left a wretched taste in my mouth.

By the time I got to the elevator to go upstairs, I was in full withdrawal. The restlessness had gotten to the point that I couldn't sit still and the spasms in my legs were causing them to twitch. I was brought to the 9th floor with a batch of miscreants who looked as bad as me and put into a dayroom while they figured out our bedding assignments. As soon as we were brought in, I bee-lined it to the toilet and started to vomit an endless outpouring of bile.

Heroin had taken over the city. Half the guys in the dayroom were kicking dope, when just a few years earlier there would've only been a couple. Needle exchanges popped up seemingly out of nowhere, catering to the masses of addicts clamoring for clean works. I'd never noticed the methadone clinics before, but now it seemed like they were packed with junkies getting their doses. The same went for the detoxes. Of course, I hadn't been to one until I'd needed to kick, but I remember seeing detox vans throughout my youth picking up drunks and taking them in for a little dry spell. After actually being in one, I found that most of the patients were there because they had a habit to smack. It used to be that heroin was the worst of the worst, only used by the wretched inhabitants of an urban

—
29

wasteland, but all of that changed by the middle of the '90s. Out of nowhere it grabbed the youth by the balls, turning them into little demons willing to sell their mom's ass for a fix.

I informed the deck officer that I needed to see a doctor and was told I'd see one the next day. It took all my will and strength to grab a mat and get to my housing unit. I was put in a unit I'd been in when I first came to the jail as a nineteen-year-old and as I entered, I saw two guys I knew from the University District. One was a Skinhead named Spanky and the other a stoner named Jimbo. Both were kicking and sitting at a table in the dayroom, doing their best to get through their personal little hell. Neither were the type I would've figured to even try heroin, yet here they were in front of me, another statistic in the world of drugs.

We stayed up talking for a bit, sharing our misery and pain, then went to our beds to toss and turn through an evening of torment. It was impossible to sleep even a minute; when I wasn't running to the bathroom to spray the toilet with puke or diarrhea, I was shaking and sweating on my mat, listening to the sounds of gang members rapping and shouting out their sets, cell doors slamming shut, guards calling names over the PA and the constant blare of *COPS* or *Jerry Springer* on the TV. It was a maddening environment and devoid of even the slightest comfort.

My name was called mid-morning and I was escorted with a cast of criminals to the court hold. I was freezing and had to sit on a steel bench with my arms inside my shirt in a vain attempt to stay warm. When the public defender spoke with me, he told me the prosecutor was offering thirty days. I asked if I had any shot at being released and was told it wasn't likely. After thinking about it for a minute, I decided to take the deal. I'd do twenty on thirty with what they called "good time". It seemed like a lifetime away, but I didn't want to take a chance on getting sentenced to more if I lost the case and just wanted to get it over with.

It took a couple of hours, but I finally made it back to my housing unit and to my bed. Both Spanky and Jimbo were gone, either to another part of the jail or home, and I really didn't care. I was left with my thoughts, the loudness, and the unbearable agony of kicking dope. I felt far worse than I had the night before; I was puking constantly, and my nerves were in shambles. Right when I'd find a position of comfort on my thin mat, I'd soon be jumping out of my skin and would feel the need to reposition myself. I'd been doing this throughout the previous night and the lack of sleep was starting to make my eyes bug out. I also knew it wasn't going to get better anytime soon.

Shortly after dinner was served, I was called for the nurse's line and made myself get out of bed to see her. I was being overly dramatic while in her office and made myself vomit—which wasn't hard to do—hoping to get some medication prescribed. She ended up buying my routine and prescribed me Clonidine for my blood pressure and Compazine for my vomiting. But she also ordered that I be relocated to the infirmary on the 7th floor to be observed by medical staff.

My initial thought was that I was going back to the psych unit, but that wasn't the case. I was put in a large cell with nothing but floor space and inmates with a wide range of medical issues. The two days I was kept there were the longest I'd ever experienced, and I was certain my being in the medical unit prevented me from going back to NERF. Sleep was but a fond desire and I hated every person in there because it was all they did, just as I'm sure they hated me because I couldn't sit still. It wasn't all bad, though. There were no thugs yelling about their "bitches" and how good they had it out on the streets, and I was given Pedialyte for my dehydration, the only thing I'd been able to digest. By the time I was moved, I was able to sit a little more still and could eat some of my food. My eyes still felt like they were going to explode, but I was feeling some sort of progress.

From there, and with only a few days clean, I was moved to a worker dorm on the same floor. They were the hallway trustees and had jobs cleaning the corridors of the jail, picking up and delivering the meal trays from the kitchen to the housing units and anything else that needed to be done. While observing the workers perform their job duties, I was immediately able to see the benefits that came with being in the unit. First of all, it was quiet and they were, for the most part, respectful to each other. Second, they were given two trays for every meal. I wasn't hungry yet, but food was beginning to look like it would be a factor in my future. And third, there was a coffee pot and it was always full. I was an avid coffee drinker and even more so after being thrown into a setting in which there were no drugs.

I was assigned to the crew that worked the 10th floor, where many of the high-security inmates were housed. Generally speaking, it was where inmates who'd been to prison, had a propensity for fighting or were looking at serious time were kept. It had a reputation for violence and riots breaking out. Whenever it jumped off within the jail, a voice would announce over the institutional PA system that there was a "Code Blue", and it was usually on the 8th or 10th floor. It was with a sizeable amount of nervous apprehension that I followed my co-workers and reported for duty.

It turned out to be easy work, however. We started by picking up trays from 10 North and East, which was where some of the inmates facing long prison terms were kept. All I'd seen of the jail thus far had been dorm settings, but there they were housed in two-man cells, with doors that were buzzed open by a deck officer when they were granted access to the dayroom. They were locked down in their cells while we did our cleanup, but I could feel the tension and saw their eyes through the food slots watching our every move.

After the trays were picked up and sent back to the kitchen, we moved on to 10 South. The inmates there were housed in a dorm setting. Most of them were there on Department of Correction's holds and were looking at going back to prison for violating their parole. We were dismissed as "punk-ass trustees" and basically ignored while we did our work, as opposed to the maximum-security prisoners on North and East who had nothing better to do but observe and plot.

It took about forty-five minutes to finish our work and the only difficult thing about the job was that it had to be done after every meal, three times a day. We had the easiest job of all the crews because most of the 10th floor inmates had been to prison and were cleaner because of it. I was just glad I didn't have to clean up the gladiator tanks on 8 North. They were all gang members who had a pension for jumping each other, and the crew working that floor would come back to the unit bitching about being disrespected.

The guys who had it the worst, however, were the ones working 7 East and the 11th floors. 7 East was where inmates with mental issues were housed, so it wasn't uncommon for that crew to be called out for special duties. Some of those duties entailed "Code Brown's"—a term the cops had coined for when an inmate finger-painted the walls of his cell with shit. Another one was cleaning up after inmates who stuffed sheets into their toilets and flooded their cells. Just about anything could happen on 7 East, and the floor workers always needed to be ready to respond.

———

The 11th floor was where disciplinary and segregation cells were located. The inmates up there were affectionately termed as "doing time in the hole". Most of them were there for breaking rules, but some were there because they were in protective custody. Rapists, child molesters and snitches were all part of the "PC" group, as well as high-profile criminals such as serial killers. They were the ones who would get stabbed or beaten if they were in general population. The trustees who cleaned the 11th floor had nothing good to say about the inmates housed there.

I'd been working the job for just under a week when I was told to roll up my property for transfer. They were moving me to a minimum-security dorm on the 2nd floor and I wasn't exactly thrilled to be leaving. I'd gotten myself into a routine and although time still crawled, it moved much faster than sitting around in a non-working dorm. Also, I had started feeling better and with that came intense hunger, which was somewhat suppressed by the extra tray I earned through my work. Down there I was going to starve.

With great reluctance, I rolled up my gear and was escorted out. In a lot of ways, it was a vast improvement: there were soda and candy machines, books, and they'd show movies from time to time. But there were a lot of people packed into a small area, which made an already loud group of people even louder. I was housed in one of the many dorms with close to twenty others and set about trying to make myself comfortable.

Right when I'd settled in, I heard the officer on duty make an announcement over the PA requesting kitchen workers and jumped on it. There were three of us who signed up, and after we came back to the officer's podium with our bedding, another cop took us to the 4th floor. It was set up the same as the 2nd, just calmer, quieter and everyone wore yellow uniforms.

The night shift came back from the kitchen at ten o'clock and as they filed into the dorm, I saw an old friend of mine from the punk scene named Joe. We used to drink and hang out at the Jesters of Chaos house in Wallingford, and he also played drums in his own band, so I'd see him at a lot of shows. As was the case with myself, he dabbled with heroin a little too much, developed a habit and ended up dropping out of the scene. The last time I'd seen him, he was selling dope in the University District, but his business went to shit and had to find a new way to support his habit.

—

33

Joe's new endeavor was bank robbery. He'd walk in and pass the teller a note asking him or her to put the money in a bag, then leave in a getaway car. He told me he never threatened them with violence or said he had a gun; that it was bank policy to hand the money over. He'd been in close to six months and his public defender thought he had action on getting out if he pled guilty to 1st degree theft. I'd thought about robbing banks before and couldn't bring myself to do it, but it sounded more appealing after talking to Joe.

I started my new job the next day. The kitchen was massive and took up a whole floor of the jail. Our shift started at two o'clock and the lunch trays from the entire jail were waiting for us when we reported for duty. More than 2000 of them, piled high on carts. There were four King County employees and close to thirty inmates on my shift and our job was to feed the entire population. I was the new guy, so I was put on the "tray-banger" crew. Our job was to make sure the food trays were empty and then pushed on a cart to an inmate who fed them into an institutional tray-cleaning machine.

After all the trays were cleaned and the work area scrubbed, they brought in coffee and cereal. The first thing I saw was a bin of Fruit Loops and I gorged myself. The other guys paced themselves and it didn't take long to see why; as soon as we were done eating, we set up an assembly line to prepare dinner trays. Each inmate was given a spot on the line: one guy handed out plastic sporks, another dealt margarine, another bread, and at the end of the line some "border brother" ladled out a nasty almost-meat slop.

As the trays were filled, they were grabbed in stacks of ten and placed on a cart until it was full, then another inmate would bring it to the elevator to be shuttled to whichever part of the jail it was going. Two hours and 2300 trays later, the boss shouted, "Last tray!" and it was then we could eat dinner. I was starving when I first got there, but after eating a mountain of cereal and drinking coffee nonstop, combined with seeing the food as it was scooped out of the pans, I was content with finding a spot to relax.

I'd just found a milk crate to sit on in the scullery when I heard someone yell, "Trays are here!" from the other side of the kitchen. My crew of Mexican tray-bangers was already on it, knocking the food out of the trays into garbage cans that quickly filled with uneaten slop the guys in the units above didn't want to eat. They worked in unison and didn't like me much because I was new, lazy, a junkie and/or white, so I ended up working by myself, hating them more than they hated me.

By the end of the shift I was burned out, ready for a shower and wanting nothing more than to lie on my rack. It was a hard job and I'd begin every shift with dread, knowing I'd have to endure another long, monotonous day. But getting back to the dorm tired and satisfied was just as rewarding as it was agonizing. My work ethic had been pathetic prior to being incarcerated. I didn't really think of it at the time, but it was the first job I had that I consistently busted my ass. All I knew then was that it made my last ten days fly by.

And then I was back out on the streets.

VIDEO TAPE BANDIT

I'd only been out a month when I caught my next case. In '96, video stores were everywhere, granting a never-ending supply for my thieving hands. I'd sell stolen VHS tapes at pawnshops or music stores during the day and in bars at night. The bars were great because I could sell them for five bucks apiece, which was practically double what the stores paid, but I'd have to hustle and would often get kicked out by angry jocks trying to impress their Barbie-doll girlfriends.

The stores I hit the most were Blockbuster and Hollywood Video, but being a resourceful opportunist, I'd steal from other stores as well, such as the Wherehouse on Broadway. It was in the same shopping complex as the Fred Meyer I got busted in close to two years prior, with only one wandering mall cop who rarely came around. I'd hit it many times in the past and my plan was to remove the alarms, fill my waistband and jacket, then make my way out the exit.

It took a long time to take the alarms out of each movie, however, and I also had to make sure none of the clerks, customers or the security guard saw me. I'd cut the packaging with a knife and conceal the wrappers of the movies behind other movies on display, but on that day the cashier was on to me. I saw her pull out a wrapper when she was in one of the aisles organizing and should've figured she'd known it was me who did it, but I was too greedy and kept at my work. Just as I'd finished loading up and was making my way toward the exit, a cop walked up behind me and asked what I was up to. Another one quickly appeared from inside the shopping complex, effectively killing any thought of running and attempting to get away. He asked if I was carrying anything illegal and, knowing I wasn't getting out of this one, I started pulling movies out of my pants and pockets. He seemed to think I'd only have a few and made a joke to his partner that the movies I stole were like a bunch of clowns piling out of a Volkswagen bug at a circus. They just kept on coming.

I was then on my way back to the county jail, feeling like the biggest turd on the planet for having just gotten out. As I was going through the booking process this time around, I refrained from telling them I'd be kicking, not wanting anything to prevent me from going to NERF and knowing the medication they gave dope fiends didn't do a bit of good.

I was brought to the 9th floor, writhing in pain and hoping I'd encounter a sympathetic judge when I made it to court. Two days later I was called out for my appearance and a realization that the slap on the wrists were but a memory. They offered me six months at my arraignment and I was told I'd probably get the maximum, which was a year, if I took it to trial and lost. I couldn't believe I could get that much time for shoplifting. My demeanor was that of a man who'd been beaten by a mob.

Having been caught red-handed, coupled with the fear of losing at trial, influenced my decision to take the plea bargain. With "good time" taken into account, I had another four months to do. I went back to my unit after court, defeated yet resigned with the knowledge I'd probably made the right decision.

When the NERF chain was called after dinner, I heard my name and rolled up my property. Despite my depression and sickness—it didn't matter if you were on a thirty-day or a thirty-year run, kicking dope in any form always made you feel like shit—going there gave me a sense of optimism. Cigarettes, a comfortable bed, good food and clean air were calling, and I knew I could do my time with ease.

And I did. Before long, I started putting meat on my bones and was able to sleep with a regularity I hadn't had since I'd started fucking with dope. My health came back and it happened fast. I'd seen many junkies get out after doing time and couldn't help but notice how great they looked, like they were different people altogether. And I also saw them revert to their pre-jail emaciated look as soon as they picked up the spoon with an alarming rapidity.

I'd hit twelve-step meetings from time to time, and one night a junkie I knew from the streets named Cherokee came in to speak. We'd met in '91 at my friend Dan Hazard's apartment on Capitol Hill. Dan's place was a dope house and I saw all kinds of crazy shit go down there, the craziest being when four of us were robbed at gunpoint and stuffed into a closet while they ransacked the apartment. Before that had happened, Cherokee would come over to score, sell or shoot his drugs, depending on whatever it was he had going on at the time. He'd been doing heroin long before I was born and it showed; his body was scarred from abscesses and he had a multitude of other health problems stemming from his drug use. I'd met and known plenty of junkies from all the time I'd spent on the streets, but he was the first where it registered that he was sick because he didn't have any dope. When I saw him on the couch one morning, his large frame curled in a fetal position, shaking and sneezing nonstop, I knew there was a heavy price to be paid.

I hadn't seen Cherokee since that day when he was sick and he looked like a new man. He wasn't the first dope fiend I'd known who'd broken free—there was that old junkie at Ace Pawn, I knew he wasn't still on the nod, and that black girl at the food bank, she used to sell dope on the Ave, she quit. And that other guy, the one who had a job picking up drunks off the street and taking them to detox, he was a gnarly hype and he got clean, but I wasn't tight with any of them. I shot my first dope with Cherokee, so his being clean hit me like a blast of good ether coke.

I'd been at NERF about a month, passing the time by working in the kitchen and listening to music in the library, when I heard there was a signup sheet for the work release program. From my understanding of how the program was run, I'd be let out for work during the day then report back to the jail at night. My assumption was that they'd get me a job and I'd be able to save up some money, so I jumped on it. Within a few days, the coordinator of the program interviewed me, told me I qualified and said I'd be picked up from NERF the following week.

True to his word, I was transported back to County a week later. When transferring to another facility, the procedure is the same as when you're released—you dress out of your jail attire and put the stinky, mildew-ridden clothes you came in with back on, then you sit around on steel benches and wait. But after they run your name to see if you have any warrants or holds, you're released to the custody of the transferring agency as opposed to being escorted toward the exit.

The King County work release facility was located two blocks west of the jail, on the top floor of the King County Courthouse. There was an elevated, enclosed walkway between the buildings, high above the downtown sidewalks. I doubted many of the people walking the streets knew or realized that 100 feet above, inmates were being escorted back and forth between the courthouse and the jail. If there had been windows on the walkway, anyone bothering to look up

—

would've seen a defeated man in baggy, dirty clothes with handcuffs around his wrists, being escorted by two overweight cops.

The length of the tram spanned two city blocks, straight to the holding tanks for the inmates going to Superior Court. Most of the men waiting in those cells wore red and the atmosphere was significantly more solemn than the Municipal Court holding tanks in the jail. Many of them made it a point to stare and mean-mug me as I was being escorted past and into the actual courthouse building. Once inside, I was led to a bank of elevators and brought up to the top floor of the courthouse where the work release detail was housed.

The jail had been built in 1931, using the top three floors of the courthouse, and was used as the main jail until the new one was constructed in '86. There were certain structural changes, such as the kitchen being torn out and the modernization of the officer's station, but the cells were basically the same as when it had first been built. The housing units were set in rows on a tier, with old-fashioned steel bars separating them from the walkway. The cells themselves were relics from the past…two steel bunk beds on one side, enveloped by scarred concrete walls, with an ancient porcelain sink and toilet giving them a cosmetic flourish (all modern jails and prisons now use stainless-steel because porcelain can be broken into shards to be used as shanks). I conjured an image of what it would've been like fifty years ago—inmates with nothing but time on their hands, locked down in their cells, using mirrors to see who was walking the tier, and relaying information to each other via notes or coded phrases.

I was able to wear my own clothes but that was where my gratitude ended. The cops told me I wouldn't be allowed to leave until I saw my case manager, and that wasn't until the following week, meaning I was stuck in the familiar position of having nothing to do with my time.

The week waiting to see him was spent watching baseball games and whatever movie they'd show on TV. The only other thing to do was hang out in an open-air dayroom. We were ten floors above the streets, but it didn't stop us from yelling obscenities to any girls or guys who happened to pass below. We yelled to the ladies that we loved them and told the men they could suck a dick. It was all good fun until a guard heard us or we were reported by do-gooders on the street, then we'd be banned from the dayroom for the evening.

By the time I saw my case manager I was ready to go. Unfortunately for me, I was told that I wouldn't be able to leave on job search. Work release was set up for men who were employed prior to being incarcerated, something that clearly didn't apply to me. But he did tell me about a new program that had just taken off called the "Boeing Crew" and that I was eligible for it. I said yes, of course—I would've signed on to a crew cleaning seagull shit from the top of the Space Needle if given the opportunity. We'd leave in a county van after breakfast, Monday through Friday, and on to the Boeing airfield or wherever else we were dispatched to clean weeds and brush.

The work was hard, and I had no idea what companies profited by using the county's "free" labor, but it did get me outside. One of the days working was spent on the side of the King County Jail, next to the entrance of the facility. When we were done and putting our tools away, I saw my friend Trish, a girl I'd known since I was a little shit hanging out on the "Ave". She was standing by the visitor's entrance waiting for her boyfriend Paul to be released. Seeing her set off an internal lust to get loaded. Quitting had entered my mind while being locked up this time, not seriously of course, but right then I knew I wasn't done. I was about to ask her if she could hook me up, but my supervisor walked over before I could, and I knew it wasn't to be. I briefly wrestled with an impulse to run, but wisely opted instead to bide my time.

It was about a week and a half later, after a long day of digging in the sun, that I was called to the officer's station and told the case manager in charge of home release wanted to see me. I walked up the ramp to his office and encountered a giant wood desk that had no business being in an office so small, with an intense and animated little man sitting behind it. Being that I was technically homeless, I was taken by surprise when he said I was eligible for home detention. I jumped on it and told him I was living with a friend in the city, and within an hour I was walking out to the streets from the courthouse with the few belongings I owned.

My case manager gave me the office number and told me to call it from where I'd be staying, and said I'd randomly receive calls from a computer. It would be able to detect slurring and any other characteristics associated with getting loaded and he told me not to fuck it up. He also said I'd have to report to the courthouse every

—
40

morning starting Monday to work on a crew handling various details throughout the city.

When I said I'd be staying at a friend's, I did so on a whim. The truth was, I had no idea where I was going to stay. I just wanted to get loaded. I decided to call my friend Slim and told him my situation, minus the wanting to get high part. Slim was a solid dude—we had met in San Francisco in 1990 at a convention for a skateboarding team we were on called the Jak's. He had moved to Seattle in '92 and lived in a house on 31st and Union with his wife Jamie. I didn't think he'd be cool with it, but with no hesitation at all, he told me I was more than welcome on his couch.

After that was taken care of, I called my dealer. I felt the drug calling my name in a way a serial killer might have for blood. The longing to get high was insatiable and the consequences of my actions were absent from my thoughts. The minute my caseworker told me I was being released it'd been all I could think about. My connect told me to meet him at 8th and Virginia and I spent the next thirty minutes standing on a corner like a fat kid waiting for the ice cream man. I had to beg him for a front, and then went into a bathroom to fix. When it was all said and done, I achieved the nod I was shooting for, but the clarity of my predicament was staring me in the eyes—I'd be going back to jail.

Deep down inside, I knew that to be the case if I got loaded. I knew I was to report by phone and that I'd give the address of where I was staying when I did so, and that there was a good chance the SPD would come get me when they discovered I'd gotten high. With that knowledge being present, I had no choice but to admit I was fully insane. It would be one thing if I liked jail or didn't care—that there is an entirely different type of crazy—but that wasn't my story. I hated being locked up and everything about it: the concrete, the metal doors, the safety glass, getting visits and talking through a phone, the nasty food, sharing a bathroom with a bunch of men, being woken up by guards, sleeping on a hard plastic mat with no pillow, the loudness in the cell, the smell of ass, the daytime TV programs, the stress of going to court, kicking dope…the only thing I liked about jail was being released.

By the time I made it to Slim's, I'd basically accepted that it would be just a matter of time before I was back in County. I think most people, if they were faced with such a dilemma, would right the

---

ship, or at least attempt to, and walk the line. But then again, most people weren't criminals. People such as myself were prone to run, but I buckled down and made it a point to at least stretch things out over the weekend. Slim was happy to see me. Both he and his wife Jamie came down and visited me when I was in jail, and I felt good around him, like he really gave a shit. They weren't thrilled I'd gotten high before coming over, but they both seemed to take it in stride. He told me I was a dumbass for doing so, especially knowing I had to report come Monday, but he knew I was a knucklehead and likely expected at least some kind of bullshit to go down.

Slim really went out of his way to make me feel comfortable and told me I deserved so much more than the life I was living, but in a manner that wasn't condescending. I'd always thought that as long as I wasn't hurting anybody, I should be free to use without consequences. My perspective had been shaped by a self-centered, egotistical mindset, one that didn't take other's feelings into account, and I justified it by feelings of low self-worth. I started to realize that weekend just how much of an impact my using had on others.

It was a far cry from an intervention, but Slim invited some friends to his house over the course of the weekend, and those impromptu visitors made me miss the life I'd known before becoming a low-grade hype. I thought my friends had given up on me, but they expressed their love, thankfully, without leaning too heavy on the emotion. But it was the words of a little girl that hit me the hardest. Jamie was a nanny to Frances Bean—Kurt Cobain and Courtney Love's daughter—and I guess maybe the kid had heard about my fuck-ups because little Frances jumped into my lap and told me not to steal and that jail was a bad place. Her tone was that of innocence, a four-year-old angelic voice stating a simple truth—I was a loser. Knowing how her father had died, her words dialed a direct line to my heart, and the knowledge that my drug use impacted others, whether subtly or grandly, burrowed into my soul.

The efforts by my friends to show me I was genuinely missed and loved, while certainly heartfelt and emotionally provocative, wasn't enough for me to tear the blinders from my eyes, however. When I was left alone I immediately started feeling sorry for myself and when Slim went to band practice Sunday night, I went out and scored some dope. I spent the evening nodding out on his couch and when he came home later that night to find me in a stupor, he never said a word. He didn't need to; the look of disappointment and disgust was written all over his face. The next morning, suffering from the guilt of the night before but not enough to do my drugs elsewhere, I did a fat shot in the bathroom and came out of a healthy nod to Slim banging on the door and telling me to leave. I left his house feeling like a piece of shit and deserving of the nothing that awaited me.

I caught the bus back to the courthouse loaded and fooled myself into rationalizing my actions. I told myself that Slim would understand, that he'd do the same thing if he were wearing my shoes. As soon as I got to the jail, I was put in a cell away from the others in work release and told that I needed to submit a urine analysis. The cops knew I was high the minute they saw me—the UA was just procedure at that point. Even if I denied it and refused the UA, I was going back to jail.

Sitting in that cell, coming out of a tail end of a nod, I started to wallow in remorse and to reflect upon the self-realization that I was destined to fail. How could I get high knowing I was going to get caught? Was I so ignorant that I thought I'd get away with it? Did I feel unworthy of anything positive in my life? Or could it be that I was conditioned not to care...

The hardest punch thrown at myself, however, the one that drove into my solar plexus and filled me with pain, was thinking about Slim. He'd opened his arms to me, knowing I was a fuck-up, and made me feel welcome in his home. The friends I had went out of their way to take me in and show me a better way of life, and whenever they did, I'd shit on them. It was just starting to dawn on me how self-centered and manipulative I'd become. I felt it was only a matter of time before they gave up and left me to my ruin.

After sitting in that cell for a couple hours, reflecting on the self-inflicted rift I was creating between myself and the people who loved me, two cops came to escort me across the sky bridge to the main jail. I sat there for a few days and was eventually brought back to NERF to finish my sentence. By the time I was released, the regret for my actions had withered away like a mirage in Death Valley, leaving a barren and cracked landscape that knew only one form of rejuvenation—a needle and a spoon.

YAKIMA AND RJC

In the winter of 1997, on an evening like any other in many respects, I went into a bookstore in the heart of downtown to steal some movies. I'd stolen from there many times before and knew they were getting hip to me, but desperation spoke loudly to my junkie heart. My method for that store was to take the videotapes to the bathroom, sit in one of the stalls and take the alarms out. When I was finished and the movies were concealed, I walked out to see a uniformed cop stalking the aisles with his eyes on me. I quickly went back to the bathroom and took the movies out, then stacked them in a pile behind a toilet, angry because I had to abort the mission, but grateful that I noticed the cop.

As I was exiting the store, he pulled me aside and asked if I had anything on me. With feigned indignation, I told him that I didn't and "assumed the position". When it was evident that I didn't have any stolen merchandise, he decided to run my name to see if I had any warrants. I'd been caught stealing from a Blockbuster Video a couple of months prior but had posted bail and hadn't missed any court dates, so I felt secure knowing my name would come back clean. When he told me to put my hands behind my back, I was genuinely shocked. My initial thought was that I should've run when I had the chance and the second was wondering what the warrant was for.

The previous summer I'd been hitting Blockbuster's like a madman. Their loss was so extensive the company hired a private investigator to find out who was stealing the movies. Two months prior, when I'd been arrested, they got their name—William S. Hayes. The investigator looked into the stores reporting substantial losses and criminal reports that were made when the police were called. He scoured over an endless array of security footage in which I was seen concealing movies, running from stores and getting chased by clerks. There was enough tape that I could've starred in my own reality TV show of *The World's Dumbest Criminals*. There were fliers posted in stores telling their employees to keep their eyes peeled for me, "The Video Tape Bandit", so when they discovered my identity, all they had to do was file a case with the police department.

44

Within a few hours, I found myself back in the all-too-familiar setting of the King County Jail. Cold concrete, the sound of metal doors slamming, and the stale odor of lockup were there to welcome me back, and the kick was much harder this time. In each successive trip to detox or jail, it seemed the suffering increased and intensified. I tipped the scales at just over 130 pounds and couldn't put weight on because I couldn't hold down a meal. The diarrhea and cramps were relentless, but the worst was the lack of sleep. When I did, it would be for a period of no more than ten minutes, and I'd wake up sweating profusely, often catching a glimpse of a dream in which I was out on the streets.

Three days into my kick, when I was at my worst physically, a man I was in court with the day prior transferred to my unit on the 9th floor. He was a heroin addict like me and the only reason I remembered him was because he told me he had some dope, but couldn't pull it out in the court hold because he had it in the "safe". I dismissed him as a blowhard and wished an agonizing death upon him, a million times over. But when I saw him walking into my unit, it was like seeing the second coming of Christ. The hope that he held the remedy for my pain swelled from within and I knew that if he was still holding, I was going to get well.

It turned out I didn't even need to ask. He saw me when he was bringing his mat in and took a spot on a lower rack. He already knew I was sick from seeing me in court, or it could've been that he was worried I'd snitch if he didn't kick down, but he motioned me over to his bunk as soon as he got settled in. I was asked the standard questions a guy holding might ask: How many times a day did the cops walk through? Was it "hot" in there? Were there any inmates he needed to worry about? And then he told me to keep point.

While I was watching the door, his hand went inside his pants to his backside and like a magician, he conjured a chunk of heroin the size of a golf ball covered in layers of plastic wrap. Seeing a piece of dope that size was like laying eyes on the Holy Grail. He broke me off a half gram but then told me I'd have to figure out a way to do it—he didn't have a needle.

I had two choices: I could put it in one of the plastic sporks, add some warm water, mix it with my finger and snort it, or I could stick it in my ass—I chose the ass. It wasn't that I liked giving myself a prostate exam, but heroin in the rectum goes straight to the

---

bloodstream. I went to the bathroom, sat on the toilet and stuck that piece of dope up my ass as far as it could go.

When I started doing heroin, I'd fix it in my vein and the effect was instantaneous. It would hit shortly after I pulled the needle out of my arm—I'd feel the heat drive straight to my brain and it would hit like a brick…the ultimate numbness. Within the last year, however, it became a struggle to find a vein, and because I'd often fix in public restrooms and time was of the essence, I started "muscling" my shots. (Muscling is when you inject the drug into your muscle as opposed to a vein. You don't get the rush you'd get from shooting it and takes about ten minutes for it to hit, but you feel it basically the same.)

The anticipation for the drug to hit was like waiting on the corner for my dealer to show or anticipating a release from jail when I was sick—they both took forever and were beautiful promises. I prayed for the elusive warmth to hit, fantasizing about having a smoke to compliment my ritual of waiting, just like I did when I was muscling it, but it was of no avail. The pain started to subside and that was it. The euphoric bliss that would take me out of this concrete hell, at least mentally, never came.

I did manage to sleep a few hours, though, and when I arose from my short-lived slumber, the first thing I realized was that I felt like shit and second, that my savior was nowhere to be seen. He'd apparently made bail, much to my displeasure. I had formulated a plan in my mind to be his right-hand man, that I'd hook him up with my food trays and even offer him protection if he'd keep me well. I was desperate and delusional. The only reason anyone would have for getting me well was because they felt sorry for my pathetic ass.

The two weeks leading to my pretrial hearing were spent in agony, but by the time I made it back to court I was starting to feel a little better. When I got arrested and went to my first hearing, my arraignment, I'd been offered 270 days and quickly turned it down. When I came back to court for my next hearing, my public defender told me they were building a solid case, but if I pled guilty that day the prosecutor would recommend 200 days. My mindset at the time was bound to the path of a defeated dope fiend who didn't have shit to live for. I was certainly not institutionalized, but I looked at the time spent in jail as a consequence, albeit a rather severe one, to the freedom and release drugs gave me from dealing with life. The risk/reward factor

---

still pointed to drugs being a viable solution. Having done the math, I figured to get out in four months with "good time" and the time I'd already served. My decision to take the plea bargain was influenced by the knowledge that doing time was inevitable, and that I'd get screwed if I took it to court.

Within a week of my sentencing, I was back on the 4th floor working in the kitchen again. At this time in King County, prisoners were being transferred to Yakima County for overflow; the jail had reached maximum capacity and they were in the process of building a new facility in Kent. Yakima was contracted out and used to alleviate crowding until the new jail was finished.

Every Tuesday a trustee would go around the dorms to the bunks of inmates who'd been selected for transfer. The transferees would then roll up their property and disappear. The inmates whose names weren't on the list breathed a sigh of relief somewhat comparable to those avoiding the death train to Treblinka.

I'd seen this transpire twice and was one of those expressing gratitude each time because I'd heard all about the Yakima jail: that it was dirty, there was no program—it was rumored they didn't even have TV there—and it was far from Seattle. In my third week there, the trustee stopped at my bunk and told me I was catching the chain. I really wasn't too surprised and knew it was just a matter of time before I was on that wretched convoy.

They held us in the transfer module with our wrists and ankles shackled, and then packed us inside a county bus. We were hungry, angry and tired, and now, being driven to goddamn Eastern Washington. By the time we got to Yakima, we were burned out and ready to go to sleep, but still had to be processed. The magnitude of just how screwed we were became more apparent when we saw the Snohomish County inmates as we were being booked in. Snohomish County is directly north of King and used the Yakima jail for overflow as well. They looked happy to be leaving and would yell at us from their cells to tell us how fucked it was.

Compared to King County, getting processed was a breeze and within a few hours, we were escorted to an area of the jail called the Annex that contained six giant pods. The pods were massive concrete bunkers with huge dayrooms—two tiers in the back overcrowded with bunks and two bathrooms with a shower, a bank of sinks and a toilet. The jail was as dirty, if not more so, than reputed. The cops gave

---

47

us a mop after every meal and we were expected to clean the unit, but the cleanup duties were performed more out of ritual than of purpose.

The only good thing about the jail was the food. Yakima has a large Mexican population because of its farming industry, and we were fed accordingly. It seemed like we had tortillas with every meal, and although the food was rather bland, it was still much better than King County. The jail, or the area we were in at least, was something like 75% Latino and they were indifferent to our plight of being bussed in from Seattle every week. I discovered we shared a common bond, however. Just as most of us were waiting to be transported back to Seattle, most of them were waiting on a ride from La Migra (Immigration Customs Enforcement) to take them back to whichever country south of the border they were from.

The "border brothers" congregated in the dayroom and the bottom tier, and those of us from Seattle held court in a row of bunks along the back wall of the top tier. We'd talk about everything from girls, to music, to baseball…anything to help us escape our "Little Tijuana". It was so boring I requested a transfer to a unit across the hall called the "God Pod" because I'd heard they had access to TV and books. I lasted twenty minutes. I was cool with the cavity search given upon admission, but a preacher came in and started talking about the gospels of so and so, and fuck and fuck. The only books they had were bibles; it was slow death from boredom. I'd rather be nailed to a cross than listen to that shit, so I split.

Just as Tuesday was the day inmates from King County were transferred to Yakima, it was also the day we were transferred back. Late every Monday night, we'd sit together and listen for our names while an officer read from a small list, hoping we were one of the lucky ones on the chain. And every Monday night we'd end up telling each other there was always next week. It was rather humorous, in a twisted sort of way, and we made the most of it by laughing at our misfortune. One of our crew was a Vietnamese crackhead from the International District in Seattle. We'd pump him up all through the week, enough that he'd practically drool when he expressed his love for crack cocaine and how he missed Seattle in his Vietnamese accent. After not hearing his name on the transfer list, he'd sit on his bunk, broken and sullen, mumbling "next week" to himself. When he said "next week" it came out "neck wee" because of his accent. We delighted in this and began calling him "neck wee" because of his dejected Vietnamese mumble.

Being in that jail and doing absolutely nothing for close to two months made it feel like time had stopped, but the day finally came when we were called for transfer. After the guard read our names off his list, our little section of Seattle criminals started cheering and dancing in such a manner you would've thought we were being called for release. I had no idea no how many of the Mexicans in Little Tijuana knew English, but I'm sure they knew what we were excited about—we were going back to our homeland.

We were escorted to the transfer module to wait for the transport bus the following morning. While sitting in the cell, I picked up on the rumor we were being brought to the new jail in Kent, just south of Seattle. It made sense, being that they pulled all the Seattle guys out of the pods. There were over twenty of us in total, and we'd have the dubious distinction of being the first inmates in the new facility. Within a couple hours, we were all sitting on a bus, shackled from head to toe, and travelling west on an institutional journey. In a crazy sort of way, it felt like a field trip—we were leaving a place we hated and going to a place nobody knew anything about. Those two things, combined with the quickly spreading rumors, led to feelings of excitement and anticipation.

We drove back over Snoqualmie Pass then took a highway toward Kent, so I couldn't see the skyline of the city I dearly missed, but I was still happy to be back in King County. The bus drove through a massive portal and after we were in, a giant door closed behind us, securing us inside. I saw right away that where the jail downtown had height—it was twelve stories tall—this one did not, but it made up for its lack of height in area. It covered several city blocks, with corridors inside that stretched every which way. As we were being brought in, I noticed electric golf carts sitting intermittently throughout its halls, lending testament to the size of the corridors that sprawled within.

We sat in various holding cells in the booking section and after a length of time, were escorted to one of the many housing units in the facility. As we walked down the main corridor, a newspaper crew took pictures of us as we shuffled past to put in their paper. I never saw it, but I imagine it read something like "THE FIRST INMATES ARRIVE AT THE REGIONAL JUSTICE CENTER—WILL IT IMPACT YOUR SAFETY?"

———

It was strange being in a brand-new jail. There was no graffiti scrawled on the walls or etched into safety glass, no brooding stench of junkie, no shit, no piss or funk of a crackfiend coming off a two-month run. The guards were excited and curious; the ones working here were all veterans and had put their time in at the old jail or the courthouse, so the setting was new to them as well. Everyone was taking in their surroundings and exuded a calm demeanor I hadn't seen before.

We were assigned cells and when my door closed, there was a warm mechanical click, leaving me alone to adjust to my new temporary residence. I'd never been housed in a cell before, they'd always placed me in dorm settings, so I found the solitude discomforting at first. In dorms, you always had to deal with the activity and movement of other inmates, their loudness and uncleanliness, and the smell of other men's shit when you used the bathroom. I quickly found that in cell living I had privacy—a place to tune out the chaos within the concrete walls.

There were about eighty cells in each unit, in a two-tier system that circled a monstrous dayroom. Two dayrooms really, separated by an officer's station. One was carpeted and the other tiled with linoleum, and both had cable TV. From a door in one of the dayrooms you could go to an outside recreation area—enclosed within the unit, of course—with a basketball hoop and an open area permitting sun, and rain, to come through. It was a different method of confinement, certainly more progressive than the old system.

The two months I had left began to fly by, and even more so when I started working. I took up my reliable position of working in the kitchen, and when I had three weeks left, I transferred to laundry. My new position was great because I was able to go to all the units and see who was in jail. Because we had contact with other inmates, drugs and tobacco were more readily available to us. We had a dorm laundry room set up in one of the offices in the unit that, besides being used for our work activities, we'd use to stash our goods and smoke cigarettes. One of the guys came up on some crack from someone he knew, and I talked him into giving me a rock to smoke in the solitude of my cell.

My plan was to smoke it that night, so I went back to my cell and put the rock, a tinfoil pipe and some matches behind a card I had on my desk, then went out to the basketball court to shoot the ball

---

around. Leaving the drugs in plain sight was careless and lazy. The officers did random searches from time to time, but not enough to warrant suspicion that they'd hit my cell. But that's exactly what they did.

The afternoon shift change took place when I was out on the yard and in a circumstance best described as being on the shit-end of the luck barometer, one of the cops coming on decided to look in my cell. I can only imagine the look on his face when he looked on my desk and saw my stash in plain sight. I never got to see it, but I did get to see a contingent of officers converge on me. There were four of them and they came at me quick. They put me in cuffs, searched me and then sat me in a chair while they conducted a more thorough search of my cell. When they did, they also found $37 I had hidden in a book. (I found that money as I was folding clothes in the laundry room. I had felt something in a shirt pocket, reached inside and, to my surprise, happened upon the money. Cash was illegal to have in jail, which meant someone would've had to have snuck it in and forgot about it, giving me the opportunity to find it. Being that it was contraband, it was confiscated, but I was pleasantly surprised to find it on my books upon release.)

It took close to an hour and when they were done stripping my cell and bagging up my property, I was escorted to "the hole". We walked the long corridor past the many housing units, then down another corridor to the solitary confinement unit. The arrangement was similar to general population, with one-man cells on two tiers, except it was much smaller and all the inmates were in their cells. I was brought through the unit to an area in the back that was designated for problematic inmates. It was behind a wall of safety glass so the officer on duty could see if anyone attempted suicide either by hanging or slashing his wrists. The cells were the same size as the ones in general population, but I wasn't allowed any property and could only come out an hour a day.

The highlight of my day was when I was able to spend my hour outside the cell, and that was spent showering, using the phone or in the mini-yard where I was able to shoot a flat basketball around and breathe fresh air. Because I only had an hour, I'd often stay on the court and shoot, skipping the shower and taking a birdbath in my cell. I also found that the main part of the unit, the section on the other side of the safety glass wall, was designated for segregation inmates. They

---

51

were in protective custody because their crimes were too heinous to be housed in general population. It made sense because none of them got up to see me when I was escorted in, whereas everyone in the hole made it a point to see the new guy. They rarely looked my way during my hour, but when they did I gave them a look that reflected a hatred for their kind.

Five long days after I was brought in, an officer came to my door and told me I was going to my violation hearing. His words were like honey because I was stressing that they were going to file a possession of a controlled substance case on me. The hearing was held in an office inside the unit and I sat down at a desk, nervously awaiting my charges to be read. The officer conducting the hearing didn't appear too interested in the circumstances leading up to my infraction—he just wanted to know how I pled. To claim innocence would've been absurd; the only plausible defense I would've been able to muster was to say it was planted and had been set up, and that just wouldn't fly. So, expecting the worst, I entered a plea of "guilty" and waited for him to make his decision. It didn't take long, and I wanted to do a celebratory dance when he told me five days loss of time. I'd anticipated a loss of at least thirty days, and that, I thought, was a best-case scenario.

I went back to my cell feeling like I'd dodged a bullet, and within an hour I was told to roll up my property for transfer back to general population. For obvious reasons, I wasn't allowed to go back to the trustee unit and was placed in a unit with guys who weren't allowed to work because of either the severity of their charges or were prone to getting into trouble. When I told them I'd just gotten out of the hole, I received a touch of respect from just about everyone there. Not in the sense that they thought I was a badass, but because they looked at me as a fuck-up like them who got caught trying to get over on the man.

It was there that I did the rest of my time and I swore to myself I was done—a 200-day sentence was enough to curb my appetite for drugs. The final stretch moved rapidly after being in the hole and passed without incident. I was awoken in the early morning on the day of my release by the mechanized sound of my cell door being buzzed open and then went to the release tanks. The process was much more efficient than in Seattle, and about two hours later, I was walking down a sidewalk and breathing crisp morning air.

I had to catch a bus to get downtown, and because I didn't have any cigarettes and it was over an hour wait until the next bus came, I decided to walk to an AM/PM. As soon as I got to the store, the thought that a beer would taste great and was certainly well deserved popped into my head, so I picked up an ice-cold tall can of Budweiser with my smokes.

I drank the beer in an enclosed bus shelter, thinking how good it was to have my freedom and knowing I was finished fucking with dope. I only had a few bucks and had nowhere to go, but was extremely grateful to be out of jail. The knowledge that I could enjoy a positive, meaningful life without using any drugs was in my grasp, but as I got on the bus and inched toward the city, my will began to dissipate. The longing to stay clean was replaced by the old familiar hunger, and when I got off the bus in downtown Seattle, I knew exactly where I was going. I was going to score.

THE HOLE AND PAIN

My intent when I got off the bus was to get high just once, but, keeping with personal tradition, I was strung out within a week. In the few years I'd been using habitually, there had been numerous attempts trying to get clean in detoxes, none of them successful. As soon as I was discharged from whichever detox I was in, I'd hit the nearest payphone and call my dealer. I knew plenty of hypes who weren't delusional about their drug use—they were committed and had no desire to stop. But I did, at least to a certain extent. I didn't want to live as a junkie and experience all the pain associated with the streets, I just wanted to get high occasionally. That was my dilemma time and time again; the longing for that one fix would carry into two days and on my third, the beginning of a habit would be present and I'd open up the throttle, jumping into a sea of molasses and getting stuck.

That summer I began a new enterprise toward supporting my habit—selling heroin. My friend Trish (the one I'd seen outside the jail when I was on the work release detail), her boyfriend Paul and I were staying together, and they happened to have a dealer who had good product and would sell to us in quantity. For a business to thrive though, you need capital to tide you over while you broaden your clientele. That was how I became a viable partner. I generated much of the cash to keep us going while our business expanded.

By 1997, Seattle was teeming with several chains that catered to the now-flourishing music scene. There had been plenty of music stores before the chains moved in and I'd stolen from most of them, but on a petty level. Small stores were good for some guitar pedals or microphones here and there, but they knew their inventory. To hit them too hard would've been a bust because they'd notify every pawnshop in town once they realized they'd been ripped off. But the newer, larger stores were stocked with all kinds of goods that wouldn't be missed, at least not right away. I was like a pervert in a sex shop. I knew the value of the instruments and accessories, and I also knew what the pawnshops and music stores wanted. They had a variety of sound rooms you could privately play a guitar in, and at the same time stuff gear down your pants, making the stores a free-for-all if you had the balls. The staff were negligent as well, consisting of progressive-rocker types who didn't pay much attention to what was going on because they were too busy practicing scales or paradiddles. Not only that, but it was also perfectly natural to walk around, check out new products and not buy anything.

With my new hustle, I was in a position in which I could afford to keep us well until we had enough customers and money coming in to make it worthwhile. It was a great trade-off because they let me stay in their apartment and before long I didn't have to boost anymore. Our business did so well that we split up and I set up shop downtown at the Commodore and St. Regis hotels, both nefarious dwellings well suited for the drug trade.

By the winter of '98, I had an incredible interest in the scourge of Belltown—crack cocaine. While my earnings were modest compared to many of the other dealers I knew, I was still setting money aside, spending what I wanted without consequence, my rent was paid, and most importantly, I didn't have to pay to feed my habit. All of that disappeared when I started hitting the pipe, and it happened fast. By April of that year, I was homeless and hanging on by a thread. I still had my business but often needed my customer's money upfront before I could hook them up. They'd have to wait for hours at times while I met with my dealer and then bring them their dope. Any profits I made were sizzled up in my pipe and I'd wake up broke and desperate, calling my clients and repeating the cycle.

On a rock-fueled evening in April, I went out on a mission to score. I'd been staying at a customer's house on Capitol Hill and his girlfriend gave me a bottle of Klonopin, a benzo that mixes well with heroin but also makes you lose it if you take too many. I naturally overshot the mark and left their place in a blackout. Out of my mind and needing a hit, I somehow came across a car with keys still in the ignition. It was a stick shift and I have a few memories of the car stalling as I worked my way downtown, ending up in a 7-Eleven parking lot on 4th and Virginia. I had an extensive history of blacking out with pills, but it was a strange feeling to come out of one realizing I'd stolen a car.

I stepped away from the car like it had a bomb in it and speed-walked to the St. Regis hotel to find some crack. My money was gone fast and I spent the rest of the night sleeping on busses. I have no recollection of what transpired over the evening, but the next time I

—

55

came to it was in the morning and I was inside a music store in Fremont, trying to stick cymbals down my pants. The drum salesman was all over me and I ended up dropping the cymbals to the ground as I ran out of the store. They must've been incompetent or lazy, or maybe my desperation to get away outweighed their desire to catch me, but I managed to jump on the bus to the University District before the cops came.

Benzodiazepines (Klonopin, Xanax, Valium, etc.) have an extremely long half-life and it's not uncommon to have lingering effects from the drugs. It was because of these lingering effects that I again blacked out and was subsequently arrested. However, the arrest didn't come from my attempted music store heist, stealing the car or from being a passed-out vagrant. I was awoken from my next slumber by two cops grabbing me from my seat and bringing me off the bus. Being that I was in a daze, I didn't notice my pants were down and was shocked to hear I was being arrested for public indecency. I can neither confirm nor deny the charge; my recollection of the event is non-existent, but the police said they received a call stating I was making suggestive gestures, with my pants down and my hand on my dick, to a UW student. I still find it hard to believe that's how it went down, but who was I to say? I was certainly out of my mind and therefore capable of doing such a thing.

Regardless of what did or didn't happen, I was going to jail and booked for possession of heroin from the residue left in my scale. The time in the precinct and the booking process in the jail passed me right on by. By the time I regained most of my senses, I was lying on a mat on the 9th floor, trying to put everything together. I'd once seen a guy in jail wake from a Klonopin haze to find he was in for 1st degree robbery. He was in total shock and I now knew how he felt. Because it was a possession charge, a red outfit adorned my skeletal frame. There was an element of fear associated with being charged with a felony, but I'd been around long enough to know they didn't have much of a case.

It turned out they didn't have a case at all, and the DA rejected it outright. When it comes to drug possession, it's impossible to get a conviction if there aren't any drugs. The residue left in the scale wasn't enough, so their only action would've been to try to get me for attempted possession or a trumped-up conspiracy charge, both of which being a waste of revenue. And because they hadn't yet filed a public decency charge, I knew I'd be released that night.

Any positive feelings I had about being released were overshadowed by the intense sickness I was experiencing. The time crawled at a snail's pace and by the evening shift change I was still waiting for my name to be called. The only thing I'd found to help for kicking in jail, at least somewhat, was taking showers, and that's exactly what I was doing when the guards did their walk-through. They told me I had one minute to get out and go back to my bunk and I refused, knowing I was due to be released at any moment. They didn't take kindly to my inaction, and after I got dressed, they cuffed me up and took me up to the 11th floor. The hole.

Common sense has often eluded me at the most inopportune moments, and this was certainly one of them. As I was standing in that elevator, still cold and wet from the shower, I started to realize the magnitude with which I'd fucked up. My release was suddenly in peril. Remembering my previous experience with being in the hole and having to wait until I had a review before being let out, I couldn't help but wonder if the same thing would occur this time.

The first thing I noticed about the 11th floor was how dark it was. There were only dimly lit fluorescent lights, some of them flickering sporadically, making it look like a setting for a horror flick. It was deathly quiet, and as we passed each cell I had the feeling I was being watched. In my mind's eye, I visualized scenes in which inmates were beaten by vicious guards and wrists being slit by guys who couldn't take it anymore. My depressed state brought forth the feeling that ghosts were reaching out to me, beckoning me to share their pain.

They escorted me to a cell at the end of a corridor, where I was un-cuffed and given a bedroll. The hole here was much filthier than the one at RJC. The faint fluorescent overhead exposed the scrawls of people's names, bible verses, gang sets and cockroaches. I lay down in the quiet and then voices from other cells crept through the door. I heard a man begin begging for forgiveness, giving another prisoner cause to scream at him to shut the fuck up, which started an avalanche of insults, threatening each other with violence if given the opportunity.

I didn't sleep at all that night. Not that I would've been able to anyway, but the cacophony of voices and the ones in my head made it

---

57

impossible. Early the next day, however, a magical voice spoke from the intercom telling me to roll up my property. Within thirty minutes, I was back in the elevator and on my way down to the release tanks. My concept of time had been torn asunder and I was shocked to realize it was already seven in the morning. I'd never been released in the day before and was pleasantly surprised at how much more efficient the process went—it took about an hour. As I was walking out of the jail and turning my pager on, I swore I'd lay off the crack and pills and stick to heroin, a promise as empty as a junkie's bank account. I ran my business as I had before—in a blackout and fiending for crack.

One of my customers worked as a maid and would pilfer the medicine cabinets of clients, hauling in a cache of pills from time to time. She called me looking to trade an assortment of pills she'd stolen for some dope. Being that I was a pill aficionado, I came straight over and worked a deal that lined my pockets with Xanax and Ativan. I was in a blackout by the end of the night. I can recall meeting with my dealer and buying a quarter piece of heroin (6.25 grams), going downtown to meet some customers, having over $500 in my pocket, and the rest was a mystery. I woke up in Harborview the next day wearing a hospital gown, dazed and bloodied from a concussion, with all my money gone.

I remember very little of that night, but I certainly remember waking up in the hospital. I had a faint recollection of my dad standing over me sometime the night before, coming to the hospital to see his firstborn son on a gurney. Or was it my imagination? My grasp on reality was tentative at best, a vision distorted by satisfying a lust gone awry. It seemed the only time we spoke was when I was in jail...he'd listen as I swore, again and again, that I was done. He'd tell me he loved me and that I deserved so much more. And he'd also tell me he couldn't watch me run my life into the ground.

My friends and family were becoming distant memories, illusions held together by a fractured mind. I couldn't remember the last time I'd seen my brothers and sister, and my mom had recently moved to Los Angeles. I'd reached a level of depravity I didn't think possible. But I still couldn't stop using.

Besides whatever pain medication they gave me, I was given nothing for withdrawals. My cries for Methadone were met with Clonidine, a blood pressure medicine, and I left the hospital with nowhere to go. I caught a bus to Capitol Hill, a short ride, but with everybody on the bus staring at me it felt as far as Canada. I looked like a vampire. I was haggard and gaunt. Making matters worse, I was dressed in a hospital gown—my clothes had been destroyed. The feelings of loneliness and despair weighed heavy on my heart, but all I could think about was calling my dealer and asking him for a front so I could get well.

He hooked me up, but I was soon cut off. I didn't have a pager, had no money coming in and was smoking crack. My habit was substantial and with no income, I took up what I knew best—boosting.

DVD's had just hit the scene. I loved them, and it wasn't because I'm a movie aficionado—if I had a TV I would've pawned it. They were flat and easy to steal. I discovered you could pop the anti-theft cases open with a key or a knife, making them easy to take out, and the alarm sensor was usually on the surface of the packaging. I could have twenty movies concealed about my body within minutes. But the best thing about DVD's was that they were worth more—stores would buy them for ten bucks a pop, meaning a quick little lick would usually payout around $200.

In November of 1998, I went to a Hollywood Video on Mercer Island and filled a bag with movies, set it on the counter, walked through the alarm sensor and when the cashier was busy, pulled the bag to me along the counter, circumventing the alarm system. Unobserved, I made my getaway and went to a bus stop to wait for the Metro back to Seattle. Mercer Island is an affluent suburb of Seattle with a police force that strives to keep out the riff-raff. The riff-raff in this case happened to be myself. While sitting on a bench in the bus shelter, my attention focused on removing the packaging from the DVD's, I didn't see the squad car roll up on me. It didn't take a genius to figure out just what it was I was doing, so I was put in the backseat of the cruiser.

They tried slapping me with felony larceny because of the value of my stash, and instead had to settle with a possession of stolen property charge. The cops went back to the store to look at the tapes from the security cameras and to talk to the employees but couldn't get any footage nor get a statement to back their claims I'd stolen anything. I swore up and down that I found the movies at the bus stop and, even though my claim was ridiculous, they couldn't prove otherwise.

———

I had a warrant for violating my probation, so I came up with an idea to use a friend's name from my street days on the "Ave", thinking I could possibly get cited and released. It didn't work, they ended up booking me anyway, but I didn't want to tell them my real identity—I thought that maybe I could skate without getting a new charge. That also didn't work. Everybody gets fingerprinted in booking and they run your prints through the National Crime Information Center to check your identity and see if you have any holds. I spent three days under the pseudonym "Adam Staubach", but they soon discovered my identity. When I heard William Hayes being called over the PA, I knew I was fucked.

Two strange things happened when I was in under my assumed identity. The first was when a detective from the Mercer Island PD came to see me on my second day in. He wanted me to work with him, busting dealers as a middleman. This was before the NCIC check and he kept referring to me as Mr. Staubach, even bringing up Adam's criminal record and telling me it was in my best interest that I work with him. He told me that he'd get my charges dropped and to call him when I was released. I pretended to weigh the principle of snitching in my mind and with a dramatic flourish, told him I was onboard. A pager would be put in my property so he could contact me, and all I could think about was how stupid he was. I've never been much of a long-term planner but I'm an ace at the "here and now". I saw it as a shot at getting out and an opportunity to get a free pager out of the deal.

The second was Adam Staubach himself. On my fourth day in and after they'd discovered my identity, I saw Adam sitting in a chair waiting to see the nurse. The chances I'd see him in jail weren't too slim—he was also strung-out—but seeing him right after I'd used his name was a shocker. I wondered what would've happened had we been in the same unit when I was still using his name. I'm pretty sure it wouldn't have gone well. He had no idea. He was just trying to work some pills out of the nurse to help with his kick. I kept my cool and talked to him for a minute, never letting him know I'd used his name. Seeing him was painful. We were practically inseparable as teenagers and we had both succumbed to the needle. I felt like a piece of shit, like I betrayed him, but I wasn't about to say anything. My self-centered ass had an agenda—making it out of jail.

I was released after a few weeks, but never managed to stay out more than a month between November of '98 and September of

'99, being booked four separate times. I'd become a regular to such a degree there wasn't an area of the jail I hadn't been, and I knew practically all the cops, if not by name than certainly by face.

The public indecency charge from the year prior came up and slapped me by way of a warrant; the police ran my name when they saw me on a corner waiting to score and off I went. I only did thirty days for it but, to put it lightly, it was a huge inconvenience. And even worse, because of the charge, the classification unit banned me from ever going back to NERF. After getting out for that one, I was picked up again for having drug residue in a spoon. The DA rejected it, but right before I was to be released, I was slapped with a warrant over the Mercer Island incident. 120 days later, I was out on the streets, picking up a misdemeanor criminal attempt charge. This was at a Blockbuster Video on Lower Queen Anne. Luckily for me, I saw the cops roll up and took all the movies out before they grabbed me. When they first approached me in the store, a stack of movies I'd prepared to steal at my feet, they asked me what I was doing. "Just looking at movies, officer." When they took me to the back of the store, I noticed a flier with my mug shot on it, with the bold letters "CALL THE POLICE IF YOU SEE THIS MAN" posted below.

Stealing was something I did every day. If I could sell it and thought I could get away with it, I'd steal whatever it was or go to jail trying. By this time I knew all the buyers of goods, the ones who'd buy stolen merchandise then go around and sell it like it was legit: a Middle Easterner who bought cosmetics, batteries and tobacco; I knew a couple vendors who had a thing for Kerouac, Bukowski and Burroughs novels; clothing stores that bought Levi's and "vintage" clothing; LP's, CD's, VHS tapes and DVD's were sold to a store on the "Ave", and if they were closed I had bars I could hit where people bought my goods; I even had dealers who would trade dope for clothes, shoes and other items.

And then there were the music stores. Not the ones that sold records and CD's, but instruments. If I could've stolen only musical equipment I would have, but it just wasn't possible. There weren't enough stores and even though most salesmen at first seemed indifferent to me walking around in their stores, they began to take notice when they saw me come in. It wasn't long before I began to have salesmen tailing me, asking if I needed any help. I had to be selective on the stores I hit and the times I hit them.

When I'd first started boosting equipment, I stuck with floor pedals: distortion, phaser, digital delay, wah—anything guitar oriented. But as availability dwindled, I began stealing other items. Cymbals were basically flat and easy to steal as were certain pieces of rack mount equipment. I wore baggy pants with a belt I could cinch tight in a moment's notice, and I'd wear a snowboarding jacket that covered any bulges.

With time, and outright balls, I started boosting guitars— walking into music stores with a subtle limp, entering one of the many rooms with guitars mounted on the walls and going to work. My belt would be loosened and within seconds, I'd have the neck of a $2000 guitar stuffed down my pants and running the length of my leg, much like a splint.

The hardest part was getting out of the store. Standing in place, you really couldn't tell I had a Gibson Les Paul down my pants, but once I started walking it became more obvious. First off, I had to walk slow enough so as not to change the position of the guitar too much; the body of the guitar would have to rest flat against my stomach— any change and bulges would become very apparent. Second, I had to talk to employees when asked if I needed any help. Avoiding eye contact and manipulating my body so they didn't look at me too hard was crucial. And third, I had to do all these things and keep my cool. I'd pick up and check out items as I worked my way to the exit, peruse catalogues by the front counter, then slip out the door. After that, I'd have to find a place outside of the store where nobody would see me pull the guitar out. It wasn't uncommon for this whole procedure to take over an hour. All this knowing I had no chance of getting away if someone caught on to my act.

I'd sell the boosted merchandise to either music stores or pawnshops. Music stores were best, because they paid more, but I was known as a thief, so I had to find someone else to off the goods. I didn't like paying people to help me, though. The main reason was because I wanted all the cash for myself and there was a chance they'd short me on the return.

The worst stores were the pawnshops downtown. They paid a fraction of what the item was worth, but they did buy anything they could sell. I didn't have to worry if something was too hot nor did I need anybody with ID, I could just walk in and unload. There wasn't a pawnshop in the Seattle area I hadn't been in to either sell or steal musical equipment, and that included Bellevue to the east, Lynnwood to the north and Tukwila to the south.

If I had to get rid of my goods at a pawnshop, I usually went to one on Capitol Hill. They paid the best—even though they knew the shit was hot. In the five years I'd been selling guitars, pedals, cymbals and whatever else, there were a few instances in which I was given cash, but most of the time the item would be documented and entered into their database. And it was because of this documentation, combined with some detective work by the SPD, that I got my first felony conviction.

I was sleeping at a makeshift campsite at the time, by an old hippy bar called the Blue Moon in the University District. My eyes opened one morning to the sight of a city worker there to clean out the encampment, with two UW police escorts in tow. The cleanup man and his entourage told me I had to get my gear and go and they were cool about it, but their demeanor changed when they saw the stash of needles lying next to my sleeping bag. From that point on, we continued our discussion with my hands behind my back.

They ran my name and I was shocked when it came back with a felony hold. As far as I knew, I hadn't missed any court dates or picked up any new charges. They didn't have any details pertaining to the warrant, none they were telling me at least, but they did say it was for larceny. My mind was spinning on the drive downtown. I had no idea why I was being held. Funny thing though…I was involved in a foot race with a couple of these UW cops two days prior. I'd been cooking up a shot in a park on the side of the University Bridge when I saw a flashlight and the familiar silhouettes of the police walking my way. I ran down a bicycle path with a cooker in my hand and hid in some bushes until they split. Now, here I am on a bullshit larceny trip—karma is indeed a motherfucker.

I was booked for 1st degree theft, although I didn't learn the nature of the charge until the next day. It happened after an officer told me I had a visitor. Visiting took place on whichever floor you were housed, but I was being called to booking, so I went down nervous and apprehensive. My visitor was a detective for the Seattle Police Department and he had questions. Did I know anything about recording gear that'd been stolen from the South Center Mall? No. Did I know anything about selling stolen goods to Capitol Pawn? No, but I did make a few bucks selling gear for some guy—I didn't know him,

---

63

but it seemed all right. That was when he brought out his notebook. In it were notes relative to every item I'd ever sold at the pawnshop: from Elvis movies years ago to a Telecaster I'd offed last month. It was then that I realized the magnitude of the case. They had me. I decided to evoke my right to remain silent.

FELON

My encounter with the detective left me with numerous questions. How much did they know? Was there footage of me inside the store stealing? Was it just that store or were there others? Did they know about all the stuff I'd sold at the other pawnshops? And the biggest one: he said that he knew I had a drug problem and could get me help if I cooperated—how much time was I looking at? My mind was reeling from the possibilities and I knew it would be quite some time before I knew anything definitive.

The court system for felony cases ran quite a bit differently than misdemeanors. My initial appearance, the arraignment, was held within the same courtroom where the judge dismissed my possession of marijuana charge as a teenager, but all subsequent hearings were held in the King County Courthouse. There seemed to be so much more ceremony involved with Superior Court—the corridors were adorned with replenished marble pillars and beautifully polished floors; the lawyers and prosecutors wore finer threads; the inmates waiting in the holds were more solemn; and the judge's presence commanded more respect.

The proceedings were different as well. Besides having to sit in a holding cell all day only to be in a courtroom for a few minutes, there were also many more hearings to attend—arraignments, preliminaries, bail hearings, pre-trial hearings, motions…All of those existed in municipal court, but I never experienced them because I had always jumped on the first deal thrown my way.

My public defender, a sharp young Jewish guy named Shapiro, came to the jail and visited me when I had about two months in. Before him, the only people I spoke with were other lawyers from his office, and all they did was go to court with me to enter "not guilty" pleas and schedule future hearings. I was excited to meet with him and to hear what he thought about my case. At that point, I was still in the dark about my charges; all I knew was that they were trying to get me for 1st degree theft. He told me right away it wouldn't fly. There was no evidence that I was the one who stole the equipment. The store didn't

—

even have proof I'd been inside because the cameras, for whatever reason, failed to record anything.

He then pulled from his file copies of the police department's records of the items I'd sold to the pawnshop. In it were five years of documented instances in which they'd bought stolen merchandise. None of the items listed had previously been reported stolen, but it only took one to get the ball rolling. The item that kicked off the investigation was a digital multi-track recorder being sold for $1200, and I clearly remember where I was in the store when I stuck it down my pants, the empty box I left behind and the $200 I got for it. That one piece of equipment led to a report being made with the SPD and they quickly discovered I was the one who sold it.

With a detective on the case, it wasn't long before serial numbers were checked, inquiries made and an assessment to the loss of value realized. I was never told the amount, but the list from my lawyer's file was long. In it were over twenty guitars, all kinds of rack mount equipment, guitar pedals, cymbals, microphones, recording gear and even a flute (not to mention all the movies, video games, CD's and anything else I'd sold them). As he told me how much property was stolen, a shock of unhealthy pride rose from within— nobody boosts shit like I do. When he was done reading from the list, he looked me in the eye and told me I was a good thief and was extremely lucky. Because there wasn't a bit of evidence proving I'd stolen anything, it would be rather difficult to pin a 1st degree larceny charge on me. To get an easy conviction, a trafficking stolen property deal was on the table. It was still a felony, but one that carried less time. Furthermore, I hadn't yet had any felony convictions, which meant I was eligible for a first-time felony waiver and would only do ninety days.

I went to court the following week. Escorted through the marble corridors of the King County Courthouse, I passed by normal people—the types who had walked the halls when I was delivering packages as a bike messenger. They stared at me with curiosity and possibly a touch of fear. I must have looked like a hardcore criminal— the shackles and the red uniform, evoking unease amongst these citizens. I was fond of the attention. When I got to the courtroom it was empty—shattering any sense of falsified criminal self-importance I'd acquired along the way. There was a judge, a bailiff, two lawyers and some bitch on the steno machine—that's what my hardcore criminal shine was worth.

My public defender made it sound like the plea bargain was a sure thing, but it almost didn't happen. There was a stipulation he neglected to tell me—on top of the time I was to do, I'd also have to complete a stint in rehab and I wasn't exactly thrilled to go. About a year prior, I went through a detox without leaving and let one of the staff at the facility convince me treatment might not be such a bad idea. They got me into a place just south of the city and I lasted all of three hours. Getting clean sounded appealing, kind of, but that *Kumbaya* approach and the fake, brainwashed smiles turned me off.

That wasn't the issue, however. I'd do treatment if the court wanted me to, or at least tell them I would if it got me out early. The issue was that I hadn't been told about it beforehand. When the judge saw my reaction, he could tell I wasn't happy and was about to postpone the hearing when my counsel told the judge he needed a minute with me to discuss the situation. I was ready to take the deal but felt I should've been told I was supposed to go to treatment. With the issue resolved, the judge accepted the terms of the plea agreement and went to his quarters, wishing me the best of luck as he left. I was now a convicted felon.

I walked back to the holding tank feeling pretty good about how everything went down. With credit for time served, I only had two more weeks to do and the more I thought about it, going to treatment wasn't such a bad thing after all. It wasn't like I had anything going for me on the streets and knew it would be just a matter of time before I caught a prison term. Doing the math, I made a conservative estimate that the police recovered close to $100,000 worth of property and was fortunate there were no other stores or pawnshops involved. It seemed to me the detective could easily have found more stolen property from around the city, thereby pinning me harder against the wall.

The more I thought about it the more nervous I got. Then sure enough, one week after my court date, I got some unexpected visitors. I was sitting in the dayroom watching TV while waiting to go to work in the kitchen when I saw two men in suits walk in, talk to the cop at the podium, then walk into an interview room. I could tell they were detectives by the way they looked around taking everything in and prayed they weren't there to see me. The butterflies in my stomach

---

67

didn't flutter for long, though, because my name was called within a few seconds and I was told they wanted to speak with me.

They told me they were detectives from Snohomish County and were there because a guitar I'd sold to a pawnshop in Lynnwood had been reported stolen. Where did I get it? Did I know it was stolen? Had I ever been to music stores in Lynnwood? I told them I sold it for some guy I'd met on the bus, that I had no idea it was hot, then went out on a limb and said I'd never been to any music stores in Lynnwood.

They left unconvinced of my self-proclaimed innocence and told me I'd be hearing from them soon. I don't know if they really thought I'd confess but they did manage to shake the shack. My nerves were shot during the rest of my stay and I thought for sure I'd be summoned to booking and slapped with an add-charge. But besides being on edge, my time passed without incident.

My release date was December 21st, 1999, and as was usual for scheduled releases, I sat in a holding cell for a few hours until midnight rolled around to be set free. While sitting in that cell, I contemplated life and my current situation, wanting to be done and knowing I deserved more. I was tired of being sick, running the streets, courtrooms, jail and its drama, the guards…all of it. I figured if I went to treatment and got a job after I completed, I'd have a chance to live a semblance of a normal life. Being just twenty-seven, I knew I had a shot at it. I wanted to skate, I wanted to play music and I wanted my friends and family in my life. In my head I formulated an idea—I'd go to the welfare office first thing in the morning and see a caseworker to come up with a treatment plan and get set up with food stamps while I was there. I really didn't have anything to work with and the welfare office was as good a place as any to start.

At 12:01, just after midnight, I was a free man but had nowhere to go. I walked outside thinking about the hundreds of people who'd surrounded the jail three weeks prior, waving signs and demanding that political prisoners be set free (a World Trade Organization protest/riot had occurred by Seattle's Convention Center and turned downtown into a military zone, with cops moving in and throwing many of the participants in jail). I was still riding my firm resolution to not do any drugs, so I went back into the jail lobby until they kicked me out and then rode the night-owl busses around the city wasting time until morning. I felt lost with nowhere to go, and I was looking forward to the noisy and crowded confines of the downtown county office.

———

It was a long six hours of wandering aimlessly before I made my way back downtown. I got off the bus feeling strangled by all the nine-to-fiver's and walked to the county office on 2nd and Blanchard, right in the heart of Belltown and what was then crack central. It was impossible to walk those streets and not see the effect the drug had on that part of the city. The only people who couldn't see it being sold and smoked were the blind, and they'd certainly smell it, hear it and quite possibly taste it.

My will up until then had been surprisingly strong, but somewhere along the way it began to dissipate, giving way to the notion that getting loaded would make all the shit going on around me all right. The longer I sat in the office, the stronger the whisper became, until finally it was a voice screaming in my ear. I spent the entire day there, taking what I thought were positive steps toward improving my life, and by the afternoon I somehow justified getting high again. I decided I'd sell half of the food stamps and get a well-earned chunk of heroin.

My last splash turned out to be anything but that. After selling my food stamps to my favorite Korean on Pike Street, I went up to Capitol Hill to score and ran in to my friend Pat. Pat was selling both heroin and coke and offered to put me to work delivering to his customers. It sounded like a good plan and might've worked had it only been heroin, but with coke in the mix, shit was bound to unravel—what started as me making runs, ended with being locked in an apartment looking for veins and the elusive white heat.

I only "worked" with him for two days and on the third, he said he had to meet his dealer and never came back. I was left in the apartment with his girlfriend and a phone that wouldn't stop ringing, in a room barren and broken with syringes and burnt spoons lying everywhere—telltale signs of ghosts on never ending quests to still diseased minds. Three long hours later, I came to the conclusion he either got busted, robbed or was doing a bunch of coke somewhere and wasn't coming back any time soon. Waiting in that apartment was agonizing; I needed a shot of dope to shut my brain up. My mind was possessed with guilt over getting loaded again and I felt trapped in the world of drugs. His girlfriend was freaking out and seemed more than just a little unstable. Her ranting like a lunatic, combined with the bleakness of the setting and my need to get high, forced my next move—to hit a music store.

—

I elected to go to one I'd hit many times before in North Seattle. It wasn't a chain store but that hardly mattered. I'd stolen numerous guitar pedals from them over the years and even a '73 Stratocaster that I got $550 for. What I didn't consider was what happened when I went there last. About a month prior to going to jail this last time, I'd gone in and stolen a mixer for recording. The guy working the counter was suspicious of me, but I stuck it down the front of my pants and walked out of the store anyway. I expected him to say something as I was leaving and figured the only reason he didn't was because he was on the phone with the cops.

My stomach was in knots and by the time I got off the bus darkness was setting in. I walked in attempting to look as inconspicuous as possible and trying to exude a calm I certainly didn't feel. The man working the register didn't look like the guy from before, but I couldn't be certain and I made it a point to avoid making eye contact with him. I was nervous as hell but needed money badly, so I decided to go for broke and roll the dice. In the guitar room I saw a Pignose—a small-body guitar with a short neck and an amp built into it—sitting in a corner. I managed to stick the neck down my pants and cover the body with my jacket, leaving me with just one more task—getting out.

I limped my way toward the front of the store and when I got to the door, the clerk looked at me suspiciously and asked if I needed any help. I knew the gig was up, but I didn't have any other options at that point. It wasn't like I could pull the guitar out and apologize so I kept walking, feeling tied down and wishing I could run. I limped across the parking lot with the goal of pulling it out and running as soon as I got around a corner, but as I got there a large man flanked me and asked where I was going. Not waiting for a reply, he grabbed me and told me I was busted. He then ripped my coat open, revealing the body of the guitar, and told me to take it out. I did so, intending to run when I gave it back to him, but by that time the guy who initially spotted me was holding on to me as well.

A junkie who knows he's going to jail is like a man not ready to die on his way to the executioner's chamber in many ways. As they were taking me back to the store, I was cooperative at first, telling them how sorry I was and that they'd never see me again if they were to let me go. But as the entrance to the store loomed large, and the certainty they'd lock me inside until the police arrived, I became more desperate and began to try and break free of their clutches. I would've had a chance if it were just one guy, but with two of them I was fucked. The harder I fought, the more aggressive they became, until one of them put his arms around my neck and almost choked me out.

They never did manage to get me back in the store, but only because the police showed up before they could drag my thrashing body inside. I knew better than to fight the cops and once again found myself in the backseat of a squad car, on my way downtown and at the mercy of the courts.

While sitting in the car and waiting for the police to finish interviewing the employees, I noticed a paramedic pull into the parking lot. My initial thought was that I didn't need any medical attention, but then I noticed the man on the ground. While they were struggling to subdue me, one of the guys, the one who noticed something funny about me as I was leaving the store, had suffered what appeared to be a heart attack. The medics put him on a gurney and were wheeling him to the transport when the cops came back to the car and told me the news. With great deliberation, I was told I was being booked for grand theft and it was possible I'd be charged with something more severe if the victim's condition worsened.

The magnitude of my predicament weighed heavily on my mind as I was brought back to the jail I was just released from. I felt terrible for my actions, especially because a man I didn't know was going to the hospital, but more than anything I wanted to be back in my self-induced tranquil womb. And it didn't look like I'd find any sort of tranquility in the coming days. I was released just three days prior, after all. I was supposed to have no contact with the police and had probation to contend with, not to mention the treatment program I was supposed to be in. There wasn't a judge on the planet who would be sympathetic to my plight.

I'd heard plenty of stories about guys getting busted right after being released and it was always something I could laugh about. Now I was the one wearing those shoes. And to emphasize the knowledge that I'd fucked up royally, on my way up to the 9th floor one of the guards on the evening shift—a cop who'd seen me leave three nights before—gave me a look and shook his head, letting me know that he too thought I was an ass.

I had court the morning of Christmas Eve and was awoken by my name being broadcast over the PA, then joined a long procession of inmates going to see the judge. I was wearing felony red and it seemed busier than usual. By the time I made it into the courtroom, everyone had already eaten lunch and were probably looking forward to a fine and relaxing evening with their families, followed with the pleasant exchange of gifts in the morning.

After briefly speaking with my public defender, I walked into court and entered my typical plea of "not guilty". The judge, one I hadn't seen before, began to set bail at $2000 and I chose to speak up. It never did any good...you could beg and plead until you're blue in the face or escorted out by the bailiff, and the answer was invariably the same, but this time the judge listened to me. I told her about having just been released, that I was in the process of getting into treatment and asked her for a chance to redeem myself. She answered by lowering my bail to $1000—a gift in itself, but I pushed further. I told her that I appreciated her kindness, but $1000 was the same as $2000 to me and there was no possible way for me to raise that money. I also lied to her and said I had an intake date set up with a treatment center. You know, looking forward to making a positive change in my life and all that shit.

When she said that she agreed with me and was releasing me on a personal recognizance, I had a hard time believing it was true. But it was and I believe numerous factors led to my release: 1) It was busy and the prosecutor didn't dig up enough dirt to warrant keeping me incarcerated. 2) It was the afternoon of Christmas Eve and everyone was thinking about going home. 3) The fact that a man was in the hospital wasn't in the police report—probably because they were waiting to see what happened with him before they filed. 4) I gave the judge an Oscar-deserving performance reflecting my remorse. 5) The judge gave me a Christmas gift.

This was all speculation, of course, but it was the last time I was in the King County Jail.

LBC AND TWIN TOWERS

Even as the sun fades from Southern California's horizon, its rays leave a lasting impression. The summer day gives way to a crisp desert breeze, but the putrid odors of piss and food piled high in dumpsters parked haphazardly in alleys refuse to step aside. They cast a sour smell that you can taste with your nostrils. I breathe deep and watch as the beautiful people wander the streets—my bones envious, stirring up a hatred that dwells beneath the surface. They're together and tan and I'm sunburnt skin and a weak hustle. They're cosmetically enhanced and my face is scarred from hours of obsessive picking—fuck them.

I was sitting with my back against a palm tree on the corner of Broadway and Alamitos, in the city of Long Beach, waiting for my girlfriend to come back with a pack of needles. We'd just gotten back from a mission boosting DVD's in Orange County. Going there was always an all-day affair but the stores were much easier to hit than the ones in L.A. After the theft and bus ride, then having to sell them and score, we'd often have to wait until early evening to get well, but that night we realized too late that we'd left our rigs at the motel we stayed in the night before. Since we couldn't fix without needles, she went back to our dealer's to get some while I waited. I should've gone with her, she was holding the dope I'd just bought after all, but I was burned out and wanted to relax for a bit.

The palm tree I was leaning against could just as easily have been a Douglas fir, but I decided to split town after my last arrest. It was too hot up there for me—I'd burned out all my hustles and the cops were looking for me because of the latest guitar store incident. Being that my girlfriend was from Southern California, we hit the road. As far as I was concerned, I was done with Seattle, the gray skies and most of all, the King County Jail.

I'd been there about five minutes when a patrol car with two cops inside pulled up to the curb. They jumped out fast, asked me what I was doing, searched me and proceeded to go through my backpack. They asked if I had any drugs or needles and I swore with certainty that I did not. The cop conducting the search said he didn't believe me and sure enough, deep within the recesses of that filthy bag, he found one. He was not happy at all and jacked me up against his car, screaming that I could've given him AIDS. I didn't have any ID and when they asked me for my name, I gave them an alias I'd been using for some time, knowing I had a warrant in Washington. They didn't buy it for a second, and when the name didn't match anyone in their database, they brought me in.

I was taken to the Long Beach Police Department and things weren't looking good from my perspective. It was August of 2000— I'd only been in California since May and I was already going to jail. They told me they were going to print me so I might as well tell them my real name, and if I didn't, they'd book me under John Doe. I decided to comply and then waited to hear the details about my warrant. To my surprise, Washington State wouldn't extradite me for it. This meant two things. First, it wasn't as serious as I thought. If anything had happened to the clerk of the guitar store during my attempted theft, they most certainly would've gotten me. And second, it meant that if I'd given the police my real name, I likely wouldn't be going to jail. I was torn between laughing and crying.

I was booked for a misdemeanor charge of giving false information and after I was printed and put into their database, they took my belt, the laces out of my shoes and brought me to the top floor of the building where the city jail was located. The jail consisted of multiple holding tanks separating felons from petty criminals, and another section for females. Each tank, or dayroom, had a battery of about ten cells lining each side of the unit, and the cells had four bunks with the standard stainless-steel sink/toilet within. My cell had only one other guy in it, a rather obese man who sounded like a hog when he snored, and he didn't bat an eye when they popped the cell to let me in. I was given a ratty wool blanket and curled up on my bunk to sleep, wishing for another life.

At five in the morning, I woke to the sound of all the cell doors being opened at once, with a guard yelling at us to get in the dayroom. The room slowly started to fill with a mixture of drunks, crackheads, junkies and gangbangers in jail for misdemeanors. It appeared every race was present, but whites were by far the minority. After everyone had filed into the dayroom, a group of trustees came in and sprayed all the mats in the cells, then wiped them down with rags and took our blankets. When they were done with their work, the cell doors were slammed shut and we were forced to stay out in the dayroom. I looked at my cell with a longing I didn't know was possible and tried making myself comfortable at one of the steel tables.

It wasn't long after that breakfast was served, so we all got in a pathetic little line to await the slop. I hadn't yet started to really get sick and my hunger was fierce. I managed to weasel three breakfasts from guys who wouldn't or couldn't eat, knowing I'd be in the same condition soon enough, and after eating found a concrete patch in a corner by the bathroom to lie down. Half of the inmates—the crackheads, winos and junkies—were already lying under tables or in random places like my own to sleep or at least try. The other half, the gangbangers, sat on the tables and surveyed each other, told stories, talked about their cases and gossiped about what was going down in their neighborhoods.

The entire day was spent in the dayroom dwelling on my past and regretting every minute of it—if only I'd done this or if I'd done that. I was thinking about my girlfriend and if she was okay. Endless scenarios of her turning tricks for dope money and getting popped for boosting shit DVD's was making me crazy. I was the brain of the operation and she was nothing without me. The TV was the same as King County, with its endless barrage of talk shows and courtroom drama. Besides lunch and dinner, the only action was when people went to court or when the gangsters told the crackheads to shut the fuck up. Finally, at seven o'clock, the cells were opened again, and we shuffled into our respective homes for the night. I was in full withdrawal by then and didn't have a chance of sleeping the slightest bit, but the thin mattress and the even thinner blanket waiting for me were an invitation to at least some form of peace.

When the cells were opened the next morning, I made my way out to the dayroom with no sleep and one full day of sickness under my belt. The night had been hell and I felt a long way from any type of relief. I lined up for breakfast on legs that barely supported me and wouldn't have if it were up to me, but the cops made us. I tried to eat some of the dry cereal on my tray but gagged with every attempted bite. A hungry tweaker became the fortunate recipient of my food because of it. I took up the same spot on the floor as the day before, knowing I was in for a fucked-up ride.

My name was called for the court line and with it came a glimmer of hope. Ten other people and I were taken out of the dayroom, shackled together in one long chain and escorted through a corridor under the building that connected with the courthouse across the street. When we made it over to the court building, we were unshackled and put in a large holding cell. The cell might have looked the same—a large concrete room with steel benches and a sink/toilet unit—but the demeanor of the inmates was a huge contrast. Almost all the guys in there were Mexican, looked like they'd been to prison and they surveyed their surroundings with cautious eyes. In Seattle's jails, about half of the inmate population was white, there were only a handful of Latinos, only a few had been to prison and it was much more relaxed. I got the impression right away that L.A. didn't fuck around.

It took a little while for me to notice, but there were no black or Asian inmates in the holding tank. I found out later the tension between the Blacks and Mexicans was so high the deputies segregated the races to avoid hostilities. And the same went for Asians. Their situation was quite a bit more serious. The Mexicans had supposedly put a "green light" on them over an incident in which an Asian gang had killed some of their people at a party (a green light meant that, regardless of the situation, anybody aligned with the Mexicans had to "take flight" on, or attack, Asians whenever possible). Asians were housed in their own units to avoid conflict and repercussions for an act most knew nothing about.

I was finally called out and brought into a busy courtroom to see the judge where I met my public defender, a badly dressed man with a bow tie and sharing an uncanny resemblance to Gene Wilder. All I could think about was the movie *Stir Crazy* while he was talking to me about my case. He told me to plead "not guilty" and that he'd try to get me released on an OR (own recognizance). The judge briefly looked at my case and then denied the OR, saying I didn't fit the bill because I lied to the police and was a transient. He then set my bail at $500 and told me my next appearance was in three weeks. I went back to the holding tank utterly dejected and prepared myself for a trip inside L.A.'s jail system.

The tension in the tank was palpable. There were guys fighting serious shit and I didn't feel too inclined to talk about my petty misdemeanor charge in front of them. The bus taking us downtown to the jail showed up around six o'clock, and a group of deputies came into the cell wheeling a cart laden with handcuffs and shackles. After we were cuffed together in groups of four, the deputies then brought us down to a parking garage beneath the courthouse where the bus was waiting. It was basically a school bus, but silver with black and white trim instead of yellow, with the words "Los Angeles County Sheriff's Department" emblazoned on its side. I'd never seen anything like it; the ones I'd seen and been on were basically nondescript, but this one made it obvious to all the outside world what its purpose was for.

Inside the bus were pens separating different seating sections. The first division was set-aside for inmates who were kept separate for their own protection—single occupant cages for the snitches, rapists and transgender. The black and Asian inmates occupied the rear. I took my place in the middle with the white and Mexican prisoners. Even though there was a cage separating us, I thought there would be friction between the Blacks and Mexicans, and half-expected to hear threats of violence between the groups, but everybody minded their own business. The only threats I heard were toward the guys in the front of the bus. Not the gays so much, they'd just get teased a little and asked to show their tits, but the others endured words so foul and looks so venomous, I knew they were glad to be safe in their cages.

The ride downtown was hell. Everybody was yelling over the oldies playing on the radio, not just at the protective custody inmates in the front, but at the people we drove by on the freeway as well. The gang members threw up their signs and shouted allegiance to their sets, and everyone got into the action when we drove by any girls. The only way you could look out the window was if you were standing up and because we were chained together, I felt a constant tug at my handcuffs whenever the guy sitting next to me got up to check out the scenery. As soon as he sat down, another guy would pop up and yell about some "fine-ass bitch" or "punk-ass buster" driving by, causing everyone to get up and more jerking of the chains. I just sat there while they played their little games, hating them all and in my own world of shit, concentrating on not throwing up.

It took over an hour to get to the Twin Towers Correctional Facility. The buildings rise from the ground on the edge of Chinatown, down the street from Dodger Stadium, and were opened in 1997 to lessen the population of the Men's Central Jail next door. The sheer size of the facility was imposing—two massive concrete buildings dominated the landscape, each one as large as the King County Jail. We pulled in and waited for a monstrous barricade door to open, then drove up to an unloading bay where three other busses were

—

77

sitting. The deputies took the PC inmates off the bus first, whisking them off to wherever it was they were kept, then came back and offloaded all of us. We were then escorted through the first of many doors within the facility.

Four deputies just inside the entrance worked in unison to remove the shackles and once they were off, we were put into a cell with trash strewn all over the floor. We were told to take everything out of our pockets and leave it on the ground, excluding court papers. The cell held about fifty people and you had to stand or be stepped on. The veterans were jockeying close to another door, anticipating it to open, and when it did most of us made it through to the next holding tank. The drunks lying down and the people in the back were screwed until the next unlock. This cell was larger in area and its only purpose was to siphon guys into yet another cell. It was a systematic and crude procedure not unlike the locks of a shipping canal.

Finally, when the deputies were ready, the next door opened, and I got to see the deputies in action. They were on us like drill sergeants in boot camp. Their job was to demoralize the inmates and show them who ran the jail, and they did it for hours on end. We were told to march along a strip of tape along the base of a wall and to set our court papers and shoes in front of us at our feet. When we were standing shoulder to shoulder, and when the wall directly opposite of us was full, two lines of hungry and angry inmates facing each other, the door closed and the fun began. They told us to turn around and face the wall, and as they patted us down, they began yelling about respect and that they were to be addressed by two names—deputy and sir.

While we were being searched, I heard one of the inmates cry out in pain. We were told to look straight ahead at the wall, but out of the corner of my eye I saw a Chicano getting hit in his back by one of the cops. All the deputies were Mexican and seemed to have it out for the other Mexicans. Every time the cop would hit him, he'd follow it up with, "Where you from? Your gang ain't shit..." After getting hit a few times the kid made the mistake of telling the cop to fuck himself. Right then, two of the other deputies jumped on the scene and joined in the fray while the fourth kept watch on the rest of us. They whooped his ass right there, then cuffed him up and threw him in another cell to be dealt with later. The deputies demanded respect and had no qualms about delivering brutality to achieve that respect. They resumed searching us without missing a beat and when they were done, we were bustled through another doorway and on to the next location. While leaving the cell, I saw a group of trustees standing by with garbage bags and aerosol spray cans. They were there to clean up the tank and get it ready for the next batch of prisoners to walk through the revolving door.

We were told to follow a line on the floor to another cluster of holding tanks that must've contained close to 200 people. Jail identification bracelets had been put on by whichever police department arrested us, and a deputy scanned each of our bracelets as we walked by his station. The bracelets had a bar code and booking number that registered our booking information into their database. As we passed a trustee, he gave each of us a sack lunch containing a peanut butter and jelly sandwich, cookies and an apple, along with a small carton of sugar juice, affectionately known as Jim Jones. The last thing on my mind was eating so I gave away my sandwich, tried to drink the Jim Jones and wished I would die.

Everybody in this cell was waiting to see one of the classification officers directly across the hall from us. There were three long stainless-steel benches filled with inmates straddling them "nuts to butts"—a term used by the deputies to get men to pack together—and it became apparent that the man closest to the door would be the next man out. After figuring out the order, I straddled the backbench and waited my turn to be the man by the door. It didn't take as long as I thought and after about twenty minutes of being sandwiched between two grotesque street urchins, I was able to cross the hall and get classified. He asked me if I was affiliated with any gangs, if I'd been to prison, if I had any problems with any particular groups, as well as questions pertaining to education and military experience. When he was done with his subtle interrogation, he directed me to the next cell down the line. It was half full and almost all the inmates were ones I'd seen in various phases of the booking process. Nobody was straddling benches here—they were curled up on the concrete using sandwiches, rolls of toilet paper and anything else they could find for pillows. I found a section of wall I could prop my back against, kept my eyes open and waited for what was next. I had no idea what time it was, just that it had to be early in the morning. None of us had showered for days and when anyone took a shit in the no-privacy-to-be-had toilet sitting in the corner of the cell, the smell of turd would linger in the air.

—

79

We were in there over three hours before a deputy finally came to the door with a stack of cards in his hand and started calling names. Thankfully, my name was one of them and he gave me my card as I walked by, and then told me to go into one of the many cells in the next room. It quickly filled and I found myself sitting shoulder to shoulder with ten other men in an 8' by 12' cell. When all the cells were filled, a deputy closed the doors and it soon became hot, sticky, and stunk 100 times worse than the previous cell. Another deputy came by and opened the cells, gave us plastic bags, told us to strip naked and put our clothes, along with the cards we were given earlier, into the bag. The doors were then closed again, locked up butt-ass-naked with ten other men who were as miserable as me.

There was a line of six deputies outside of the cells doing nothing but watching us. The display of force was likely meant to show us how deep they were, but I couldn't help thinking they were there because they enjoyed looking at vulnerable naked men. After enduring thirty minutes of man-musk permeating my nasal cavities, they opened the doors and directed us toward a shower room close to 100 feet in length, passing a group of trustees along the way who gave us towels, soap and blue jail uniforms. Before locking us inside, we were told we had five minutes. It had the feel of a Nazi death camp and I wouldn't have been terribly shocked if Zyklon-B had started seeping out of the shower heads. All that came out was water, of course, but right after I'd lathered, the water was cut off, forcing me to have to wipe the suds with my towel.

It seemed everything the deputies did was calculated and with a motive of malice behind their actions. We'd been locked in the shower room for about an hour with the water shut off when two deputies opened a door on the far side from the one we'd entered from, telling us to shut the fuck up and listen for our names. When they were done with the roll call, we followed them to a large caged room. There was a trustee sitting behind a gate. He passed us beat-up, black Kung Fu shoes. I noticed that many of the gangbangers were given brand-new pairs. My pants were falling apart at the seams and my shirt, a much lighter blue than my pants, was missing its pocket, but the gangsters were given blues that matched and so new they looked pressed. It appeared there was a pecking order in L.A. County and strung-out white boys weren't on top.

Next to the shoe cage was another enclosure, caged also, with numerous inmates lying about on the concrete. Many of them were the type you'd see at the welfare office or in a downtown park, unkempt and wild-eyed. We walked by them and to another large area with steel benches everywhere. In the center of this room was a large podium that must've had ten deputies working there, some doing paperwork but most just lounging about and yelling at inmates every so often. At the base of the podium were a dozen gay inmates. Many of them had breasts and were kept separate from general population because of L.A. County's policy of segregating homosexuals. Some would look our way from time to time, responding to catcalls from some of the guys in my group, but most just sat there, sad and tired, awaiting a move to their next destination.

We were told to straddle a bench and slide up nuts to butts, then began a multi-day foray in what I discovered was the medical wing. Movement was slow—first you were seen by a psychologist, then an x-ray tech who checked for TB and another nurse who checked vitals. I felt like death by this point. I couldn't sleep, but all this activity amid no activity was wearing me out and I wanted to lie down. I told the nurse I was dope sick to hopefully get something prescribed to help with my kick and found myself being sent to the enclosure by the shoe cage.

If you were currently taking or requesting any medication, you were destined to spend time "in the cage". The cage was where inmates went and were forgotten about. It was about 30' by 50' in area, with inmates packed within. I took a spot on the floor and waited for my name to be called, not knowing how long I'd end up staying there. Most of us were there because of drugs and/or psychiatric issues; men with broken arms, heart conditions or any other kind of "normal" ailment were the minority. Outside the cage was a TV that played the same movie over and over—I've never been an Adam Sandler fan, but after watching *Happy Gilmore* close to twenty times, I can honestly say that I hate the man. I also saw the group I came in with, the ones I went through the beginning part of the booking process with and who didn't have any medical issues. They were straddling a bench just outside the cage waiting to be escorted to their housing units.

I stayed in that holding tank for four days. The only time I came out was when a nurse dropped by to take my vitals and when a doctor finally talked to me. He gave me the standard fare for junkies at the time: Clonidine, Robaxin and Thorazine. So now, instead of feeling like shit, I was a zombie feeling like shit. I'd been in the system over six days by then and was past the initial stages of kicking—the part when medication could've helped.

After seeing the doctor, I was moved to a housing unit. With days of nothing but peanut butter and jelly, Jim Jones and Happy Gilmore under my belt, I was ready for the change. However, there was a kinship that had developed among us in the cage. We were the Damned—pissed on by a correctional system devoid of progressive policies and destined for failure. But I quickly forgot about them when I heard my name called for the transfer line. I went out to the bench, sat nuts to butts, and prepared myself for the Men's Central Jail.

MCJ

Men's Central Jail, or MCJ, is located across the street from the Twin Towers. It was built in 1963 to house 3,323 inmates, but its capacity has since skyrocketed to hold as many as 23,000. To accommodate the steadily rising numbers, the jail had to do a number of things to compensate. Some of the methods included adding bunks in what were already small cells, implementing triple-rack bunks, putting bunks next to each other in dorms with no spacing between them, housing inmates in churches and dayrooms, having inmates sleep on the roof and also having inmates sleep on the floor. It is a dark and dirty dungeon of a jail that is constantly under scrutiny by various advocacy groups and will cost as much as 1.7 billion dollars to replace.

The journey from IRC (Inmate Reception Center. It encompasses the ground floor of the Twin Towers and is where inmates are booked, released and transferred to other facilities) to MCJ was one long hallway with holding cells intermittently placed along the way. I was in a group of over fifty people, and we walked in single file from the benches in front of the cage, over an elevated sky bridge connecting the two facilities, then split into groups and put into cells toward the end of the hallway. In each of the cells we passed were inmates going to other L.A. County facilities, waiting on prison chains or other counties to pick them up—it was a turnstile of criminals. We were kept in those cells for a couple hours and then brought to our last holding cell: a room about 100 feet in length, really just a hallway with steel benches and a toilet inside.

The contrast from that cell to the ones in IRC was sharp; IRC's holding cells were modern while this one, most certainly, was not. Flickering fluorescent lights revealed dirty yellow/white walls and a steady stream of water leaking from the broken sink/toilet, evoking images of ancient catacombs. We were there about thirty minutes when three deputies came in, exercising their power by yelling at us to shut up and having us stand on the benches. The room was packed, and I had to squeeze myself in to gain a foothold, but when we were all standing on the bench, one of the deputies started calling names from a stack of deck-cards in his hands. We were all going to different areas of the jail and our names were called out accordingly. When my name was called, I lined up with a group going to an area called the 5000 Floor.

We filed out and made our way into the interior of MCJ, passing a group of trustees along the way. They gave us bedrolls, L.A. County sack lunches and "fish kits"—named so because we were considered new fish in the pond. They came stock with a micro-toothbrush, toothpaste, soap that was just a step up from worthless and a razor that was fully worthless. After receiving our illustrious care packages, we continued down another hall with murals depicting a Western scene and cops running in the desert, then turned a corner toward a bank of escalators. As we went up the escalator, groups of guys peeled off to their designated floor assignments. Many went to the 2000, 3000, and 4000 Floors, and the rest of us went to 5000.

5000 was all dorms, and each dorm was numbered 5100, 5200, 5300 and so on. I was put into 5200 and by the time I made it there, my group had dwindled to four other guys. It was early in the morning, so most everyone in the unit was asleep. I grabbed a mat by the entrance and made my way toward one of the empty racks, setting my mat down on top of it. Right after I did, a white inmate came up to me, told me to grab my mat and to follow him. His tone was solemn and serious, telling me I couldn't just walk into a dorm and sleep anywhere I wanted. He kept calling me "Wood" and I could tell he didn't like me. I'd put my stuff down on a Mexican rack, apparently, and he felt inclined to enlighten me on the potential ramifications of my action, being that he was the shot-caller for the Whites. He then began to fill me in on L.A. County politics.

Race dictates prisoner interaction and that is close to absolute, at least as far as general population is concerned. Prisoners adhere to a strict code of rules and regulations called "politics". On any given prison yard, each race has a designated section where they exercise, play cards or shoot the shit. On most yards, depending on the size and/or racial tension, Whites, Southsiders (Mexicans from Southern California) and Native Americans share areas in truce, while Blacks, Northerners (Mexicans from Northern California) and Asians share others. This is a general rule and there are exceptions, but Whites and Southsiders are prohibited from exercising, eating or playing sports with Blacks and Northerners, and to violate that rule is tantamount to a severe beat-down or worse.

84

Politics are passed down from the prison system to the jails and we were obligated to abide by them. Blacks and Mexicans are an overwhelming majority within the L.A. County Jail and are often one small incident away from full-scale war erupting between them. To keep it at least somewhat peaceful, the Blacks had their own area in the dorm and the Southsiders had theirs. Because of politics, and because we were drastically outnumbered, the Whites and Paisas (any Latino that was from south of the border) rolled with the Southsiders. The Black's section of the dorm was off limits; we weren't allowed to walk through it nor were we to shower at the same time. I'd never experienced racial tension on this level and the shot-caller for the Whites didn't seem to believe me when I told him so.

With my newfound information regarding race in the system, I grabbed my mat and went to my assigned bunk. I was on a top rack and went out of my way to be as quiet as possible when I made my bed. I was worn out and full of fatigue, but I knew sleep was a long way off. Even if I hadn't been kicking dope, I wouldn't have been able to sleep because I was scared that I'd get jumped when I closed my eyes. There were only a few guys awake, as far as I could tell, and they were up by a TV set in the front of the unit watching *COPS* at close to full volume, but I imagined them slinking toward me as soon as I got comfortable and stabbing me.

My mat was only two-inches thick and when I lay on my side, I could feel the steel of my rack against my hipbone. My next court date was two-and-a-half weeks away and I wished I could curl up in a ball until then, but that obviously wasn't going to happen. I'd left a shit stain in the toilet and it was my job to clean it, so when the lights came on in the morning, I got up like everyone else and prepared myself for the day. Most of the inmates got up slow, but the Southsiders were all out of bed quick, saying *"Buenos Dias"* to each other. It quickly became evident they were a disciplined force in the jail.

There must've been 120 inmates in the dorm, and we filed out by race when the deputies opened the door. I counted close to ten other Whites and jumped in with them as they lined up. We had to walk in single file with our hands in our pockets, shirts tucked in and saying nothing on our way to the cafeteria, and there were plenty of deputies in the hall to make sure we abided by the rules. The cafeteria was filled with stainless-steel tables, and after grabbing our trays we were told to

85

eat fast and not say a word while doing so. We were given about three minutes and then, table by table, told to get up and leave. All movements were coordinated in a timely manner; as we were going back to our dorm, another group of men were coming in.

Most of the dorm went back to sleep after breakfast, which left me lying on my rack wishing I could. At 10:00, representatives from each race sounded off with "Good Morning!" in various dialects and from that point on we were prohibited from sleeping. Anything having to do with food was the high point of the day. I had about a week clean at this point and I was always hungry. Dinner was handled the same way as breakfast—we marched out single file to the cafeteria, where we ate a horrid concoction of lima beans and processed turkey bits that everyone referred to as eraser tips.

When I'd started going to jail, I wasn't exactly concerned with my personal hygiene. I'd usually take a half-ass bird bath in a café bathroom, then put on some clean clothes I'd stolen from a second-hand store, and if I was doing well I'd clean up in whichever shitbag motel I stayed in. That being said, I'd come in smelling foul from my bad habits and would need to clean up or hear it from the other inmates. The Whites had a "hygiene kitty" (a supply for inmates who didn't have soap, shampoo and so forth) under the shot-callers bunk and we were expected to use it. After dinner I got the shower slippers, some soap and shampoo, then took a shower, but forgot that my girlfriend had polished my toenails black a week prior to me getting arrested. The guys in the shower noticed this and when I made it back to the shot-callers bunk with the slippers, he told me I had to remove the paint somehow or I'd be "regulated".

I ended up scraping the polish off with one of my worthless razors but was ostracized after that; the nail polish threw them off and they didn't know what to think. The next few days were basically spent on my rack until one morning when my name was called for transfer to a worker unit. I left without saying a word and was moved upstairs to 9200—a kitchen worker's dorm. It was about the same size in area, but they packed more people into it by pushing the bunks together; they were so close I could've rolled over to the bunk next to mine.

I went to work the next day and was assigned a job with the elevator crew. I still hadn't really slept and had very little energy, but the job was great because it kept me out of my head. My crew's assignment was to clear one of the many service elevators filled with

—

shit from the floors above. The trustees on each floor packed the elevator with trash, water and piss-soaked sheets, uneaten jail food and anything else they could fit in there, then sent it down to us to clean out. We'd pull the wet bags and bundles out, watching rats and roaches scurrying about as we worked, then throw it all in a room to be sorted and sent to the trash pile or laundry room. There was no telling what was sent down and it wouldn't have shocked me to have found a body wrapped in a blanket.

Besides keeping me busy, the job had another huge payoff—I could eat as much as I wanted. When I wasn't busy pulling mountains of the nastiest crap in L.A. County out of the elevator, I was walking around the kitchen on an endless quest for food. To call it just a kitchen was a massive understatement because it was the size of a city block. Everything was stored down there: rooms full of sandwiches and juice, an endless supply of the jailhouse slop, boxes of cookies, even the food cooked for the deputies. It was all there for the taking as long as you looked like you were staying busy and didn't get caught.

Inmates weren't as high-strung, either. The politics still existed but I didn't feel like I'd get my ass kicked if I talked to the wrong person—the deputies had weeded out validated gang members and inmates with high-security levels. There were quite a few guys who were waiting on the prison chain, but none of them were going up for anything too crazy and because of that the environment was much less stressful.

The tension between inmates was less evident, but with the deputies it was still in full effect. Every night, while the cops were conducting their head count, somebody would be rolled up and put back in general population—usually for something as small as eating on the job. I didn't last long. After five days I was sent back for joking around with another inmate. There were a few deputies who were cool, but most were uptight assholes who didn't appreciate my good humor.

I was sent to a transfer dorm in 5500. It was empty compared to the other dorms I'd been in, about half-full and much quieter. It wasn't until I got to this dorm that my medication caught up with me. I had almost two weeks under my belt and didn't really need it by then, but I wasn't the one to refuse pills. The combination of Thorazine, Clonidine and Robaxin had me doing the shuffle, and the shot-caller for the Whites wanted me to roll up my property because of it. It was more due to me not fitting the traditional convict mold, I'm guessing, and he'd give me shit every time I came back from taking my meds.

It was just a matter of time before he or someone he appointed fucked me up, but luckily that day never came. Three days into my stay, a deputy called all the Whites to the front of the dorm. After checking us out, he pulled me aside and asked if I knew about Nazi Low Riders and the Aryan Brotherhood, then went on to ask if I had any affiliation to either. I assured him I did not, and after he checked my arms for gang tattoos, he asked if I wanted to work as a trustee in the "high-power" module. I wasn't exactly sure what that meant, but I was more than willing to do it.

He escorted me out, then down the escalator to the main floor. We walked through a wide corridor with rooms for visiting and other functions before stopping abruptly at a nondescript door with the number 1750 stenciled above and a sign to the right of the door stating "ALL PRISONERS SHALL BE HANDCUFFED BEYOND THIS POINT". Upon entering, I was stripped and checked to make sure I wasn't bringing anything in. He had me open my mouth and wiggle my tongue, run my hands through my hair, then bend at the waist and cough while he shined his flashlight into my ass. Content I wasn't hiding any weapons, drugs or messages, he showed me where my living quarters were and went to his office.

As soon as I walked into the dayroom I knew I had it made. There were two couches, a TV, a coffee pot and a kitchen with all the food I could eat. The sleeping area was a separate cell with only six bunks and double mattresses, a private bathroom, a light switch and it was quiet. I couldn't believe my luck. Compared to what I'd seen of the jail thus far, it looked like a little piece of heaven.

There were six men on the crew and all the guys were white, so racial politics weren't an issue. We were split into two-man shifts and we didn't have much to do. I was put on graveyard and our job was to make sure the place was clean and to serve the food brought up from the kitchen to the inmates.

Serving the food was an interesting task. It was a high-power module, which meant all prisoners housed there were either validated prison gang members (Nazi Low Riders, Aryan Brotherhood, Mexican Mafia, Black Guerilla Family, etc.), convicted of heinous crimes or had high-profile cases. It blew my mind to think the Night Stalker, O.J. Simpson and the Menendez brothers had been there at one time.

Because of the prison gangs, the deputies had us cover the info on our booking bracelets with tape. They were concerned that, should one of the prisoners get upset with us, retribution was a possibility. When we passed out the food we were to avoid eye contact and prohibited from talking to them. The food was dished out on Styrofoam plates so they couldn't make shanks and kept in portable storage containers. The containers were the size of refrigerators and wheeled from cell to cell as we did our rounds. Their purpose was twofold: to keep the food warm and to shield us from any cell-made spear attacks or shit-bombs thrown our way. A deputy walked with us as we passed out their food and he'd walk behind the container as well.

I never had any issues while on the job, but one of my co-workers did. He was a huge Italian jock from Venice with an affinity for steroids on the streets. His story was that one night, after leaving a bar, he'd been accosted by a man and a fight ensued. When all was said and done, a lifeless body was left lying on the sidewalk. The DA had offered him an eight-year term for manslaughter, which he declined, and was waiting to see if his lawyer could get him off or at least lessen the time he had to do. The day before I came to the unit, a Mexican had tried stabbing him with a rolled-up newspaper strengthened by soaking it in oatmeal—a spear, and the tip was probably dipped in shit and piss. The spear by itself can make a decent-sized puncture wound, but if the shit or piss gets into the bloodstream it can create all kinds of issues, hepatitis being just one of them. I had no idea why he tried to stab him, but after hearing the story of what happened my danger sense was on full alert.

Nobody famous was there when I came in, just your average group of high-power prison gang members, but on my second day they did bring in someone who achieved at least some notoriety. His name was Damian "Football" Williams. When the L.A. riots kicked off in '92, they started on Florence and Normandie, and the world watched as Reginald Denny was pulled out of his truck and then beaten to a pulp by a group of men. The choppers filmed all of it and one of the guys who smashed a brick into his face was recorded throwing up his set to the crew above. When the cops looked at the footage, they discovered it was Williams, that he was a member of the Eight-Trey Crips and it wasn't long after that they caught him. He was in for another charge this time around and while he was in 1750, he'd yell at

---

the deputies constantly, asking for a one-on-one with any cop who came near his cell.

Being a trustee in 1750 was easy time and it wasn't long before my court date came around. A deputy got me at five in the morning and told me to report to the court line. The court line cells were in a corner of the jail on the main floor and were packed with inmates going to see judges all over L.A. County. It was a beehive of activity, with deputies carrying chains and prisoners shouting names. I went to the Long Beach cell and tried to act like I was comfortable but was far from cool. Being a trustee in high-power was like being in a protective womb and I'd already forgotten the activity and insanity that took place in general population.

The drivers of the Long Beach court bus finally came and got us, bringing with them a brief respite from the jailhouse stories of pimping and the conquest of bitches. We were brought out to an open-air parking lot, enclosed within massive walls and containing over thirty busses. There were more busses leaving there than the Los Angeles Greyhound terminal and the coordination it took to get everyone to their destinations in a timely manner was mind-blowing.

After loading us on the bus, we navigated the roads surrounding the jail and jumped on the freeway to Long Beach. We were all court returnees, dressed in county blues, and many of the guys going back to court were fighting serious shit, so the feeling on the bus was solemn and subdued. We drove into the loading dock beneath the courthouse and were immediately separated by race when we were put into the court holding tanks. The cell I was put in had no more than five Whites and what must have been at least thirty Mexicans, most of them gangbangers. If there was any anti-white sentiment present, we'd be goners for sure.

Fortunately, nobody was in a "Kill Whitey" kind of mood, and I was pulled out of the cell for my afternoon court appearance without a hitch. I had the same public defender as before, the man who looked like Gene Wilder, and he told me if I pled "guilty" I'd be let out that day. I wasn't overly concerned about picking up another conviction, so I jumped on it. The judge said "time served" and then sent me back to the holding tank to wait for the bus back to county.

Within a couple of hours I was stepping off the bus with my entourage of criminals and walking back into MCJ. Because we'd already been through the booking process, we were brought to the

—

90

main jail and bypassed the Twin Towers. Coming back to the jail was bizarre. After our chains had been removed, we were put in one of many cells having turnstile entrances; you could go in but couldn't get out. It was jail, so there was nothing strange about that, but the turnstiles reminded me of an exit seen at a zoo.

We were all tired from sitting in cells, waiting to go to court and the stress associated with it. The cell was close to full when I walked in, but they kept putting more people in until it was standing room only, then were finally called out and told to form a line outside of the cell. Forty of us were told to take off our clothes, turn around and kiss the wall. Butt-naked men, standing shoulder to shoulder, was a sad sight, but it paled in comparison to what was next: they had us face them and rake our balls with our hands like we were actors in some twisted gay porn fetish flick. We looked like a line of men who had a thing for massaging our nuts in a group. And after they were done checking out the front, we turned around so they could check out the back.

First, we had to lift each foot and wiggle our toes and then came the fun part. One of the cops, some jerk a lady had the misfortune of marrying, yelled at us to bend at the waist, grab a butt cheek with each hand and to spread 'em wide. He was the "asshole overseer", I guess you could say, and there were two "asshole checkers" who shined their flashlights into our anal cavities to see if they could spot any goods. While the "checkers" were walking down the line, literally looking at a bunch of assholes, the "overseer" yelled out every so often to spread 'em wider, initiating a round of laughter from us each time he did.

When the visual check was done, the asshole overseer yelled for us to squat and cough. "1,2,3…Cough!" After doing it a couple times, the overseer yelled, "Harder!", sending us into another fit of laughter. We coughed four or five times, then put our county blues back on and left the asshole checkpoint as quick as possible, finding laughter in our misfortune, but ultimately feeling violated by their depravity. We received a handoff of two burritos from some trustees as we walked passed them on the way to our housing units. The burritos were given to us because court returnees rarely made it back for dinner, but they could also be perceived as a reward for enduring such degradation.

The entrance to 1750 wasn't far from where we'd been booty checked. I went through another strip/cavity search upon arrival, then went back to my quarters to get some rest. My experience with getting out told me it would take all day and sure enough, it wasn't until late in the evening when my name was called. While cleaning one of the corridors, an officer came and told me to roll it up for release.

I was given a pass and told to report to IRC. The long walk to the Twin Towers was eerie; I could hear deputies shouting commands to a group of inmates who were approaching from the opposite direction. As we passed, both prisoners and deputies glared at me. Maybe it was just my head, but they seemed to know I was being released and hated me for it. I walked for an eternity and finally came to an officer's station where they scanned my bracelet and sent me down a hall to the release cells.

The release cells were a strange place. People go from being cautious caged criminals to creatures wild with excitement and anticipation for the streets. The truth comes out there—the ones claiming to be players lose their bravado when they put their ratty clothes back on and ask the jailer for bus tokens because they don't have any money; the bible thumpers hiding behind religion forget about their Lord and toss their sacred bibles aside; the drunks going in and out of jail because they can't put the bottle down cry because they know they'll be back; and the junkies such as myself, tired of the streets and what they bring, will begin plotting and scheming to get his next fix.

The process took a few hours but was surprisingly efficient and after being moved from cell to cell, putting on my clothes, getting fingerprinted and checked for holds, I was let out to the streets at around four in the morning. There was a line of cabbies out front and I'd heard a few stories about them and their hustles. These yellow-cab leeches did everything from selling cigarettes for a dollar apiece to giving girls and guys rides and having them pay their fares with a blowjob in the backseat. They were sitting on their hoods like vultures waiting for the dead. I walked to a Denny's down the street. The restaurant had a reputation as a dangerous place—gangs supposedly patrolled it, looking for enemies who'd just been released—but being that I was only a dirty dope fiend, I wasn't too worried about getting jumped.

I'd spoken with my girlfriend a couple times while locked up and told her I'd probably be released that morning, so we agreed on Denny's being the place we'd meet, either there or in Long Beach. I sat there over four hours, bumming cigarettes, watching for her car and fiending to get high, and finally had enough, deciding to jump on the Blue Line to Long Beach and wait at the Denny's there. It was a better location as far as people watching was concerned—the one downtown was between the jail and the Hollywood Freeway with nothing else in-between. But it was more of the same: sitting in one place watching for her car and hoping she'd show up.

The self-pity I felt by this time was in full swing. My disposition had changed from one feeling excitement over being released to feeling worthless with nowhere to go. My clothes were dirty and ragged, I didn't have a pot to piss in and all I could think about was getting loaded. With a few hours of sitting on the corner of 5th and Long Beach Boulevard under my belt, I decided I'd had enough. The workers in the restaurant kept eyeballing me, as did the cops driving by, and I knew a record store down the street that was ripe for the taking. So off I went.

ORANGE COUNTY

About a month later, in October of 2000, my girlfriend and I left our motel on Pacific Coast Highway in Long Beach, journeying into Orange County to boost DVD's. I found her the day I got out of jail. I guess I should say she found me, and it just so happened to be when I was waiting on a corner for my dealer to show. She'd been driving by in a car her mom bought for her, probably wondering how she was going to get her next balloon, and there I was. The gods of smack saw to it that we reconnected so we could further our junkie activities together.

Her car had died the week before, and with it her usefulness, so we were at the mercy of public transit. I'd been secretly dieting on Xanax bars and had no idea how we got there, just a vague recollection of different busses, but we ended up at a Blockbuster Video in Buena Park. I had her wait in a Carl's Jr. across the street and went into the video store with a plastic bag and the intention of filling it up. That store, for whatever reason and unbeknownst to me, only sold previously viewed movies and I knew I'd have to steal a shitload to make the boost worthwhile. I don't know the exact count of movies I put in the bag, but before I left the movies-for-sale aisle the bag was full. I walked up to the counter like the *Grinch Who Stole Movies* and when the clerk began ringing up a customer, I heaved the bag up on the counter and walked through the alarm detector. I then walked around the counter and, while the clerk was busy, grabbed the bag, effectively circumventing the alarm system.

The heist went smooth and I made it back to Carl's Jr. unscathed, sat next to my girlfriend at a table and started removing price tags, alarms, and stickers from the movies. With the Xanax and heroin in my system, this seemed like a perfectly good decision to me. My girlfriend didn't think so at all. I didn't take the lunch crowd into consideration and when I started opening the cases, she insisted that we leave. When I ignored her advice, she began begging and pleading with me, telling me that she was sure someone would call the police.

I finally took heed of her warnings and had her call us a cab, but by then it was too late. Two cops walked in and they weren't there for cheeseburgers. They approached our table and asked me what I was doing, and when I didn't give them a satisfactory response, they

---

put me in the backseat of their cruiser. I told them I'd found the bag with the movies already in them but they didn't buy my bullshit. A simpleton could've figured out where they were from. They were plastered with Blockbuster stickers—with the store's address—so the police went there and spoke with the clerk. He told them he didn't see anything but when they looked at the footage from the video cameras, they found all the evidence they needed. The film clearly showed me setting the bag on the counter, then walking around the counter and grabbing it.

I went to the Buena Park precinct in a blackout and would snap out of it periodically, only to return to my incoherent state a short time later. All I remember was the jailer being a dick, the nurse telling me I was going to the Orange County Jail because I might need medical attention and the cop driving me there, telling me I needed to get my shit together. OCJ was in the heart of downtown Santa Ana, amid a grouping of various government office buildings. Booking took place in an area called "the Loop" and was like any other large city jail—inmates going through a succession of cells while getting fingerprinted, classified and so forth.

The deputies were even bigger assholes than the ones in Los Angeles and they all looked like rockabilly posers. Most of them wore fresh ink on their arms, with slicked back hair and sporting fades. Social Distortion and Sublime were being cranked out of portable stereos all throughout the Loop while they did their work, which was primarily talking shit and hemming people up. They reminded me of the frat boys who hung around in the University District and I did whatever I could to stay out of their way.

Going through the Loop was fucked, but still not as bad as IRC in L.A. I'm not sure how long it took because of all the Xanax in me, but by the time I was dressed out I was knocking at the door to sickness. When the crew I was with finished dressing, wearing orange jumpsuits with O.C. JAIL printed on the breast, a deputy escorted us upstairs to our housing units. I was brought to a dorm with close to eighty inmates, and assigned a top rack with a Mexican bunkie. I was starting to get a grasp of jailhouse politics by this time and was reluctant to bunk with him, but the shot-caller told me it was okay and that I'd be moved to a white rack soon enough.

I went to sleep knowing it would be the last I'd get for some time and woke up to lights blazing and being told by another inmate

—

95

to line up for chow. We packed into a staircase outside our dorm and I was able to check out the other inmates, quickly noticing there were no black inmates among us (I found out later black prisoners were put in separate housing units from general population for their own "protection"). I already knew about the racial disparity in Orange County, but it still took me by surprise. Most Whites hailed from Huntington Beach and the coastal areas south of there, while most of the Mexicans were from Santa Ana, Anaheim and Garden Grove, and they all said, "eh?" at the end of their sentences, much like Canadians.

We sat in the staircase for a long thirty minutes and when the door was opened, we walked out in single file to the chow hall. It resembled the cafeteria in L.A. County and we filled the tables after grabbing our trays. The food was better than L.A.—something everyone called "Red Death", a red meat sauce over potatoes. We were given five minutes before the deputies called us out row by row yelling, "Pick it up! Next row pick it up!"

I didn't eat or sleep for some time after that. I'd stay in bed when chow was called, relishing the short-lived quiet when nobody was in the dorm. With three days in, I went to my first court appearance, my arraignment, in North Court in the city of Fullerton. The holding cell we waited in was freezing cold, so I curled up in a ball underneath one of the benches in a futile attempt at keeping warm. I had the runs so bad that when I wasn't under the bench like a wino, I was sitting on the toilet, relieving myself of liquid poison. Whenever I sat down, I'd hear a chorus of, "*Agua!*" "Put some water on that shit!" and "Drop one, flush one!" from the other guys in the cell, accompanied with looks that reflected they'd have no problem regulating me if I didn't comply. I was thrust into a world where even taking a shit had rules.

Nothing much happened in court—I pled "not guilty" and was told my next hearing was in two weeks. The stress over wondering how much time I'd get was eating me up and I became that annoying guy who'd ask everyone what he thought of my case. Most thought I'd get sixteen months because of my lengthy misdemeanor record. The stress of not knowing was eating me up and I was dying for some resolution.

My girlfriend came to see me before court and I was thrilled. We met in one of those visiting booths with the glass windows and the telephone receivers. We were having our conversation, looking at each other through the safety glass, when she told me she'd started turning tricks. I couldn't believe what I was hearing, but I also knew the desperation that came with the lifestyle. I wished more than anything that I could've been out so she wouldn't have to again, but I knew it wasn't to be. She put some money on my books—probably earned by sucking cock. I felt a certain amount of guilt in that, a feeling that was overshadowed by the candy I'd buy. When it came down to it, I didn't care what she did as long as the money kept rolling in.

By the time my next hearing rolled around I was starting to feel better. I went to North Court expecting the worst and was surprised when my public defender told me there was a five-month deal on the table. I'd have to plead "guilty" to a felony count of commercial burglary and would be on probation when I got out, but I'd only have to do 100 days after "good time" was taken into account. I took the deal that same day, grateful I didn't have to go to prison and that I didn't have to come back to court. Something about the whole court process takes a toll on your mind and body, leaving you feeling drained and insignificant. I'd heard plenty of stories about men taking deals just so they could be done with the constant shuffling through the courts and jails, eager to get to prison and start doing their time.

With my court and sentencing done, I set my release date in my mental calendar and began counting days. I figured I had just under ninety days to do and did my best to stay out of my head. Depression overrode my thoughts much of the time, thinking about my girlfriend and where she was, what she was doing, and missing the time we spent together holed up in some dive for the night. I wondered if I'd ever see her again and if we'd continue living as we did. Getting clean was the furthest thing from my mind and I was constantly obsessing over the shot of dope waiting for me when I got out.

I'd been moved to a white rack by then and the guy next to me was an older man who kept a big bag of commissary under his bunk. All throughout the day, I'd watch with envy as he pulled out candy bars and honey buns, smacking his lips while he kicked back on his rack and ate like a pig. I seethed with anger strengthened by hunger each time I heard him digging in his bag to retrieve a snack. The crinkling of the plastic wrappers foretold the sounds I'd hear from his mouth while he ate, and it began to eat at me. I became so angry and resentful that I justified formulating a plan to steal some of his candy while he slept.

It was risky, to say the least. Getting caught would guarantee a severe beat-down but I was willing to chance it. I still wasn't sleeping well so I had no problem staying up, and around two in the morning I reached over, quietly pulled his bag toward me and took out two Snickers. I was extremely nervous because there was never a moment in a dorm when everyone was sleeping. They may appear to be, but each race always has a designated man keeping point in the event a riot jumps off and to prevent early morning ambushes. With this in mind, I stashed the candy bars and put the bag back as quickly as possible, then ate them with my blanket over my head, greedily savoring each bite like a kid after a Halloween score hiding his candy from his mom.

When the old man pulled his bag out the next day, I could tell he knew something was up. After looking in his bag and taking inventory, he looked around suspiciously as if to assess who might've stolen from him, then pulled some candy out and ate it quietly in a sad sort of solitude. He probably suspected me but never said anything, and the thought somehow entered my head that I could steal from him again. That night I took even more items, saving a honey bun and a couple of candy bars to eat later.

When he woke, the first thing he did was look inside his bag. It was like he knew a jailhouse gremlin was there to strip him of his goods. He looked at me knowingly, and then went about cleaning himself up for breakfast. A short time later I did the same, all the while walking in fear of repercussions. My fear turned out to be valid, for when I returned to my bunk, there were three Southsiders rifling through my shit, with the old man's property set off to the side.

I was fucked. He was angry about getting robbed and went straight to the Mexicans. They were the dominant force in the dorm and with their strict politics he probably felt they'd dispense a fitting punishment. The three Southsiders who found the stash talked to their shot-caller, and within thirty seconds I had a group of ten homies surrounding me, telling me we needed to go to the bathroom and "talk".

I had a fear something like this would happen and stole from him with a veil of denial covering my eyes. Thievery was unacceptable within the jailhouse, but I still thought I'd somehow be able to talk my way out of getting regulated or that nobody would really care because I was stealing from an old cantankerous man. The thoughts I'd once

---

98

held were irrelevant though, because I now had a small platoon of Mexican foot soldiers ready to do me in.

As they walked with me to the bathroom, much like a phalanx of guards making sure their prisoner won't escape, I pled my innocence, telling them I bought the items from the store and had a receipt to prove it (I did have a receipt, but it was from the week prior. The items I'd bought were long gone). They didn't hear a word I said, and their shot-caller told me to quit acting like a little bitch. In these circumstances, inmates are always guilty until proven innocent, and if someone is found to be innocent, it's only as an afterthought at best. My old receipt wasn't going to save me.

The bathroom was situated between the sleeping area of the dorm and the dayroom, out of sight from prying eyes. I was consumed with fear but didn't have time to dwell on it—as soon as we turned the corner into the bathroom they were on me from all directions. I was pummeled. They laid into me for thirteen seconds—a predetermined time frame used by the Southsiders—and I was rewarded with knots atop my head and bruises on my arms, legs and torso. I warded off many of the blows and escaped without any significant head injuries or blood loss and was fortunate to have been in a dorm that didn't have any hardened convicts in it. If there were I would've been smashed—they don't tolerate thieves.

They scattered like rats in an alley after handing down my "regulation" except for the shot-caller. He stuck around long enough to tell me I had to roll my shit up, that they didn't need any punk-ass thieves in the unit. That was the hardest part—rolling up my property and standing by the door in shame, while everyone in the dorm stared at me with evil thoughts running through their minds. There wasn't anyone in the unit who I considered to be a friend, but there were quite a few I'd played cards, shot the shit and ate with. The shame was a heavy load and I couldn't look a single person in the eye.

The wait for the deputy to open the door was eternal and I felt the weight of the world lifted from my shoulders after I made it out. The cop gave me a look of disgust and then escorted me out into the main hallway on the floor where I no longer had to endure the thousand-yard stares and hear people calling me a punk. I sat in the hall for over an hour before being moved to a unit next door. As soon as I was brought in, I was hit up by the shot-caller for the Whites, wanting to know why I was being transferred. I lied. I told him I was rolled up because a guy claimed I'd stolen from him but that it wasn't me. They'd already gotten word I was coming over and that I was a thief, but my story was close enough that I was given a break. He told me I was on probation and if anyone had anything come up missing, I'd be held accountable.

I'm certain the only reason I wasn't regulated again was because the dorm was much more laid back. Politics certainly existed, but not at a level in which tension was present every which way you turned. Everybody seemed to get along and there wasn't any particular race trying to dictate how things needed to be done.

Later that evening I was walking to the dayroom and saw Gabby from the Cadillac Tramps exercising in the bathroom. I'd met him in '94 after a skateboarding contest in Vancouver—his band played after the event and had started to gather a following. It was strange seeing him in a jumpsuit doing pushups and burpees in the county jail…the last time I'd seen him he was onstage pulling down his pants and mooning the audience, then leading a Conga line through the crowd. I'd always known them to be a sober band, so it was somewhat shocking to hear he'd started doing drugs again and picked up a case. It was another reminder that nobody was immune from drug addiction.

I'd been in the unit a week when I was transferred to a minimum-security facility in Irvine called the James A. Musick Jail—the Farm. I was escorted to the Loop with other inmates set to make the journey and after we were shackled, we boarded a bus and were driven to an expanse of property donated by a sheriff long ago.

I was assigned to a crew that prepared the deputies meals in the kitchen. We were able to cook and eat practically anything we wanted, but the drawback was we had to work with deputies standing behind us and watching our every move. The same cops who treated us like pieces of shit became angels when we cooked their food, providing the ingredients for a strange relationship.

My time at the Farm passed quickly. We were able to play basketball, softball and volleyball, and there was also a separate tent used as a pool hall. Besides the sports, there was a decent library, a barbershop and a constant supply of tobacco coming in. Visits were conducted in an open room and one of the guys I hung out with would get a "package" from his girl when she came to see him. He had to stick it in his ass to get it back to the yard, but that was fine by me. It was funny watching him walk back to the tent knowing he had a buttload of tobacco in the "safe", but the best part was when he had to take it out. The extraction took place in a bathroom with two of us keeping point, and after pulling it out, he'd run to the sink with his hands in front of him like a mummy and a look of disgust plastered to his face.

His little trick kept us smoking until the day his girlfriend stopped coming to see him. I was sure there was more to it than just that...she could've gotten busted, hooked up with another man or possibly fallen into the category of girls who jump ship as their man's release date approaches. Who knows what was really going on, but it was right around then that I got a piece of mail every inmate feared— the Dear John letter.

My girlfriend had been arrested shortly after coming to visit me, then jumped into rehab after she got out. According to her letter, she had an epiphany while there. If she was going to stay clean, she'd have to get rid of her junkie boyfriend. With the help of the U.S. Postal Service, the heartbreak and long, drawn-out fights associated with breaking up were negated and she'd be able to move on, relatively pain free. I could picture her dropping the letter into a mailbox with a feigned dramatic flourish and could also picture her sucking her new rehab boyfriend's dick right after. It saddened me but only a little. I knew our relationship wouldn't last and that it was our love for drugs that bound us together. What bummed me out was that she was the one who'd ended it and that she did it while I was in jail.

When I had two weeks left, I spoke with a pre-release counselor and was told about a rehab called the Cooper Fellowship. They took inmates straight from jail, got them jobs and transitioned them to a sober-living. I had absolutely nothing going for me and was more than willing. She said they'd be there to pick me up when I was released, lifting a heavy weight off my chest. Up until then, I had no idea what I was going to do.

The guy who picked me up was one of those twelve-step preacher types, taking great satisfaction in dropping lines from whichever page of his sobriety bible he thought was relevant to my situation. He had a quote for everything and said, "thy will be done" constantly. He reminded me of the fanatics who passed out religious pamphlets on the "Ave" when I was a kid. I'd been around long enough to recognize his fervor for what it was, so I just nodded my head when he talked about God and being "rocketed into the fourth dimension". Besides, he did come down to the jail to pick me up and I knew I'd be hitting him up for a smoke when we got to wherever we were going, so I figured being respectful was in my best interest.

The treatment center was in Santa Ana and seemed like a nice enough place. Twelve-step literature was strewn across tables and stocked the bookshelves, and with my brief experiences of rehabs in Seattle, I knew I was in for some long days full of counseling sessions, awareness groups and twelve-step meetings. Despite the bad taste treatment had left in my mouth, I was grateful to be there. I had a bed to sleep on, a break from the chaos on the streets and there were girls. With a sense of peace and the knowledge that everything was going to be okay, I settled in and reflected on my state of being.

My state of being was that I needed to get laid. The thought of getting high hadn't occurred but I did think about the girls and if I'd have any action with them. Without ever even seeing who was there, I started thinking about where we'd fuck when the time came. I'd spent the last ninety-seven days with nothing but men around and because I was clean, my drive for sex was in full swing. I needed sex to fill the void within, the hole that was empty with heroin out of my life.

I went to the cafeteria in the morning with the vigor and excitement of a young boy going back to school after a long summer to see my ex-girlfriend sitting at a table. She was sitting with another girl and did a double take when she saw me. The possibility that I might show up after being released had never entered her mind and she was visibly flustered. The rules stipulated that conversation with the opposite sex be kept at a minimum, but we talked long enough for me to know we were done and for her to give me the number to the pay phone in her dorm. Apparently, she thought it was important to tell me why she'd sent that letter.

I told myself I wouldn't call her but did, feeling the pain and loneliness associated with heartbreak seep into me after seeing her. It's easy to tell yourself that you don't love someone, or that you'll be better off without them, but the thoughts formulated in the brain are entirely different than those felt in your heart. I called her later that night, clinging to the hope she'd realize she made a mistake and that we should get back together, but she maintained her position. She told me how much she loved me, some crap about always being in her heart, and that she needed to move on so she could focus on her recovery. I couldn't understand where she was coming from, nor did I want to. All I knew was that I was left in the cold.

I'd gotten her out of my mind after receiving her letter but seeing her in person made me realize I missed her companionship. The feelings of longing and sadness changed to betrayal and anger only three days later, however. I was getting accustomed to my program, going to classes and meetings, when I saw her sitting out on the patio with her belongings. I tried to find out what happened, which is difficult when the person you're talking to won't look you in the eye, but all she told me was that she was being discharged. I knew she didn't want me asking questions and hanging around, but I felt an obligatory concern over where she was going and what she was going to do. And I was also secretly hoping she'd ask me to go with her.

I told her to call me and shortly after, watched with dismay when a Skinhead came by to pick her up. I found out later they'd been seeing each other for a couple of months, which meant they'd been fucking around before she mailed out the Dear John letter. Her claim that she wanted to end the relationship to protect her sobriety felt like a slap in the face.

That same day was also the first in which I was able to leave on pass without supervision. I'd been served with an order to pay child support while I was at the Farm, so my first pass was to go to the child support office to handle the matter. It was strange because I didn't have any kids and was served under my little brother's name—an alias I'd used in Seattle on occasion. The kicker was, the one who owed child support was a black man. It seemed to me the whole situation could've been avoided with some investigative work, but they wanted me to report to the department personally to clear up the matter. After going there and dealing with all the idiots from their office, I spent the rest of the afternoon at the skatepark across the street, feeling down on myself for not being able to skate and because my girlfriend had left me.

They didn't drug test me when I got back to the Coop, so I decided to test the waters. Because I could now leave the facility and felt that I could get away with it if I was careful, I formulated a plan to get loaded. I went on a pass for a job search the next day but instead of filling out applications, I went to a video store and filled my pants with movies. After stealing the movies, I caught the bus to Long Beach, sold the DVD's and scored some dope. When I returned to the

Cooper Fellowship, I did so without arousing anyone's suspicions. I was nervous the whole time, knowing that if I was drug tested my probation officer would be notified and I'd be going back to jail.

My fear of getting caught kept me clean for the next few days, until the obsession overrode my fear and directed me back to the spoon. I did the same thing as last time but overshot the mark as far as getting loaded was concerned. This time when I went back to the Coop, I did so on a supreme nod, and to think nobody would've been able to tell was indicative of just how loaded I was. I would've been better off if I'd decided not to go back because they called my probation officer.

One of the staff members suggested that I check into detox so my probation officer would see I was at least trying to do something positive about my situation, as opposed to running like a rabbit. They were adamant that I leave the facility right away, and after calling the detox to get a bed set up, one of the staff members drove me there. Having only used that day and four days prior, I knew I wasn't going to be sick, but I didn't want to go back to jail and it was my best option toward keeping my freedom.

The detox was a non-medical facility in the city of Stanton. I had to attend a barrage of meetings and was worried my P.O. would scoop me up, but the food was plentiful and there was a supply of tobacco. Groups of people came by and visited us every night to tell us how the twelve steps had changed their lives and how they could work for us too. Most of them sounded desperate to convert us to their way of life, much like the Jehovah's Witnesses who'd dropped by different places I'd lived over the years, spreading their unsolicited gospel. I didn't put much stock into what I perceived to be empty words, but I did take up a man's offer when he said I could stay at his sober-living if I completed detox. I was certain my P.O. would give me another shot after seeing the proactive steps I was taking.

I moved into the sober-living, one of those shitholes that packed each room to full capacity, then caught the bus to downtown Santa Ana the next day to report. The probation office was like any other city, county or state office I'd been in—filled with the poor and destitute awaiting a decision from someone or something that would benefit them or, as is more often the case, screw them. A lady who looked like she was at war with the world told me to have a seat and that I'd be called shortly. I don't know what she meant by "shortly", but I spent half the day sitting in the lobby, wondering if I was going back to jail.

My probation officer finally came and directed me toward his office, walking close behind me. As soon as I turned a corner, he ordered me to stop and face the wall. Within a matter of moments, I was in handcuffs. He told me what I already knew, that I was going back to jail, and after doing some paperwork, he put me in his car and drove me to OCJ. I'd been pleading with him the whole time I was in his office and he appeared to listen to me when I told him I went to detox and got into a sober-living, but ultimately my words fell on deaf ears.

Because I was booked during the day, the process moved rather quickly, and I was upstairs sleeping in a dorm by the evening. Going to jail without a habit was new to me and I took full advantage of the fact I could sleep, and three rest-filled days later, I was transferred to the Theo Lacy Jail in the city of Orange.

The deputies got those of us who were going into shackles and drove us about fifteen minutes north of Santa Ana. The jail was across the street from the skatepark and child support office I'd been in the week prior—it was a more modern version of the Main in Santa Ana and was also the largest lockup facility in Orange County. After being offloaded, we were moved around to different holding cells throughout the morning, eating sack lunches that were thrown into our cells from time to time, then split up and put into whichever housing unit our security levels designated us to—the unit I was assigned was the size of a massive warehouse.

I went to probation court a few days later in Santa Ana, thinking I had a shot at getting out early. A representative from a treatment center in Laguna Beach showed up on my behalf and told the judge I had a drug problem and should be released to their program, but the judge wasn't having it. She followed the probation department's recommendation—another ninety days in jail. I caught the bus back to Lacy a little bummed but not at all surprised, knowing how the judicial system worked. You might be lucky enough to catch a break here and there, but to get your hopes up too much was setting yourself up for debilitating pain from unrealistic expectations.

The good thing was that the next day I was transferred to the Farm. This time I was placed in a cabinet building program. We did close to nothing and its real purpose was to fool taxpayers into thinking that some of their money was being spent on rehabilitation. By having us in classes and training programs, it justified the sheriff department's exorbitant use of funds, thereby allowing them to allocate, or demand, more revenue from the annual budget. When it came down to it, I had no problem with not working. It made for a long day, but that was fine by me.

Being in the cabinet shop did have its moments, however. The shop was across from the softball field and twice a week the girls were brought down to play. They were terrible and only a few of them had enough skill to hit, catch and throw, but they looked great trying. We had to watch them without being seen but they knew we were there and would tease us—I saw more than one set of tits from girls willing to throw us a quick flash. The coach was also watching and would bust us for "fraternizing", so we both walked a delicate line of flirting with each other and not being noticed.

That was the excitement at the Farm. When I was two weeks from being released, I signed up to go back to the Cooper Fellowship and was surprised when they said they'd take me. A different guy picked me up this time and I liked him right away. He just stared at the road while he was driving, occasionally commenting on how everything was changing. He reminded me of a David Lynch character. He didn't preach at all and toward the end of the ride, told me the program had changed his life and was there for me when I was ready. Sitting with him was much better than riding shotgun with a guy I didn't know for shit, listening to him preach about the virtues of being a slave to a program and praising God at every opportunity. I could believe him and his silence, which was somehow enticing. It didn't mean I wanted to stay clean, but his coolness implied that all twelve-steppers weren't bible-thumping kooks.

There was a whole new crew of residents at the facility from when I was there three months prior. I was put into a different apartment, right next to the girl's dorm. Being that I was just there, I knew the staff would be keeping a vigilant eye on me. And they weren't the only ones—I had a neighbor who was checking me out as well. I didn't know her story, but at the same time I did. She'd poke her head out of her window and talk to me when I was on my patio smoking, her dark and beautiful eyes dancing about, always on the lookout for staff members who'd write us up for talking to each other. We never talked for long, but long enough to know we shared a love for heroin. I didn't need her to tell me about the abuse she endured as a child, and she didn't need me to tell her about mine. We were attracted to each other not just physically, but also from the pain we shared.

I'd been there close to a week when she came back to the facility on a nod. She was brought into the office and sat with them for about an hour, then escorted out with her belongings. I was crushed. I barely knew this girl but had already established a bond with her—in my mind, at least—and was getting up the nerve to ask her if she wanted to hangout or go to a movie. Anything. I just wanted to sit with her and listen to her tell me her story. I'd sit on the patio and smoke, missing our little chats and knowing she was out there getting loaded. With her gone, it changed everything.

The very next day, a guy who'd gone through the program some time before came to the facility to find a client willing to help him move some furniture. I was the first person he saw and when he asked me if I could, I jumped on it. It was a full day of work—I'd get fed and would be paid cash when we were done. All I had to do was help him move some shit into his garage. It was easy work and when we were done, he broke out a bottle of Jägermeister. We only had a couple shots, but I thought it was odd that a guy who'd gone through a treatment program would be offering me drinks. It wasn't exactly enjoyable because I half-expected him to start making moves on me.

Nobody at the Cooper Fellowship suspected anything when I came back that night, and with my slight buzz and pocket full of cash, I decided to score the following day. This time I had a plan: I peed in a bottle and hid it in my closet to use later if they got suspicious and wanted me to test. I knew the likelihood was high, whether they were suspicious or not, so the first thing I'd do when I got back would be to get my pee and get it ready. I also made sure I had a condom and after filling it, would tie it inside my pants to my boxers, then use a safety pin to poke it when the time came.

It was a long night of anticipation and longing for my drug but eventually daylight came. I took to the morning with longing and couldn't wait to be reunited with my old friend. I went out for a "job search" and was on my way to Long Beach by nine o'clock. It was still another three hours before I had the dope in my hand, but once I did, it was all worth it. Much like a climber reaching the summit of

Kilimanjaro, scoring the drug gave me a sense of accomplishment. I was king.

I did the dope in a gas station on Broadway and Alamitos—the same corner I was arrested when I first arrived to Long Beach—and spent the day along the dirty little beach and in Belmont Shore, oblivious to the world. When the sun began to set, I made my way back to Santa Ana. I went straight to my closet and filled up a condom with the clean urine I'd saved, tied the excess rubber to the elastic band in my boxers, then went to the office to tell them I was back. They didn't seem too concerned but they did want me to test, so I went with one of the staff into a bathroom and did my thing. I was in luck because the man testing me didn't stare at my dick—I pricked the condom with the safety pin and filled the cup successfully. The only issue I had to contend with was that I put too much pee in the condom, so after the cup was filled, I had a runoff of piss soaking my crotch.

I thought I'd pulled it off but the cup's thermostat proved to be my undoing. I was called back to the office and told the test was invalid because the pee was cold and would have to test again. He knew exactly what I'd done and used the word "invalid" just to be diplomatic. He then asked if there was anything he needed to know and when I told him I was clean, he told me to have a seat in the office until I was ready.

It was nine in the evening by then and I had no idea how to overcome my current predicament. My decision was to stand strong with my proclamation of innocence, hoping they'd believe me and that all of this would somehow go away. When it became apparent that my fantasy wasn't going to come true, I started to get scared.

The rehab was going to call my P.O. in the morning and after my last encounter with him, I knew I'd be violated. My decision was clear—I wasn't going to report. I made up a bullshit story, called my mom and told her I was being kicked out, and she told me I could stay with her in Los Angeles. Living with her didn't bother me at all; in fact, it sounded exciting. Up until then, most of my time spent in Southern California had been in Long Beach and now I'd be close to Hollywood and Santa Monica, places that in my mind embodied L.A. culture. I told the staff I was leaving and they took me to the Transit Mall in Long Beach. Because it was midnight by then and the train wasn't running, I took a seat at the station and settled in, nervous yet excited about my future.

PRISON BOUND

I woke up to a scream and when my eyes came into focus, I saw my mom standing over me with a look of panic on her face. It took me a few seconds to realize just what it was she was screaming about, but when I saw the needle in my arm it registered. She had screamed because she thought I was dead.

My memories of the night before began to creep into my consciousness, and I pieced them together like an ill-fitting and very dark puzzle. I'd gone downtown to score and while there, picked up some Klonopin on 5th and Broadway. I took the pills and caught the bus back to my mom's, then cooked up a fat shot when I got there. I vaguely remember searching for a vein and spending a considerable amount of time stabbing myself with the needle searching for blood. The Klonopin laid me out, inducing a blackout and putting me to sleep. If I had found a vein, I'm certain my mom would've woken up to a corpse on her floor.

I took the needle out of my arm and saw there was an abundance of liquid black tar still in the rig, then ran into her bathroom before she could stop me. Even if she hadn't been pounding on the door, I wouldn't have had a shot in hell of finding a vein that early in the morning, so I stuck the needle in my ass cheek and pushed down on the plunger. The sting associated with muscling a shot of dope brought forth simultaneous feelings of joy and pain, then I was off and running. When I opened the door, I could hear her voice coming at me from another world, telling me I had to leave and to never come back. I really didn't care at the time, I just knew I needed more drugs, and left her house not even bothering to grab the small bag of clothes I owned.

This was in June of 2001 and in the two months I'd been staying with her, I managed to get my habit back to a level in which I was boosting every day to support it. I had tried staying clean at first but soon discovered how easy it was to score downtown. Up until then I'd been scoring from a dealer in Long Beach, which I had no problem doing, but when I went downtown all I had to do was get off the train at Pershing Square, walk over to Broadway or Spring Streets and everything was there. Mexicans with mouths full of balloons whispering "*chiba*" filled the busy sidewalks. On 5th Street, between

Broadway and Spring, I could buy needles and pills from street hustlers, and if I wanted crack, the Brothers were selling that on Main. I could buy anything I wanted within a couple city blocks and it was all dirt-cheap.

My mom stayed on the west side, between the abundance of video stores in Santa Monica and the drug-rich haven of Pershing Square. When I took to boosting again, I did so subtly at first, but it wasn't long before it became a daily occurrence. As the stores in West L.A. became too hot, I moved on to stores in the South Bay, particularly Torrance and Redondo Beach.

It was to Long Beach that I went after my mom kicked me out. I spent the days boosting, scoring and doing drugs, and the nights sleeping in the bushes along the bluffs on the beach. I'd been hitting a particular Hollywood Video in Lakewood, enough that they began to recognize me, and in the week following my "eviction", I began to hit it even more. With a confidence boosted by benzo's, I went inside with two shopping bags and loaded them with DVD's. I grabbed a used VHS movie that was for sale and walked up to the register with my two bags, placing them in front of the counter where the clerk couldn't see them. I then bought the movie and did my reliable rip-off tactic, which was to walk back through the alarm detector with the movie I'd just bought and grab the bags I'd left there. Everything was going according to plan, but this time I was either too loaded to pull it off smooth or he was just suspicious of me, and he told me to stop as I was going out the door.

He grabbed my shirt but I kept walking, shaking off his grasp with a little junkie juke. I heard him yelling for me to come back but it was the furthest thing from my mind. With the jump I had and the abundance of bus lines in the area I might've gotten away, but made another bad decision that I fully blame on the Klonopin—I stopped running and hid behind an IHOP around the corner from the video store to take the DVD's out of their cases so I could sell them at a store across the street.

While cracking each case open with a knife, nodding out as I was doing so, two security guards responding to the clerk's call happened upon me. They came at me with pepper spray canisters drawn and when I stood up to run, one of them doused me. Blinded by the fiery pepper solution I didn't have a chance, but I still tried fighting them off when they grabbed hold of me. In many ways, it was similar to a man trying to get away from the cops in a high-speed chase; there was no way I was going to be successful, but the "fight or flight" defense mechanism running my brain said otherwise.

At some point a deputy pulled into the parking lot, jumping out of his car and running in to help. When I saw the billy club in his hand I became cooperative and gave up. I was cuffed, thrown into the backseat of his cruiser and then I was off to jail.

The Lakewood substation was a sprawling police compound used by the L.A. County Sheriff's Department. It reminded me of North Precinct in Seattle because of all the cop cars surrounding it, but much larger. I had a few Klonopin stashed in the small pocket of my jeans that the cops didn't find, so when I was put in a cell, the first thing I did was take them out and eat them. My state of awareness after that was one in which I was in and out of reality—coming to in different cells on my journey through the booking process.

I must've told them I'd be kicking dope because the last time I came to, I was in IRC in the Twin Towers. I have no recollection of being booked in, all I knew was that I wasn't butt-raped or beaten and slowly coming to my senses in the showers. There was a vague recollection of getting busted and as what transpired became clearer, I knew I'd be looking at some time. I was sure I had a warrant out of Orange County by then but that was the least of my concerns. The likelihood I'd be sent to prison loomed over my head like a wicked thundercloud. Anticipating the kick that was well on its way didn't help my mental state either, but I did as all the other inmates…I filed in line and went to the next cell.

The next few days were spent in "the cage", waiting to be seen by a doctor. After getting arrested and going through the intake process, it was hard to find anything positive about my predicament. Being surrounded by violence, angry deputies and an assortment of other issues, it was easy to feel the only light I'd see at the end of my tunnel was from another train, bearing down on me to take me out. I felt like walking death, stuck in a concrete hole with no escape, and knowing I wasn't going anywhere made that hole even deeper.

When my time in the cage was up, I was escorted to the Men's Central Jail. This time I was housed on the 3000 Floor. It was a dark and dirty habitat, consisting of various modules containing four rows in each. The rows were designated by call words: Able, Baker, Charlie,

Denver, and each row had thirteen cells with either four or six-man capacity—depending on which row you were on. I say capacity loosely because most cells had an extra occupant who wasn't assigned a bunk. He'd be given a mat and the floor sleeper would take up a spot under one of the bunks or in the space between the bunk beds.

I rolled into a four-man cell, tired from constantly moving around and glad to have made it there. The cell consisted of Southsiders and I was told I'd have to sleep on the floor. They didn't fuck with me but let it be known they controlled the cell and that Whites were a minority on the row. I didn't want any problems, I just wanted to do my time and hit the streets again. To question any rules or jailhouse policies would've been futile.

The cell was tiny—about 10' by 14' with four bunks, a payphone and an old stainless-steel toilet/sink unit. There was a sheet that was unrolled from a line spanning the walls for privacy when you had to take a shit and that was all you got. Whenever it was used a steady succession of flushes would ensue to try and alleviate the odor. At any given moment along the tier you'd hear gruff voices telling their cellies to "put some water on that shit!" in response to the smell of turd. The toilet got ice cold when you flushed it, freezing your butt cheeks, and would also spray your ass with water—a crude jail bidet. We had no toilet paper and had to use strips from our sheets to wipe, but it wasn't so bad because of the toilet's bidet effect. It was mandatory that you wiped the toilet and sink down after using it; to not do so would be cause for a regulation, which the homies were more than willing to administer.

There was a PA announcement at six in the morning telling us to get ready for chow, and a few minutes later our cell doors rolled open to a tier full of inmates. I only saw a few white guys—Mexicans and Blacks were the overwhelming majority. The talking between prisoners was kept to a minimum; at that time in the morning, everyone was focused on getting their food and making it back to their cell. When the cops were ready for us, they had us file into the main corridor on the floor to get our food. There was a cafeteria on 3000 but it wasn't used; we got our slop from a group of trustees who scooped it onto our trays from containers in the hall, then went back to our cells to eat. After we had all made it back to our cells, a deputy said over the PA, "Watch the gates. Gates closing." followed by the sound of all the cell doors rolling on their mechanized tracks and slamming shut.

The trays were made from soft plastic and when we were done eating, they were placed outside our cells and counted by a deputy to ensure none were stolen for the purpose of making shanks.

The module returned to silence after everyone had eaten his breakfast, but all of that changed at 10 o'clock. I didn't know which cell it came from, but I heard a Southsider yell out, *"Buenos Dias*! It is now program time! Brush your teeth and shake your sheets! Sound off when you're done with the mandatory routine! *Gracias*!" at which point every Mexican in the module stood at their bars and answered back, *"Buenos Dias*!" and *"Gracias a ti*!" when the one who'd started the shout-out was finished. The Blacks were next and though they weren't as demonstrative as the Southsiders, they did make their presence known. Someone from down below hollered, "Blacks! Throw down with your set!" which was met with, "Playboy Cuzz!" from one cell, "East Coast Cuzz!" from another, "Insane Crip Gangster Cuzz!" carrying on until the sets of everyone locked up were yelled out, concluded by shouting *"Asante*!" in unison. And last were the Whites. We were so few in number that our shout-out sounded pathetic. A white guy down the tier announced, "Good morning Wood Pile! Have a good day and respect the tier! Thank You!" I couldn't have heard more than ten chants of "Thank you!" in response, but I did hear calls of "Cowabunga!" and "Dude! Where's my car?" from other races making fun of us.

From that point on it was a madhouse. It was designated quiet time from 10 P.M. to 10 A.M. and then inmates were expected to program. Each race was different but the Southsiders took to their routine like soldiers. All of them had a mandatory workout they had to do and would shout out a cadence as they did so. The four Mexicans in my cell rolled with the Southsiders but were just residents in their neighborhoods, meaning they didn't run with any gangs on the streets, but were still expected to run a program inside the jail. They did the bare minimum as far as their routine was concerned, huffing and puffing through 113 burpees. When they were done they shouted out to the tier who they were, that they did their routine and sent out a loud and proud, *"Gracias*!"

The Blacks and Whites had separate rules as far as workout routines went, so many of us stayed in bed. I heard some of the more vigilant black gangsters shout out to their homies, and the skinheads to their comrades, but most of us without brown skin didn't do shit.

113

We obviously couldn't shower in our cell and were only let out for showers every other day, so the way we cleaned ourselves was to take birdbaths. The same sheet drawn for privacy when taking a shit was put up, and then the sink was filled and used to wash off your funk. It was a crude yet effective way to clean up after a workout, or in my case, to rinse the sweat of sickness seeping through my pores. It was a chore because of the time spent on your knees mopping and drying the floor when you were done, and if it was up to me I would've just laid in my filth, but my cellies were on my case, telling me that I stunk and needed to clean myself daily.

Sack lunches and Jim Jones juice containers were brought to our cells for lunch and dinner was carried out in the same manner as breakfast—we'd walk out in single file and return to our cells. The days were long and monotonous, devoid of even the smallest bit of excitement. If you didn't have a court, medical or visiting pass, you'd spend all your time in the cell. Showers were given every other day at best, a tier at a time, and were five minutes tops. Five minutes was usually about two and were cut short if anyone was heard talking. Most people took birdbaths to avoid the hassle and nobody wanted to wait to take a shower after working out.

It was a long week spent in that cell until I had to go to court. I was excited yet nervous because after going I'd have an idea at how much time I was looking at. It was held in Cerritos, a much smaller courthouse than Long Beach, but I didn't learn shit. I spent the entire day sitting in a cold concrete cell just to enter a "not guilty" plea and to be given a court date for the following week in Downey.

I was starting to feel better by the time I went to my next appearance. Certainly not 100%, but good enough that I was able to sleep a couple of hours throughout the day. The hearing was called an early disposition and its sole purpose was to put a plea bargain on the table. My public defender told me they were offering a year in the county jail, which I was willing to take, but then went on to tell me about my warrant in Orange County. The time I was sentenced to in L.A. wouldn't run concurrent with them.

He did, however, offer a reasonable solution to my predicament. I could plead guilty to grand theft and take a sixteen-month term, which would eat up my O.C. probation violation. I'd have to go to prison, but I'd get out relatively close to the county time they were offering because I'd only have to do half of the sixteen months. I was better equipped to separate fact from fiction by then and knew doing time in prison was better than doing it in the county, so I jumped on it.

The judge called my name and after hearing my plea, I was sentenced to a term of sixteen months in the California State Prison system. I was told that I'd be sent forthwith and was now considered to be a ward of the state. It didn't really hit me until I was on the bus back to County, and when it did, I started realizing the magnitude of my situation. While running the streets I hadn't given it much thought, but while sitting in jail I was privy to a whole new perspective. I kept thinking about a book I'd read in the King County Jail. It was one of those "Convict to Christian" stories that was hard to relate to, but the convict was a three-time loser who couldn't stop doing drugs and robbing banks. He finally quit but only after he'd had enough. He also had this thing about finding God but that wasn't until the end, and by then I'd read enough. What was striking about the book was how the character's desperation and level of depravity increased as the story unfolded. Was I doing the same thing? Would I get out of prison and find myself doing more serious crimes as time progressed?

Having been to prison was a badge of honor in many ways. I'd seen the respect given to those who'd just gotten out and to those inside. Even though my experiences on the streets and in jail had been extensive, I had never exuded the demeanor of a convict. Underneath the feigned image of the convicted I was now forced to portray, I was a twenty-nine-year-old little boy and I was scared. I grew up hearing tales of riots, violence and brutality in prisons like Walla Walla, San Quentin, Folsom and Attica. I heard what happens if you don't stand up for yourself—that you'd be labeled as a punk and taken advantage of by gangbangers. There was a mountain of mystery and fear associated with what went on behind the walls, and I knew it was in my best interest to show I was ready for it.

We got back to MCJ by the early evening and went through the ritual of spreading our butt cheeks, then went back to our housing units. The following morning after breakfast, I heard my name being called in a PA announcement, telling me to roll it up for Wayside. There were around twenty of us and after grabbing our property, we went out to the 3000 Floor corridor and were escorted to IRC. We were packed into four different holding cells with guys from other areas of the jail who were also going to Wayside and waited for the transport deputies. It took a few hours, but we heard them and their chains being wheeled in from afar and jumped to attention like animals at the zoo hearing the keys of the zoo keeper at feeding time.

The deputies opened the doors to the cells and demanded absolute silence, telling us we'd be left there until the next day if they heard so much as a single word from us. They called us out by name and when we were all accounted for, we filed out in a line down to the transport bays. We were then chained together in groups of four, boarded an L.A. County Sheriff's bus and were on our way.

The bus crawled its way north through the daytime Los Angeles traffic and got off the freeway just past Magic Mountain in Castaic. We drove onto a huge tract of land owned by the Los Angeles Sheriff's Department called Pitchess Detention Center that was used as overflow for the jail system. Pitchess had opened in 1938 and was at first a minimum-security facility known as the Wayside Honor Ranch. It was the first honor farm in California, housing about 1000 select prisoners who were cleared to work in a farm setting. The honor ranch closed quite some time ago but there were still four different compounds being used to house 8000 inmates: Supermax, Eastmax, Medium North and Medium South.

We drove into Supermax, one of the most modern of the facilities, and after the giant barricade doors closed, the deputies killed the engine and began offloading us. We were then brought to a large room with cells adorning one wall and stainless-steel tables set up in the middle. They had us line up around the tables and were told to strip and put our belongings on the tables. After doing a body visual and looking to see if we were concealing anything in our mouths, we were once again told to spread our cheeks and cough. The deputies looked inside our assholes so much it seemed like they got a kick out of doing it. As was usual, this started a contagious flow of laughter but this time the cops singled out one of the participants, handcuffing him and throwing him naked into one of the cells.

When the cops were finished checking out our assholes, we were given a clean set of county blues and ushered out to Supermax's main corridor. It stretched out in a lengthy L-shape with entrances to different housing units along its path—900 was the hole and ad-seg; 800 was medical; 700 and 600 were general population; and 500 was trustees. There were about fifty of us and we were all put into a large dayroom in 700. We were left in there close to an hour before a deputy

116

came to the door, calling us out in small groups. I walked up a long ramp with three others to 723, one of four units on the floor. It was a large dorm with an officer's station outside, set up so the deputy on duty could look into each dorm and see what was going on at any given moment.

Each unit had two tiers—a top floor lined with two-man bunks and a bottom floor with even more three-man bunks. I was assigned to the bottom floor and quickly discovered how cramped they were. After making my bed I talked to the shot-caller for the Whites. He gave me a rundown of the place. I was one of five Whites and we shared the phones and half of the tables in the dayroom with the Mexicans. I was told to stay on my toes because the Blacks and Mexicans might kick it off, and was also told that if they did, to stay out of the way.

The next morning before breakfast, I heard a commotion a few bunks down, then heard someone say, "Homies!" with a hint of tension in his voice. At those words, all the Mexicans rolled off their bunks and put their shoes on, while the Blacks did the same. They started grouping across from each other in the dayroom, and we—the Whites—gathered in a corner by the bathroom, away from the dayroom and what would inevitably be the battleground. Before it jumped, however, the deputy at the officer's station told everyone to go back to his bunk and lie down, with all the lights in the dorm coming on at once. Within a minute there were ten deputies standing at the entrance of the unit, telling us to come out in our boxers.

We were told to walk out with our hands behind our back and directed to a dayroom and then told to sit and face the wall. When the dayroom was filled, they closed the door and had us cool off. It was freezing in there and all we were wearing was our boxers. Everything had calmed down by then, for the moment at least, and it was eerily quiet while the posse of deputies tore our housing unit apart. A group of them came into the dayroom when they were done, close to two hours later, telling us how stupid we were. Being that the cops had a thing for looking into assholes, they had us strip down and go through the squat and cough routine again. Nobody laughed this time, and when they were done, they had us march back into our unit.

The place was in shambles. They'd gone through everyone's property, throwing the commissary on the ground and tearing the bunks apart. Blankets, sheets and mats were strewn across the floor, left for us to determine who had what. I didn't have any commissary,

---

but I saw quite a few guys who were pissed and trying to collect what belonged to them. They left us with a clear message—if you messed with the program, the deputies were going to show you who really ran shit.

The week following the incident passed calmly, meaning that it didn't jump. We had yard two times a week within a giant-walled perimeter, but besides that our time was spent in the unit. When we were fed, mobile trustee workers set up tables and passed us our food from an assembly line, scooping out our slop onto trays from mobile food containers. There was a TV in the unit that was controlled by the deputies. The idea was that if they were the ones changing the channels, it would reduce conflict. The problem was, they'd put on Teletubbies and other bullshit not fit for man, creating an environment that made it feel like we were in an insane asylum.

At the end of that first week my name was called for transfer and I was relocated to a trustee dorm. I noticed right away there was an abundance of Whites and that it lacked the tension of general population. I discovered later through time and experience that Whites, unless you were a fuck-up, on psych meds or fighting a serious case, were always sent to trustee dorms. My job assignment, if you were to call it that, was in the print shop. Forty of us lined up and went to work every day, but only a handful ever did anything. The rest of us were "active participants" in another training program set up to give taxpayers the impression there was rehabilitation and schooling taking place.

The days dragged but it was calm, which I preferred over the chaos on the mainline. That's not to say we didn't have issues, we still had politics and people were regulated for breaking rules, but the atmosphere was much more laid back. Even the police were calmer— I didn't go through one single cavity search during my stay.

Finally, about six weeks after being told I'd be sent to prison forthwith, my name was called for transfer back to MCJ and the prison chain that awaited me. I said my goodbyes to the crew I hung out with, gathered my short supply of property and went to the dayroom. When all the transfers were accounted for, we were escorted to a massive octagon-shaped holding tank near the entrance to the facility and waited for the LASD transport deputies to come and get us.

It was a long wait. There were over fifty of us, with tempers starting to flare because of stress, hunger, racial tension and whatever

118

else, and were there over two hours before we heard the magical sound of chains being wheeled in on a cart. The deputies came into the tank, yelling at us to shut the fuck up, then our names were called one at a time to be shackled. When we were all chained together in groups of four, we boarded the bus and began the drive down the 5 to downtown Los Angeles. The drive back to MCJ was bizarre—about half of us were going to prison and the other half home, meaning half were envious and the other half oblivious, but we all shared a gratitude in leaving the county jail.

When we got back to the Twin Towers, the guys being released were whisked off to the release tanks and the rest of us to cells inside the long IRC hallway. Most of us were put into cells with the word "Delano" scrawled across the safety glass, and the others were put into cells that said "Chino" and "Lancaster". I noticed that the deputies were much more respectful...they didn't talk shit and hooked us up with sack lunches. I don't know if it was because we were now considered state property or if we had garnered a minute level of respect by being sent upstate, but it made for good contrast.

It was close to 10 P.M. when we were put in our cells and it wasn't until 4 A.M. when we heard the chains coming for us. Some of the men slept and others sat around and shot the shit, trying to find comfort in a cell packed with men, but all of us jumped to attention when we heard the cart being wheeled down the hall. The guys having been to prison before had told us about the process. We were going to be sitting in cells all day while waiting for them to handle our intakes. When we were all chained together, we walked down the long fluorescent-lighted IRC corridor one last time and boarded the bus to North Kern State Prison, aka Delano.

DELANO

The bus lumbered out of Los Angeles, passing Wayside and Magic Mountain, over the Grapevine and into the fertile farming region of the San Joaquin Valley that Steinbeck had written about so many years ago in *The Grapes of Wrath*. But instead of a jalopy carrying the Joad family, our transport carried convicted felons.

The San Joaquin Valley stretches from Bakersfield to Sacramento, and while being one of the most arable regions in the world, it is also home to another of California's more nefarious industries: the California Department of Corrections. Of the thirty-three prisons within the state's borders, half of them lie in this region (that number doesn't include federal or privatized prisons).

There had only been a handful of prisons in California but in the late '80s and early '90s they started spreading like sores on a crackhead's mouth. Draconian drug laws, gang enhancements and three-strike laws, combined with a civilian population swept by fear, created a condition in which new prisons were being built at breakneck speed. California's answer, it seemed, was to lock up anybody who broke the law. (This led to severe overcrowding and it wasn't until recently that it was recognized as a problem, and only because the federal government identified it as such. The California Correctional Peace Officers Association, the union protecting their interests, was and is so powerful that they easily manipulated taxpayers by lobbying in Sacramento and using the media to further their aims, which was passing even stiffer laws so more prisons and prison guards would be needed.)

North Kern State Prison, or Delano, was off highway 99, about thirty minutes north of Bakersfield. I left Los Angeles excited to get on the road and to leave the county jail, but as we neared the prison that excitement was replaced by apprehension and dread. Even the men who'd been there before appeared to recognize our impending reality, giving way to a silence and solemnity that overtook the bus. Our transport pulled off the highway, driving west down a desolate road, and we all looked out the window toward our destination. Lights used to illuminate the prison yard rose high above three tall fences. The inner and outer fences were laden with razor wire and a high-voltage electrical fence was sandwiched between. Guard towers stood at intervals and I could see their occupants standing by with Mini-14 assault rifles. It was a bleak setting and it was very real.

The bus drove up to a gated entrance and after we pulled in, a California Department of Corrections officer walked up and conducted a search, using a mirror at the end of a rod to check the undercarriage of the bus and looking through the luggage compartments. When he saw there weren't any weapons or stowaways aboard, we went through another gate and came to a stop by an entrance to one of the buildings. We walked off the bus in our shower slippers to a blast of Bakersfield heat. The deputies then removed our handcuffs, leaving us with our new wards, and drove back to L.A.

There was a small force of CDC officers wearing green jumpsuits standing by to bring us in and looking like they were ready for action. They marched us inside single file and began a booking process that would take all day. We were told to strip, then were searched by an officer in a manner similar to how the deputies conducted them in Los Angeles, except here it was much more serious and there was no laughter involved; I could feel his eyes looking into my asshole as I squatted and coughed. We were handed boxers and socks by an inmate worker, then directed toward a barber who'd shave our heads if need be.

The intake process took place in an area called R and R (Receiving and Release) and went significantly smoother in the prison system. Much of that was because of the demeanor of the officers. They showed us a fair amount of respect as opposed to the deputies in County who did not. Correctional officers busied themselves handling tasks relevant to our placement, keeping an eye on us and taking mugshots. We were all interrogated after a few hours by a C.O. (correctional officer), asking us who we ran with, if we were a member of a prison gang and if we had any enemies. He also documented our tattoos. When he was finished with his inquiry, we were given orange pants and shirts labeled with the words CDC PRISONER, and put in a cell to await our housing assignments.

It was late in the afternoon by the time our escort arrived. He brought us all in a group to D Yard, where we were split into smaller groups reflecting where we were being housed. D Yard had six buildings that looked like concrete bunkers, flanking one side of a stretch of grass over a football field in length. I was put in a caged area with two others outside of our housing unit. We sat on stainless-steel tables hot enough to fry eggs on, waiting for a C.O. to let us in.

The heat outside was stifling. My previous experiences with the San Joaquin Valley's temperature had been limited to driving through it on my way to San Francisco or Los Angeles when I was younger. Being on a concrete patio without any shading in inferno-like heat offered me a perspective of what it was like in hell. I couldn't imagine anyone living in such a setting and made a mental note never to return.

We sat out there cooking until a C.O. walked out from a catwalk and told us to enter. He was stationed on the second tier, separate from the rest of the housing unit, but with full visual capabilities of everything going on below. I was able to look up into his station through a safety glass window set in his floor and saw a Mini-14 and a shotgun propped on a rack. He told us which cells we were assigned as we entered and to go straight to our doors.

In the cellblock were two tiers of cells, banking around in an elongated U-shape. A massive dayroom with rows of stainless-steel tables was in the middle of the unit, with an area lined with benches sitting beneath a TV set off to the side. Stenciled in places on the concrete walls were the words "WARNING NO WARNING SHOTS" and "*AVISO NO DISPARE.*" As we walked to our housing assignments, I could see faces in the cell windows looking out at us, checking to see what we were about. We were on the shit-end of a microscope, being analyzed by a pack of wolves.

My cell was on the bottom tier and when I walked up to it, I saw a burly Skinhead peering out the window. After the door popped open, he greeted me by helping me with my bedroll and telling me his name was Bam-Bam from Antelope Valley. He put my bedroll on the top bunk and asked me the standard introductory questions: what my name was, where I was from and how much time I was doing. I'd shaved my head when I was in R and R so he asked if I was a Skinhead, and seemed a little bummed when I told him I wasn't. He told me he was in for a hate crime and had received a fifty-six-year sentence—the number rolled out of his mouth in a manner that reflected a certain amount of pride.

His disposition wasn't one of a man having to live the rest of his life in prison and being miserable because of it, but rather, a man comfortable with his surroundings. His story was one of so many

122

others locked away in prison—being raised in a broken family with a dad who wasn't around, getting into trouble as a kid and spending his childhood in California Youth Authority, where he was taught to manipulate a broken system, break the law and fight. Everything he'd learned stemmed from fear, hatred and a sick sense of necessity. He didn't tell me the details of his case, and I wasn't one to ask, but he wore the sentence he was given like a crown. And I understood why. When a person lives their life in an existence devoid of hope, then adjusts to a setting as ruthless as prison, it's only natural, if they want to prosper and survive, to carry themselves in a manner which states they just don't give a fuck.

He was hardly impressed by my little sixteen-month sentence, but he did listen when I told him stories about my upbringing and punk rock. Like most Skinheads I'd met in the system, his knowledge of music was limited; he became a Skinhead through an ideology based on hate as opposed to going to shows, hanging on the streets or embracing the working-class culture the movement initially stood for. He had a voracious appetite for any bit of information I had about the scene, curious about a lifestyle he never had the opportunity to live.

The rest of the night was spent talking about race and relations inside prison. He schooled me on the intricacies of the Southsider's politics and how the Southern and Northern Mexicans absolutely hated each other and were at war. He said the Blacks, Northerners and Asians ran together, and that the Whites, Southsiders and Native Americans did also (this was by no means absolute, and there were always variables or tensions which might split groups). And lastly, he told me about the Woods and the Skins.

If you were white, you fell into the category of being a Peckerwood or a Skinhead. Whites ran together regardless, but each group had their own way of running their program and an occasional rift would come into play when it came to interaction with each other. The funny thing was, the term "Peckerwood" had started in the south and was used to describe poor white trash. It had always been used in a derogatory manner but had somehow been adopted by the Whites in the system. And when Skinheads first came about in London in the late '60s, many of them were black and embraced the Ska music coming from Jamaica, a far cry from the hardcore hate many listen to today. The irony of it all wasn't lost on me.

———

There were lines drawn in prison and if they were crossed, you were dealt with. Respect was everything. If someone called you a punk, bitch, lop, lame, or showed any other form of disrespect, it was mandatory you "take flight" right then and there. And the same was expected if you happened to encounter a snitch, rapist or child molester. Under no circumstance was giving information to C.O.'s permitted. To do so would be seen as being a snitch and you could expect a sharp piece of steel in your ribcage. He told me that most riots and attacks occurred over drug debts with other races and advised me to stay out of the game. If there was a situation on the yard, you were expected to stand with your race. People that didn't got handled. We were never allowed to eat or exercise with Blacks—we could talk to them and nothing more. Whites were allied with the Southsiders, but he warned me that they'd stab us in the back in a moment's notice.

His rundown of the prison world painted a dark picture and offered a stark reality of what it was like inside the walls. Years of tales gleaned from people who'd been before, movies I'd seen and stories I'd read didn't lend a fraction of truth to what it was truly like being there. He told me how I was expected to act, not from the standpoint of a Skinhead soldier (although he was quick to point out his beliefs and shortcomings of other races), but as a veteran of the system trying to steer me in the right direction and not get caught up in any bullshit. Fear of the unknown gave me clean ears to listen with, and I clung to his words out of fear for my life.

I slept a solid sleep and woke up refreshed, with my cellie telling me I needed to get up for breakfast. The C.O.'s popped the door and we stepped outside our cell, waiting for the green light to file into the dayroom. When the entire bottom tier was out, we walked in a line to a group of trustees who handed us trays from mobile containers. I was starving and the giant slab of coffee cake on my tray was beckoning me to devour it. We had to sit where they told us, filling the tables row by row—I was finally able to put faces to some of the guys I'd heard through the vents over the course of the night. Besides the morning "pleasantries" spoken at the tables, everyone ate in silence, giving the already subdued acoustics of the concrete dayroom a haunting feel. The C.O.'s gave us ten minutes to eat, then we all got up and walked in a line, dropping off our trays to the trustees and grabbing a sack lunch from a C.O. on our way back to our cells.

124

An hour later, the cell door popped open again and my name was called to go to diagnostics. Everyone coming to prison, whether for a term or a parole violation, had to go through a screening process in which blood samples were taken, vital signs checked, a physical exam performed, and questions asked pertaining to mental health. The whole procedure was asinine and left the impression it was done only to comply with state law. I assured them I didn't think I was Superman when I talked to the psych doctors and subjected myself to a barrage of poking before they got the blood they needed, and when they were done, I went back to my unit to rest.

The diagnostic's process took all day and by the time I made it back to my cell it was close to dinnertime. When the C.O.'s were ready, they popped the doors and we went out for chow in the same manner as breakfast, in a line and a tier at a time. The variety of prisoners was striking—there were many such as myself with sixteen-month terms and just as many doing sixteen years. My cellie knew practically everybody and introduced me to the Whites sitting near us by our table. One of them was a Hell's Angel from Northern California and after introductions were made, he seemed to dismiss me as a guy not worthy of his time. It became obvious a hierarchy was in place where those with time and having prison status were at the top, while first-termers with sixteen-month sentences were at the bottom.

Time seemed to have slowed to a point I didn't know was possible. We had nothing to do in our cell except read, exercise and talk shit. We were let out for yard two times a week and it was mandatory for us to go out and represent our race. The yard was an expanse of grass set between the housing units on one side and the outer perimeter fences on the other. Guard towers and catwalks between buildings offered platforms for C.O.'s to stand with their rifles, ready to quell any potential uprising. Each race had their own area staked out, with two sets of pull-up and dip bars being used, one by the Blacks and Asians and the other by the Whites and Southsiders (there were no Northerners on the yard because of past riots). Men walked together in small groups on a walking track, talking about their time while looking toward the acres of farms on the other side of the fences. I couldn't help but wonder how many of those men would never again see those fields from the other side, destined to live their lives within a kill fence.

Within my first week there, my cellie gathered the materials necessary to make a batch of pruno. He acquired a bag of apples, jellies and syrup from other inmates, and a bag of old rotting fruit that was used as a kicker (to get the fermentation process going) from one of his Skinhead buddies and started to cook. Bread was used for yeast, the jellies and syrup, even though the content was low, contained the sugar needed to turn into alcohol. It took a couple of days for the fermentation to take but when it did, the bag the pruno was cooking in started blowing up with gas and we'd have to open it to let it out or the bag would explode, spraying the cell with apple chunks and not-yet-done wine. He kept it cooking in the toilet, keeping a towel over it to keep it as warm as possible, and we'd hit the gas from time to time, inhaling it and getting a rush comparable to nitrous oxide.

After a few days of brewing, he took it out and strained the pruno into Folgers containers using a sock. That night, after the first count, we drank the horrid concoction, but it had very little effect. He seemed to think it didn't have enough sugar but after one of the tier-tenders (inmate workers who had jobs cleaning the tiers and passing items from cell to cell) drank a cup, the worker responded with an Orson Welles quote from an old Paul Masson commercial stating, "We will drink no wine before its time…" inferring Bam-Bam hadn't cooked it long enough. He then went back to work, telling all the Whites on the tier that Bam-Bam made the worst pruno in all of Delano.

One week after our failed pruno experiment, an issue on the yard arose regarding a Skinhead and a Wood. Some tobacco had come onto the yard via one of the support workers on the minimum-security yard (in prisons with high-security inmates, or in this case prisoners in reception, there are minimum-security workers available to handle kitchen, laundry and maintenance duties) that was supposed to be delivered to a Wood in our housing unit. The delivery was to be handled by a Skinhead from the San Fernando Valley who worked D Yard, whose job was to bring the food from the kitchen to the housing units. The tobacco was passed to the Skinhead in the kitchen, but he ended up taking some for himself. When the Wood got his package, he saw that it was short and knew the Skinhead had stolen from him. The Wood made sure he was out to help with the food when it was being brought in the next day and as the Skinhead was wheeling his cart in, he enacted his revenge.

126

All of this happened in our building and we had no idea why at the time, all we saw was the Skinhead getting beat and the C.O.'s dousing them with pepper spray. We watched it go down from our cell and then had to deal with the lingering effect of the pepper spray—my cellie and I were coughing and tearing up for a solid thirty minutes after the spray was used. When it cleared and both of the guys involved were taken to the hole, my cellie looked me dead in the eyes and said, "You better hope we ain't goin' to war." Because I rolled with the Woods and he was a Skinhead, the potential was there for it to get nasty between us.

Bam-Bam was a hothead. I didn't think he'd attack me because I wasn't perceived as much of a threat, but the tension in the cell was palpable. His answer to the issue, before an edict of war had even been declared, was to be ready. He looked at me again and threatened, "If you say so much as a word, I'll book you." He then proceeded to make a shank using a plastic cup, an apple and the elastic thread from a pair of boxers.

He tied the thread to an apple, holding the excess thread over his head, and spun the apple until it was a well-wound nylon cord, then used the cord to cut the plastic. He did it by holding the cup tight between his knees and sawing a three-inch pointed shard out of the cup. When he was done, he did the same thing on the other side of the cup but making a handle this time. Both pieces were then connected by cutting notches at the base of the blade and at the top of the handle, bound together by crisscrossing the cord until both pieces were locked tight. He tested its strength by stabbing it into a book and looked like a madman while doing it. As he sharpened the point against the cold concrete floor of the cell, I told myself that if I ever made it out of there, I'd give up my life of crime.

Fortunately, nothing ever came of the situation. Not long after he finished making his instrument of death, a Skinhead tier-tender came to the cell door and whispered some words to him. He then broke it apart, threw it in the toilet and flushed it down the drain. With a word from someone higher up in the chain of command, the issue was squashed. They'd have to deal with the matter between themselves when they encountered each other after they got out of the hole.

Knowing my cellie had the potential to transform into a killer in a moment's notice made me feel like there was a bomb in my cell. Much to my relief, however, I only had to endure the uneasiness for a couple of days because my name was called for transfer to C Yard. He gave me a hug and told me to "stay down" as I left the cell, then was escorted out by a correctional officer. I had no idea what C Yard was, but I was glad to be going. I knew he could've stabbed me just as easily as hugged me.

C Yard was similar to D as far as the layout of the buildings and the yard was concerned, but the buildings were comprised of dorms as opposed to cells. All prisoners coming into Delano were put on B or D Yard upon entry, and if their charges weren't excessively violent they were usually moved to C. Everybody looked my way as I walked in, some sizing me up and others just curious who the new guy was, and after I was given my bed assignment, a white man came up to help me with my property. He asked me where I was from then gave me a brief rundown of the unit on the way to my bunk. I was told to stay on my toes and if it ever jumped, to get with our people right away.

It was much louder because there was constant activity in the dayroom, but it was nice to be able to move around and not be confined to a cell. Groups of people played cards within their races at tables and there were movies shown on occasion. I was able to stay busy much of the time and wasn't as consumed by my thoughts, making the time move in a manner that made me feel like I wasn't frozen in ice. Even so, I couldn't help but think about the days I had ahead of me and hoped I'd make it out without getting jumped or stabbed in a riot. Most of the guys only had a few years to do but there were some who had over ten, and when I talked to them, I tried to imagine what it would be like to do that much time. It always made me grateful to know I had as many months as they did years.

The building didn't have any racial tension at the time, nor any knuckleheads trying to run shit. Everyone seemed relatively calm and eagerly awaiting the day they'd be transferred to a regular prison yard. The guys who'd been to prison before all said that a regular yard, or "mainline", was much better than reception. They'd tell stories about conjugal visits, getting packages sent in from the streets, personal clothes and shoes you could wear, having guitars and music you could listen to and that you were able to smoke. You couldn't have or do any of those things in reception.

I'd been there almost two months when my counselor came to see me. She was dressed like an office worker but wearing a green

CDC vest over her clothes and toting a cart loaded with different prisoners C-files. C-files were used to document all known information about prisoners, including criminal history, the controlling charge, psychiatric and/or medical issues, gang affiliations, known addresses and contacts, etc. It was information that was often helpful to police or parole officers should the prisoner go on the run or break the law after paroling, but it was also used to make a "point" assessment in deciding where and what level yard a prisoner was sent to.

After a brief and very informal introduction, she told me that I had seventeen points and would be sent to a Level 1 yard. She also said I'd be sent to a CCF (Community Correctional Facility)—a privatized lockdown unit reputed to be extremely laid back. The guys in the building had already told me that was where I'd be going, but it was still good to hear it from her. But most importantly, my "half-time" started kicking in the day she dropped by (non-violent criminals only did 50% of their time, but you first had to see your counselor).

I was called for transfer the week following 9/11. That was a strange day. I woke up to the see the C.O. on duty in shock and staring at the TV intently. We were as well. The whole dorm watched in silence, lending an eerie quality. The feeling in the unit was somber and our program was cut for a couple days, but it didn't take long for everything to go back to normal. When I talked to the C.O., I was told I was going to Corcoran, a prison notorious for riots, crooked C.O.'s and housing Charles Manson.

Anything I was bringing with me had to be brought to the officer's podium in a bag. They called it "trans-packing" and they'd hold my belongings in R and R until the day I transferred. I trans-packed on a Friday and had to wait until the following Tuesday to roll up my bedding and catch the bus, so those three days were spent nervous with anticipation and from the reputation the prison held. Knowing I was going to a Level 1 yard helped to placate my anxiety, but knowing that Charles Manson and Sirhan Sirhan had both been housed there at one time still gave the prison an ominous quality.

The rest of the week passed slowly and without incident, and on Tuesday morning I was told to roll it up. I jumped in with a group of five other prisoners from C Yard and walked to R and R with a C.O. leading the way. When we got there, we were put in a cell with other guys waiting on chains to other prisons. Delano was a transportation hub and because it was a reception yard, convicts were always being shipped to any number of prisons throughout the state.

The group waiting to catch the chain to Corcoran was a large one. The CDC transportation officers showed up within an hour and had us wait on benches while they dressed us out. They were dressed in black uniforms and carried themselves like they were a Special Forces unit. We were given paper suits to jump into, shackled individually from head to toe, then boarded a green bus with the words CALIFORNIA DEPARTMENT OF CORRECTIONS on its side. The bus was checked for prisoners trying to escape—the compartments and undercarriage with a mirror, and when they were satisfied, we were given the green light to move out. We rolled through the gate, leaving one prison behind, and on our way to another.

OLD CORCORAN

The sun began to creep over the peaks of the Sierra Madres to the east, casting a glow across the commanding landscape of farms, fields and prisons. We followed Highway 43's desolate path into King's County and on to the slow prison town of Corcoran. Half of the city's 20,000-plus occupants were its prisoners, and a significant portion of the other half worked in or around the prison industry, either as guards or staff. There was also a large contingent of civilians who worked around the fringes of the prison supplying those guards with food and gas, as well as lodging for the throng of visitors who came each weekend to see their loved ones behind the walls.

Our journey on the bus was made in complete silence—the C.O.'s made it a point to tell us no talking would be permitted. They were dead serious about this. There were three correctional officers on the bus: two in the front with their pistols locked and loaded, and one sitting behind a cage in the back with a shotgun. They exuded an ominous demeanor that commanded respect and obedience.

The ride to Corcoran was relatively short, taking about an hour. Just inside the gate, another C.O. inspected the outside of the bus, making sure our load was legit, then motioned us forward to another gate. After going through it, we drove down a service road in what was called "No-Man's Land" (an area between prison buildings and yards where no prisoners were allowed. Most cells have a view of this barren and rocky landscape) to Corcoran's R and R building.

As I got off the bus, in the shadows of the razor wire fences and guard towers, I had a surreal feeling come over me. I never once thought I'd end up in prison. From another's perspective it probably wouldn't have come as much of a surprise, but to me it was somehow shocking. My memories of skateboarding and going to shows seemed so long ago, buried by my lust for drugs. I'd opened a door to another world.

The prison itself was soaked in notoriety. Besides housing such inmates as Charles Manson, Sirhan Sirhan and Juan Corona at one time or another, it was also known for its violence. In 1996, the L.A. Times ran a front-page article stating Corcoran was the most troubled of California's many prisons. Prisoners had been shot and killed from the guards in the towers at an alarming rate and there were instances in which C.O.'s had reportedly set up gladiator matches between rival gang members (the CDC had tried to cover up these killings and it wasn't until two "whistle-blowers" went public that this violence was recognized as an issue). The dark history of the prison's storied past was enough to instill a sense of fear deep within me.

We were put into two large cells while being subjected to another booking process. C.O.'s would come to the cells periodically, taking prisoners to whichever yard they were assigned, and I had the feeling something was amiss when the other guys going to the 1-yard were picked up, leaving me behind in R and R. After some time, I was told that my warrant in Washington prevented me from being placed on a Level 1. The hold made me a potential flight risk, and CDC protocol directed that I be placed on a secure yard.

Level 1's only had fences and were outside prison perimeters, conditions optimum for a "potential flight risk" to escape. I'd be put on the 3-yard to do my time and then released to the custody of Washington if they chose to get me. I was pretty sure they wouldn't, that was the least of my worries, but I was concerned about surviving on a Level 3. I'd heard many tales of people getting shanked during riots and C.O.'s shooting people for participating in them, especially at Corcoran.

A C.O. escorted me down a service road toward the entrance to the yard, walking with me in silence through No-Man's Land. When we got to yard 3-C, he offered some sound advice: show respect and don't get caught up in any drug debts. I knew better than to compromise myself along either of those lines and nodded in agreement to his positive words, even if it was a cop giving them to me. I wanted to portray an image of a hardened convict, ready to walk any yard if need be, but I was full of fear and scared for my life. There was something wrong about a man with just over five months left in his sentence being thrown on a 3-yard with lifers and killers, and there wasn't a goddamn thing I could do about it.

He brought me to a gym that had been converted into a giant dorm, and it felt like everyone stopped what they were doing to check me out when I walked in. I was taken to a guard's office where I was given my bunk assignment and pointed to my rack. A Wood came up as I was making my bunk and introduced himself as Eric from Alameda and said if I had any issues or problems, I should talk to him. He also told me he'd need to see my paperwork. I didn't know it at the time, but guys had to carry proof they didn't have any dirt on their jacket, such as rape or child crimes. I was told to fill out a request for a 128-G (a classification chrono; it would state my charges), and then he watched to make sure it was put in the mail.

I was told that I was on probation until my 128-G arrived. After Eric had given me a rundown of the place, another Wood came up, introducing himself as Germ from San Francisco. He was a punk rocker with a Maori tribal tattoo on his chin and I liked him right away. A fellow heroin addict, he got busted breaking into a house in Potrero Hill in S.F. and was in his last year of a 10-year bid.

He gave me a heads-up on the political landscape of the gym, showing me where the White section was located, and filled me in on the Blacks and Mexicans. There wasn't any tension right then but just a few months prior, there'd been a massive riot on the yard between the Southern and Northern Mexicans. The word was the Northerners had been smashed, and if history was any indicator, they were certain to avenge their loss when the time was right.

The gym was packed with bunk beds and there was no privacy to be had. In a corner of the building was a large, open shower room, with a row of toilets and sinks adjacent to it. There was a catwalk where basketball hoops had once been, and a C.O. would step out from time to time, surveying the landscape. He had a Mini-14 and a shotgun up there with him, and the same stencils I'd seen at Delano were on the walls stating that no warning shots would be fired, emphasizing the fact there was a man trained to kill looking down on us at any given moment.

The yard on 3-C was gigantic. It had multiple handball and basketball courts, a tennis court and workout bars set up in various locations. There had been weights on the yard up until 1998, but they were taken away because, depending on who you asked, they could be used as weapons or because prisoners would parole the size of monsters. A field where prisoners could play soccer and softball—or battle if a riot kicked off—sat in the middle of it all, surrounded by a paved track where people could walk and run. The track was strange because you were only allowed to follow it in one direction, much like drivers in a NASCAR race. Because of this and a rule stating prisoners couldn't walk together in groups of more than five, guards were more visually equipped to differentiate a mob from people walking the track.

There were five buildings that housed the cell-living units surrounding the yard, as well as a long administrative building that accommodated the library, infirmary, cafeteria and offices for the CDC brass. The gym was in the middle of the admin building with a gunner's tower resting above it like a nest. He'd sit up there watching everything that went down on the yard and I wondered more than once how many people had been shot from his vantage point.

Time in the gym moved slowly and I was fortunate Germ was there to shoot the shit with. He was from the Mission District in San Francisco, so we were able to reminisce about venues and shows from back in the day, and the crazy things we'd seen. His story was funny in a fucked-up kind of way—he'd broken into a house with the intention of stealing jewelry and whatever else, and while he was there, loaded on pills and smack, he decided to catch a little nod on a couch. When he woke, it was to guns in his face and police screaming at him to get on the ground. They booked him for residential burglary, a violent crime, and he began his life of doing time in the California prison system.

He was the only one I'd really hang out with in the gym; most of the other Whites were of the white trash variety, with a penchant for listening to bands like Limp Bizkit and Nickelback. I went out to the yard by myself one morning to smoke a cigarette and walked over to an area of the yard appropriated by the Whites. I had just lit up when a big homie walking the track came up and asked if he could sit down and smoke with me.

His name was Hoss and I thought it was funny that a Mexican shared the name with a character from the show *Bonanza*, but after taking his giant stature into consideration, it made perfect sense. Our conversation started with him telling me about the riot between them and the Northerners, and how he was tired of all the politics and violence. He could tell I was a first-termer and didn't seem at all surprised when I told him I was only doing sixteen months. After a bit of silence, he told me he'd been down since the early '90s, right after the three-strikes law had been enacted, and knew he was never going home.

He was in for murdering a rival gang member in East L.A. He felt then that his actions were justified, that the guy had gotten what was coming to him and had no problem doing the time for it. He was a soldier for his clique and it was just a part of living life in the barrio.

134

But after many years maturing behind the walls, knowing he'd taken another man's life and that the yard was all he'd ever have, he began to realize the life he chose was wrong. He didn't go so far as to discredit his neighborhood or allegiance to his gang, but he did say if he could've turned back the hands of time, he never would've gotten jumped in.

When he told me his story, pain and regret were cast from his cold dark eyes, visual instruments that had once been vibrant and bright with the prospect of life. He'd passed the period of his youth when such actions were considered admirable and had since entered a stage in his life full of reflection and remorse. To this day I wonder how many nights were spent alone in his cell, with a cellie he couldn't reveal his feelings to and a head full of dark thoughts…thoughts that once embraced a position of martyrdom for his 'hood and with time being supplanted by the insight that comes with age. Wisdom wasted to reside in a landscape of fear, while the gunner in the tower grins from above.

My encounter with him was brief but the impression he left was enduring. His deportment was that of a man broken and tired. It was sad to think about…he'd been raised in a neighborhood where most were from one gang or another, prison was a rite of passage, the primary cause of death was from a needle or a bullet and opportunity rarely came knocking. I felt truly fortunate for my upbringing and swore to myself I wouldn't end up wasting my life in a prison cell.

The next two weeks passed without incident until the day I received my 128-G. I'd forgotten all about it so when I heard my name being called, I thought I was getting a letter from a friend or maybe my mom. Eric, the one who'd told me to send for the 128-G in the first place, had not, and as soon as I had it in my hand he was there to verify its content. When he was done reading it, he told me to wait at my bunk and walked off to talk to his right-hand man, visibly disturbed. They talked for a minute and I was starting to get seriously worried because Eric kept looking my way with menace in his eyes.

When they were finished discussing what it read, they both came my way. It stated that I had a "possible R-suffix" attached to my name. I had no idea what that meant but soon found that it was a designation for prisoners who'd been convicted of sex crimes. They wanted to know if I'd ever been busted for rape or anything else sex related.

I knew I hadn't but remembered all-too-well the time I'd been arrested for pulling my dick out on a bus in a Klonopin-fueled haze. Thinking fast, I told them I was arrested for public indecency, but that it was for peeing at a bus stop. I failed to mention the part about me spooking the student on her way to class at the University of Washington, knowing it was probably in my best interest to omit the details.

They told me I'd be smashed if they found otherwise and Eric went to confer with another guy on the yard about it. This was a grave matter and one that could've led to a severe beat-down or a shank in my ribcage. There were three things that worked in my favor, however. First, the chrono said it was a "possible" R-suffix. Second, I was housed in the gym where everyone was going home soon. And third, my story sounded plausible. If any one of those things had worked against me, I would've been marked.

I was ostracized by the Whites in the gym from then on. Not to the level in which I was considered prey, but to the point I wasn't acknowledged. Germ had even taken a stance by telling me he'd kick my ass personally if he discovered I was lying. I spent the rest of the evening on my bunk, reluctant to even get up to use the restroom. I was on edge all throughout the night, fully expecting to get jumped when I did use the restroom or that a crew of convicts would attack me while I was in bed.

I knew I was being watched to see if I'd make a break for the officer's station. When I awoke the next day it wasn't to fists or a knife, but rather, to another white man dropping off a couple of cigarettes on my bunk. He had apparently read my fear and despair, or quite possibly could've walked in my shoes at some point. Regardless of why, he went out of his way to make me feel better when I was more scared and alone than in any other time of my life. The compassion he showed hit me right in the heart. The fact I didn't have any tobacco was of little relevance—what mattered was that even in a place filled with cold-blooded killers, I could be shown a semblance of love. I knew then that this fucked-up situation would pass and I'd be all right.

I decided to go out to yard after breakfast and deal with anything that might come my way. But nothing did. Eric had undoubtedly talked to the shot-caller for the yard, whoever that was, and was probably told to lay back until the word was solid on the R-suffix. The propensity for violence and retribution against people who commit sex crimes on a 3-yard was extremely high. When it came to "rapo's" and "chomo's" (rapists and child molesters), prisoners with dirt on their jacket were guilty until proven innocent, and I was fortunate I wasn't perceived as such.

There was still an unseen barrier preventing others to get too close to me, but I think most people knew I wasn't in for some funny shit. Germ told me he knew I was good when I didn't "PC-up" and go running for the officer's station and when he saw me go out to the yard. Doing my time in there was still difficult, however. I felt there were those who still thought of me as a piece of shit and knew it would be the case until my name was cleared.

The day I did clear my name was also my last on 3-C. I'd been on the yard a month when I was told to report to a classification committee. We were on lockdown over an incident that happened in one of the other buildings, so I had to be handcuffed and escorted to the administration building. Inside the building were numerous offices and I was put into one with a lieutenant, sergeant, counselor and C.O. sitting around a table.

At some point, King County in Washington State had been notified I was in custody, which meant they were obligated to either file for my extradition or dismiss my case outright. In most instances, the agency issuing the warrant is notified when an inmate has somewhere around ninety days left to do in a sentence, unless the inmate files the appropriate paperwork on his or her own initiative. But in my case, because I was on a 3-yard with Level 1 points and because it was an out-of-state felony hold, King County was notified shortly after my arrival to Corcoran. And to my delight, they decided it would cost too much to get me and dismissed the case.

The only person in the committee who did any talking was the lieutenant, and that was just for the record. The hearing was recorded, much like in court but without a stenographer, and she listed off things such as my controlling case, point level, the felony hold, that I had no known enemies and lastly, her recommendation that I be transferred to CSP-Corcoran Level 1. When she was done, the lieutenant said a few things and ended, basically, by saying I was cleared for transfer and would be placed in the Substance Abuse Program because of my history of drug abuse. I had a vague idea what that meant and wasn't exactly thrilled about it, but I wanted to get there regardless. I would've done practically anything to get off that yard.

137

I was escorted from 3-C and moved to the 1-yard that same day. After the kangaroo committee finished finalizing their decision, I was brought back to the gym and said my goodbyes to the few people who gave a shit and I was off. I didn't get to see Germ because he was working, but any sadness I felt was trumped by moving to a yard where I didn't have to worry about getting killed and therefore soon forgotten.

When I got to R and R, I was placed in the same cell as when I arrived and waited for the transport officer to show. The C.O. who came was an angry little Mexican who walked with a limp, and he made his presence known by shooting me a disdainful look and mumbling something under his breath. He reminded me of an evil mastermind's sidekick from a movie—someone like Igor from *Young Frankenstein*—and it was hard not to laugh when he limped his way toward me and put me in cuffs. He drove from R and R to the 1-yard like a madman, blasting through turns with enough speed to fling me into the panels of the van. I'd been in enough cop cars and dealt with their malicious actions to know his intent, and I also knew enough not to tell him to slow down or act scared. He was a miserable little man taking his anger out on me and I just went with it.

Yard 1-A was outside the perimeter of electric "kill fences" and gun towers, a separate prison from the rest of Corcoran with its Level 3 and 4 yards and SHU program (segregated housing units). We drove through a gate and got out of the van, Igor prodding me along in an attempt at being a vicious prison guard but coming across as a lame duck. The building we walked into had the only entrance to the yard—a concrete room with an officer's station off to the side and a metal detector used to scan prisoners returning from work.

Inside the room was a line of workers in white jumpsuits standing by the officer's station. They were coming back from the prison dairy and they smelled like a combination of shit and turd. Corcoran had a massive dairy that provided the milk for the prisons in Southern California and was one of the best jobs an inmate could land through the California Prison Authority. CALPIA workers manufactured shoes and clothes for prisoners, products for the DMV and other agencies, and the dairy, of course. (PIA workers were paid well for prison standards and had significantly lower recidivism rates than other prisoners, but sadly, the state of California has cut back on PIA programs, opting instead for the warehousing of prisoners.)

138

After stripping and going through the metal detector, I was given a new set of state-issued threads and then escorted to my housing unit. The yard was set up like many high schools I'd seen; buildings surrounding a quarter-mile track with a soccer/softball field within. The largest building was an administrative one of sorts, holding the kitchen, cafeteria, library, church, offices for sergeants and lieutenants, as well as the yard entrance portal.

The administrative building, for lack of a better word, flanked the east side of the yard, with five housing units and a portable for SAP programing on the west. I was assigned to building A, the easternmost, where everyone in the Substance Abuse Program lived. The other buildings housed dairy, painting, kitchen workers and so forth.

The lack of tension was evident from the moment I walked onto the yard. The caution and distrust were still present, but nowhere close to 3-C's level. Getting stabbed by someone I didn't know wasn't something I'd have to worry about here, at least not as much. Another significant factor was that there were no guns in the towers. There weren't any towers, period. Even the barbwire fence surrounding the facility was miniscule compared to the big yard's trifecta of razor wire fences and another with enough electrical voltage to fry you on the spot.

The SAP building was a dorm setting, with four housing sections surrounding a cavernous dayroom. Each section had two floors filled with bunk beds, but everyone had a small area of personal space as opposed to the congested environs of the gym on 3-C. Just like in Delano, or any other California prison for that matter, my bunkie was a white man. He was a flavorless sort, in prison for drug possession, and he told me about the SAP classes we'd be attending as well as all the other rules we were expected to follow. It had a laid-back feel and I was truly happy to be there after all the stress I endured on the Level 3. I felt at the time I could do my last bit of time standing on my head.

The Substance Abuse Program classes were really just a means for the state of California to show that they were making some sort of attempt at rehabilitating prisoners. They were facilitated by workers employed by a treatment center called the Phoenix House and were proponents of "behavior modification" as opposed to the twelve-step program. They used methods like putting people in the "hot seat" and confronting them about issues relevant to their addiction or any other attribute detrimental to recovery. We'd have to endure daylong classes by facilitators who never had any problems with drugs, alcohol or the law. With feigned expertise, they'd tell us the virtues of "just saying no" and how to prevent a relapse.

While I believe most of the facilitators were sincere in their desire to want to help, it was hard to take them seriously because they hadn't lived the life. We were convicted felons and they were people who got their information about drugs from secondhand sources. One or two might've had an uncle or cousin doing time but the majority learned about drugs in classrooms, from the media and shows like *COPS*. I felt a little sorry for them, not because they were squares, but because they were perceived as morons who didn't grasp the subject matter. They were like substitute teachers facing the daunting task of covering a disciplinarian's job in study hall or detention.

There was one good thing about the SAP program, however. The state of California had funding set aside for inmates who paroled from SAP yards under an acronym called SASCA (Substance Abuse Services Coordination Agencies). SASCA paid for treatment and would also foot the bill for residence in halfway houses upon release. This sounded rather enticing to me because I had nowhere to go when I got out. Not only that, but I wanted to stay clean and was willing to use whatever tools I had at my disposal.

Building A was the only housing unit that had to attend SAP; the rest of the buildings on the yard had inmates doing "normal" prison time and not some candy-ass treatment program. There was a feeling among us SAPer's that we were looked upon as less-than from the others at Corcoran. I didn't mind attending the classes at first but after two weeks my tolerance began to fade. We'd have to start the day reciting an oath of sorts—something about a Phoenix rising from the ashes and moving forward despite the hardship it faced. It was ridiculous. The worst part about SAP, however, was that it was destined to fail. I was by no means an expert in how treatment programs were run, but I knew enough to know that honesty was a key component. Being that we were in prison, nobody was going to disclose their personal feelings in a group setting.

The key in prison is to do your time and not let it do you. Your choices are limited for obvious reasons, but you've got to make do with what you got. I ended up getting a night job in the kitchen, pulling me from the monotony of evening pinochle games and exchanging war stories with the other convicts. If you don't stay busy, it's easy to get caught up in the trivial issues that arise from day to day living. I had a steady rhythm moving me along—between the SAP classes, exercising in the afternoons and working in the kitchen at night, I was able to stay out of my head and not think about the day I was due to parole.

With this formula I managed to make it to my release date without incident. The knowledge that I'd soon be hitting the streets brought about an anxiety which worried me. I handled it well, all things considered, but it was still unsettling. In January, when I had two months left, I sat down with a counselor from the SAP program and we mutually decided I'd go to the Substance Abuse Foundation in Long Beach when I paroled. A driver contracted by SASCA would pick me up and take me straight there, so I didn't have to worry about jumping on a bus or train to get there. Having a plan upon release subdued the fear rising within me.

The night before I was due to be released, I received a ducat in the mail stating I was to report to the work-transfer station for release. The next morning, I had my last Corcoran breakfast then walked off the yard. The same gimpy C.O. was there to drive me to R and R and after he cuffed me up, he drove the service roads with the same reckless abandon as when he brought me to 1-A. I was put into a cell in R and R with two other guys who were also paroling. We shared the same nervous anticipation; the feeling that a life-changing event was about to occur and regardless of what the future may or may not bring, we were excited about it. In a sense, it felt strange to share that excitement because one of the guys had just done twelve years and the other eight. Both made my nine-and-a-half months seem like nothing and I couldn't help but wonder how they felt after doing such long stretches. There had to be significant fear going back to a world that had changed from the last time they'd seen it.

Regardless of the differences in the amount of time we'd done, we were being thrown back into society with perspectives twisted by what we'd seen behind the walls. It was unsettling to say the least. I was fortunate because I had a program to help smooth the transition. There were many I'd spoken with who had no idea what they were going to do when they got out and knew their chances were slim. The system was set up in a manner that failure was imminent and most returned.

The guards called us up to the podium and gave us our dress-outs. My mom had sent me some clothes I'd left in her closet when I was "thirty days to the house"—they were just shorts, a thrift store shirt and a pair of skate shoes but I felt like a king. I didn't want to wear a pair of blue denim pants or a blue button-up shirt for as long as I lived. The other guys didn't have clothes sent in, so they paroled with sweatpants and sweatshirts supplied by the CDC.

Before being shuttled to the Visitor Information Center, we were counted out $200 "gate money". The money was given to each prisoner upon release so they'd be able to purchase a ticket to wherever it was they were going and to ensure the prisoner wasn't destitute when they got there. The idea was that it was safer for the communities and for the prisoner.

We boarded the bus, without cuffs this time, and Old Gimpy drove us through the facility, getting us to the main gate intact. A C.O. posted in a gatehouse searched the exterior of the van and then we drove toward our final destination.

The Visitor's Center was adjacent to the prison compound and surrounded by a massive parking lot. Outside of the center was a small group of people watching and waiting for the shuttle to deliver their loved ones. One of the parolees, the one who'd done eight years, saw his mom, dad, wife and daughter standing among the group, and I didn't need to see the tears welling up in the corners of his eyes to feel his gratitude. It made me think that he might've been holding those tears in for the entire length of his term.

He was the first one off the bus when we pulled up to the drop-off point and was swarmed with love the second his foot hit the ground. The man who'd just finished doing twelve years stayed on the bus and was taken to the Greyhound station. I felt sorry for him but there was no need for that; he looked thrilled to be leaving.

True to my counselor's word, my driver was waiting for me when I got off the bus. I didn't know him for shit and it was a little awkward at first, but we were soon on the road. Long Beach was calling my name.

CHINO

I sat outside of a 7-Eleven on Harbor Boulevard loaded out of my mind and waiting for my phone to charge. All my worldly possessions were with me—a skateboard and a bag of filthy clothes—and I was on my way to an indigent detox in Costa Mesa called Charle Street. I was strung-out, beat up and tired, wondering how my life had fallen apart.

It was now September of 2002 and I'd managed to make it almost six months without drugs getting the best of me. The program I paroled to was laden with rules I didn't want to follow, particularly the one condemning relationships with the opposite sex. It was a co-ed facility and like any other sex-starved man just getting out of prison, I hooked up right away.

I loved being in treatment initially...I met a girl and would sneak out to her apartment in the middle of the night, but it wasn't long until the day to day tedium of going to classes and boredom with the program started outweighing the pleasure of a nice piece of ass. This lasted close to two months until I'd had enough and moved into a halfway house down the street that didn't care what I did. The move to the halfway house coincided with my reconnecting with a girl I'd been messing around with before I went to prison. She was trouble waiting to happen, just like me, and even though I knew the potential for disaster was likely, the day finally came when we made plans to hook up.

I caught the Blue Line into Los Angeles and met her downtown by the Staples Center. She looked good, but it soon became apparent she had a habit. Her being high didn't bother me—I just wanted to get laid. I told myself that if I stayed true to my intentions, I'd be all right. The plan was to jump on a southbound train and go back to her place but while we were waiting on the platform, a northbound heading downtown arrived. The desire to get loaded lay dormant in my conscience and even though I said I wanted to stop, it wasn't really the case. I'd kept secret thoughts of getting high stashed away like a kid's guilty obsession with pornography, but being with someone who was fucking around brought my lust for the drug to the forefront of my mind. By the time the train going downtown had stopped, my resolve had been broken and was replaced by an all-controlling obsession to score, and when I told her my true desire, we were on our way.

It didn't take long for the jones to manifest itself into my daily routine. When it did, I took up residence at the Cecil and Huntington hotels in Skid Row. The girl I was with would sell her ass on Sepulveda Boulevard and I took up boosting DVD's again. My familiarity with the lifestyle was striking; even though I'd been clean a little while, the transition back had been smooth. If I hadn't been sedated I surely would've been hit with similarities of my days in Seattle—a junkie Déjà vu.

The good times lasted two weeks before everything unraveled. The girl left me for one of her sugar daddies in the Valley, the places I was stealing from were getting hip, my parole officer was looking for me and I was broke. I knew if I didn't get my shit together quick I'd be back in lockup, so I called Charle Street and told them I needed a bed.

It was an old-school detox that had been around for years and only took in drunks. My plan was to down a beer right before I got there, which was the main reason I stopped at the 7-Eleven. I had a stash of Klonopin I planned to smuggle in to help with my kick, and had just stashed them in my sock when a cop rolled up on me. He was being cool and only asked for my identification, then drove off after jotting down my information. I thought for sure he'd take me in and breathed a huge sigh of relief after he left.

I took it as a sign to leave, so I unplugged my charger and was about to go into the store to get the beer when his car pulled back into the parking lot. His pleasant demeanor had disappeared and when he jumped out of his car, he told me to put my hands on the hood and cuffed me. He ended up running my name after I'd given him my ID and it came back that I had a PAL (parolee at large) warrant. Any minute chance I might've had of being let go was erased when he searched me and found a needle and cooker in my coat pocket.

I was driven to the Fountain Valley precinct and placed in a holding cell to await transport to the Santa Ana City Jail. The inevitable feelings of loneliness and self-pity were present, but what hit me the hardest was that I'd been on my way to detox. I felt that I couldn't catch a break; that all the cards in the deck were stacked against me.

144

Such is the life of the junkie, full of pain and regret. But living that lifestyle, the excitement that comes with the realization you still have drugs can't be matched. I'd forgotten about the pills I had in my sock and not only that, the cop did such a half-ass job patting me down he failed to find the cigarettes in my coat pocket. The pills and tobacco would be a godsend later, but I had to get them out of the cell to be of any use. Which meant I'd have to put them in the "safe".

I had no problem doing drugs and smoking tobacco that had previously been in another man's ass, but had yet to use mine to do the business. The only thing I had to use was the cellophane from my cigarette pack, so I mixed the pills and tobacco together and then rolled up the package as tight as I could. Cellophane isn't the best packing material for handling such tasks because of its jagged edges, but with a little hard work and perseverance I inserted the goods and was ready to roll.

I nodded through the booking process and when I came to my senses, I was in a two-man cell. The cell itself was nothing special but the facility was great compared to many of the other jails I'd been in. Most of its occupants were illegal immigrants waiting for I.C.E. (Immigration Customs Enforcement) to take them back to whichever country south of the border they were from, and the rest were inmates with parole holds who were waiting on the Chino chain. Like most jails, there was a bank of cells on two tiers, but the dayroom was carpeted and even had a couch in it. I thought that was the strangest thing and wondered if there were many fights over people claiming spots on the couch as their own.

Those brief observations were my last because of the pills I had stashed in my ass. My intention was to save them for when I got to Chino, but I ended up taking all of them and have no memory of what happened to the tobacco. I could've smoked it with my cellie or I could've traded it for food—I have no idea. Klonopin isn't known for its euphoric qualities but they work wonders for tuning out. And that's exactly what I did. I have no recollection of getting on the bus the next day, just some vague memories of being chained to someone, then pulling into a sally port at Chino. The bus had stopped in Riverside and San Bernardino before pulling into the prison, so it was filled with an assortment of ruffians, many of them as fucked up as me.

California's Institute for Men, or Chino, had been built in 1941 and was loaded with interesting history. It was California's third prison and was also the first minimum-security facility of its capacity in the country. It didn't have any walls surrounding it when it'd been built, which was unheard of at the time. All it had was an old barbwire fence, and that was used to keep cows from coming on to the property. Over time, changes were implemented to accommodate a growing prison population and the violence that came with it. The barbwire fences once surrounding the prison were replaced with electric kill fences, razor wire and guard towers.

The receiving unit for Chino, also known as Central, was a large building and contained R and R, a collection of housing units, the infirmary, an administrative wing, and an ad-seg unit. It was inundated with activity; a steady wave of prisoners from Riverside, San Bernardino and Orange counties flooded its corridors. Which meant that all those prisoners had to go through diagnostics, get evaluated and sent to a housing unit reflecting their security level.

Each unit was designated by tree names: Alder, Madrone, Spruce, etc. I was assigned to Cypress. The unit looked like it had been built long ago and its design reflected its age, with wear and tear giving it even more of a run-down feel. Each unit was self-contained, with its own chow hall on the ground floor and the tiers above connected by metal staircases. I was put in a cell on the second tier with a guy from San Bernardino who had a penchant for talking about his "old lady" incessantly. He was in for a parole violation as well and was certain his girl was fucking around on him. He was so obsessed with her that I felt a little sorry for him. But I was also wary of him because he carried the disposition of a man ready to snap.

Below us on the first tier were "dropouts"—protective custody prisoners who wanted out of their gang for one reason or another. Some drop out because they tire of the lifestyle, but most do so because they find that they bit off more than they could chew. Many of them are youngsters who come in with lengthy sentences and know they're never going to see daylight again, so they aspire to make a name for themselves by climbing the prison pyramid.

To get to the top, however, means you have to "put in work". Putting in work for a prison gang comes in many different forms: bringing information about prisoners, gang and CDC activity to other yards via kites or notes, selling and smuggling drugs, supplying weapons and murder. Other gang members are often targeted but the victims are usually people with dirt on their jacket, such as sex crimes or snitching, people who owe money and prisoners who give the CDC info about the gang they want out of.

For a man with a life sentence and a head full of hate, killing an enemy or a prison guard might seem noble, but it doesn't always turn out that way. Just like in government politics, prison politics are bound by a code of backstabbing, betrayal and secret aims. The unsuspecting get caught up in the ruse to further the gang's goals of power, then one day an order comes from a shot-caller stating that a person who may or may not have the gang's interest at heart needs to be taken out. A sociopath might not have a problem killing people on the whim of another, but even in a place as cold and heartless as prison, this ruthlessness doesn't ring true to most prisoners in general population.

The most notorious of the shot-callers are slammed down within the isolated confines of the Segregated Housing Unit, or SHU, at Pelican Bay in Northern California, and when an execution order comes down to the yard from one of them, someone from within the gang, or even a prospect, is expected to follow through with the mission. To not follow a command is tantamount to treason and out of fear for their lives, it's not uncommon for prisoners to drop out of the gang. The dropout is put through a debriefing process conducted by prison officials in which the CDC extracts information about the gang from the defector. The prisoner is then placed on a Special Needs Yard.

Special Needs Yards have been growing at such a rate it won't be long until there are more SNY inmates than there are general population inmates. Dropping out over feared retribution, the cracking down on validated gang members and placing them in the SHU, and the accruing of drug debts are the biggest reasons for this. They've grown to such a level that PC gangs have sprouted on the SNY's.

In tiered housing units there will usually be a flurry of activity between prisoners, with guys shooting lines every which way, but that wasn't the case in Cypress. Communication was forbidden with the guys on the first tier because they were in protective custody. When they yelled up to us, we were not allowed to respond nor were we to tell them to shut the fuck up. They didn't have to abide by any of the regulations we were bound to, such as having respect for others on the tier, so they yelled back and forth with impunity. And because they were PC inmates, we couldn't have gotten at them if we wanted to—whenever they came out of their cells there were guards present.

Staying in Cypress Hall was comparable to living in an apartment above a household of drunks. I found it extremely difficult to shut out the din from below and my only relief was when we were let out of our cell for the walk downstairs to the chow hall for breakfast and dinner. My cellie and I couldn't stand each other; between his crying over his girl and my intolerance for his ceaseless sniveling, it was a wonder we never came to blows. He knew he was driving me mad and seemed to take pleasure in sharing his misery with me. But to be fair, I was always bitching about how shitty I felt—I was once again going through the throes of the agony associated with kicking dope. Being locked down in a cell with another man for any length of time, constantly focusing on their negative traits and mannerisms, has the potential for creating hostility and I knew it was just a matter of time before we took it to the next level.

Fortunately for myself, and for my equally pathetic cellie, I was transferred from Central to the West Yard after a week. It was an open-air setting and on Chino property, but within a separate perimeter from Central and the East Yard.

There were close to twenty of us who came over from Central and after going through a cavity search, being given new clothes and a brief orientation, we were escorted to our housing units. The buildings were old and dilapidated—they resembled old Army barracks with open spaces where windows had once been. The units were essentially large dorms, with a TV room on one end, a sprawling living area that included a guard's office and the shower/bathroom, and another living area on the other end. Bunk beds were everywhere, lining the walls and littering the halls. It was another fine example of overcrowding in the prison system.

I was designated a top rack, over a morbidly obese man who did nothing but eat and fart. His locker was full of Top Ramen's and he'd trade them to inmates for courses off their dinner trays. Steamy summer wind blew in from broken windows, bringing with it horse flies and the sweet pungent aroma of pasture. The dorm was hot, sticky and wrought with tension; it always felt like violence was right around the corner—and it was.

On my second day, the Skinheads jumped the shot-caller for the Whites. Chino, because it was on the edge of the Inland Empire and its close proximity to Orange County, had a large population of the bald-headed Nazi types. The shot-caller was from Venice Beach and, besides the fact that there was an on-again, off-again beef between the guys from L.A. and the guys from I.E. and O.C., they decided that Skinheads from the area should be the ones running the unit. I wasn't there to see what happened, but I heard a meeting was held in the TV room and when it was over a Skinhead from the Riverside area was the new guy running the show.

After the Skinhead coup d'état, a mandate was laid down in which all Whites were to hit the yard and exercise daily. Working out had already been mandatory but I'd been given a pass because I was kicking and practically worthless if any shit went down. With just over a week of clean time under my belt, the thought of jumping into a routine didn't exactly excite me. But what excited me even less was getting regulated, so I followed suit.

I did a workout the next day, doing the minimum and going back to the unit after the first unlock. I went to my bunk after taking a shower and subjected myself to smelling my bunkie's ass rather than the militant stares of Skinheads hanging out in the dayroom. I wasn't there but a half-hour and had just finished eating my meager lunch when the dorm porter came to my bunk and told me to roll up my property. I was being released. Unbeknownst to me, my parole agent had orchestrated a COP (continue on parole), meaning my hold had been lifted.

In the blink of an eye, I went from dreading my life and predicament to feeling like the luckiest man in the world. COP's were a rarity. What usually happened was a confinement of anywhere from four to twelve months, depending on the severity of the controlling case and the type of violation. As I was carrying my bedroll out of the unit, I could feel the envy radiating from the others and did my best to contain my excitement. It wasn't until I made it to R and R that I allowed myself to smile.

I was dressed out in khaki's, a white T-shirt and Jap-flaps, then escorted to an office where my parole agent was waiting. After signing some papers, I was released to his custody and we were on our way. He bought me some food from a Carl's Jr. outside of Chino and drove me back to the precinct in Fountain Valley so I could pick up my property, then surprised me even further by giving me $10 and telling me to call him soon before driving off.

149

I couldn't believe I was free. Being released from Chino was crazy enough, but for most of the ride back I had assumed he'd put me in some kind of lockdown treatment center. And I would've been grateful having gone—anywhere would've been better than that shit yard.

As fortunate as I was, I still felt like a leper when I walked into the precinct. My dress-out attire confirmed the fact that I'd just been released and the looks I got from the cops reflected wanton anger toward me. I didn't want to be there, but I needed my clothes, phone and skateboard, so I had no choice but to endure their stares and angry temperaments. They had me wait on a bench and kept blowing me off, but I was finally given my property and sent on my way.

I had just under ten days with no dope in my system so I was still feeling a little ragged, and as I was leaving the precinct, the thought of getting high began burrowing deeper into my mind, until it became an undeniable obsession hell-bent on what would be another run. My parole agent undoubtedly wanted me to get into treatment and my plan was to report to him so we could discuss where I'd go, but all of that changed when the bus I was on passed a Hollywood Video on Westminster Boulevard.

I'd stolen from that particular store many times before but had always been loaded—boosting clean wasn't something I was used to. It took over an hour because of how nervous I was, but I made it out of the store with a small cache of DVD's. I sold them in Long Beach and with cash in hand, the resolve I once had was left to rot in the Southern California sun.

BACK UPSTATE

Boosting DVD's had once again become my full-time occupation and I dropped by a Hollywood Video in Long Beach to come up with some quick cash. I went in with two empty shopping bags and filled them up but as I was doing so, one of the workers saw my handiwork and went to the front of the store to call the police. Not one to abort a mission, and because my judgment was impaired by all the drugs pumping through my veins, I decided to grab the bags and make a break using the fire escape.

I'd done plenty of grab-and-dash jobs in the past, but I preferred to use guile and tact; a clean getaway was always preferable to the cops being called and having to hide out. I couldn't use my hands because they were holding the bags, so I kicked the door open and ran outside. My plan was to cut through the alleys to the store where I was going to sell them, but it was cut short when one of the video store clerks tackled me from behind, letting out a loud, "citizen's arrest!" as he took me down.

A small army of store workers and neighborhood heroes held me down until the police arrived, then I was on my way downtown. They booked me for 1st degree theft, housing me in the felony tank of the Long Beach City Jail. It was set up just like the misdemeanor tank, the only difference being its occupants. Most of the inmates were Black or Mexican, and they were blasted with tattoos naming their sets and neighborhoods all over their bodies. That in itself wasn't so strange because by 2003 everybody was getting inked up, but it was much more solemn and imposing than the misdemeanor tank.

I couldn't believe I was in jail again and would likely be going back to prison. When I got out of Chino eight months prior, I swore I'd get high just once, but that of course led to another run. The day after being released, I discovered I had a financial aid check waiting for me—I'd applied a few months before going to Chino. Like any competent addict, I jumped parole and booked a room at the Cecil Hotel in Skid Row. The money didn't last long, but long enough for me to get a couple of abscesses and some blood poisoning that almost killed me.

151

I ended up being admitted to a hospital and called my parole agent while I was there. I had a sincere desire to quit and he must've believed me because he got my PAL hold lifted and into rehab. Everything was going great until I got my first pass. I left with the intention of going shopping but was soon overwhelmed with the all-too-familiar urge to stick a needle in my arm.

While I was downtown, to go along with my routine order of heroin and pills, I made the curious decision to buy some black hair dye. The staff probably would've figured out I'd gotten loaded regardless, but I ended up painting the bathroom black as I was dying my hair, all kinds of fucked-up, and my roommates ended up ratting me out. I was escorted to the office and asked to provide a urine sample and when I refused, I was asked to leave.

I was picked up the next day in Culver City for having drug paraphernalia and found myself back in the county jail, but not for long. My parole agent came to the rescue again and within a week I was released to a treatment center in San Pedro. I stayed at the rehab for ninety days and completed the program, then moved into a sober-living after I did. I managed to get five months clean and a job in Gardena working as a plumber's assistant, and I was feeling good about the direction my life was taking. And then I broke my elbow skateboarding.

When I went to the hospital, I did so with a friend and a fierce determination not to take any narcotics. My resolution began to dissipate the longer I sat in the emergency room and as the intensity of the pain increased, however. By the time the nurse called me into the X-ray room I was ready for any kind of painkiller she was willing to offer. She came at me with a shot of morphine and I was off and running. The drug brought out my lust for my demon love and within a week I was back on the streets and on the run.

* * * * *

152

Coming to in a cell was always a horrid thing. It wasn't until the effects of the pills wore off and the dope sickness kicked in that I realized just how good I had it and how bad the choices I made were. I slept horribly the first night but clung to my nightmares knowing it was only going to get worse. The cold sweats, muscle spasms, bone pain, diarrhea, vomiting, restlessness and intense depression made it so I wished I was dead, and I gladly would've killed myself if I wasn't so goddamn scared of making the move. My thoughts were torn between the longing for death and obsessing over the cure to my malcontent. I knew a fix was a long way off and the court was going to fuck me, leaving me to wrestle with a mind bent on self-destruction and no means to escape from my anguish.

Three torment-filled days later, I went to my arraignment and pled "not guilty", then was shipped off to the county jail and the mad parade of insanity within. I learned to tell the nurses I was going through alcohol withdrawals instead of heroin and was rewarded by being prescribed Librium, a mild benzo that helped very little but was better than nothing. To get the Librium, however, I had to sit in the cursed cage to await my medication and housing assignment.

Sitting in the cage was hell, especially after enduring days of moving from one cell to another and longing for a comfortable place to sleep. While lying on a spot of concrete I commandeered for myself, I was approached by an older white man having the look of a well-seasoned veteran of the prison system. He told me he had some meth stashed in the "safe" and needed me to keep point for him. We then walked over to one of the toilets and I kept an eye out for deputies while he sat on the toilet and pulled out the goods. Within a minute he had a shard of crystal in his hand and we were getting high.

It goes without saying I would've much rather been doing heroin but being a drug aficionado, I was welcome to ingesting anything. He broke off a healthy chunk of the glass and smashed it into a semi-fine powder, then snorted two monstrous lines apiece. The burn was intense and had me spinning from the pain, but I noticed right away I didn't feel sick anymore. The speed gave me an energy I found difficult to harness; I certainly wasn't going to exercise or start cleaning, but I couldn't sit still and would pace back and forth to stay occupied.

Despite being fully on edge the time moved quickly, and I was still spun when my name was called for transfer to MCJ. I was brought to the 3000 Floor again, but this time housed in a dayroom full of bunks used solely for the purpose of accommodating inmates impacted by overcrowding. Most everyone there was still awaiting trial and I could feel the tension immediately. Of course, I was coming down from speed and was exhausted and feeling sick again, so I'm sure I contributed to the sentiment in the unit as well.

The cell was filthy. At one point it had been used as a dayroom for the inmates on the tiers, but those days were a distant memory. The stand where a TV had once sat was now used for pull-ups. There were bunk beds strewn in a manner using every inch possible, maximizing the number of prisoners housed there. The shower room was outside of the unit and we were only able to use it every other day, so there was a makeshift birdbath set up by the sink and toilet. The result of this was a water runoff and dampness that was always present due to its constant usage. They were deplorable conditions but I found solace in knowing it was only temporary; I knew I'd be transferred to a different shithole at some point.

I did the courtroom shuffle over the next few of weeks, going to court to enter "not guilty" pleas, then brought back to the labyrinth of concrete and steel after seeing the judge. On my third court date, about four weeks after getting arrested, I was offered sixteen months. I wasn't exactly enthused about going back to prison but was tired of being shuttled back and forth between downtown L.A. and Long Beach, and also knew I couldn't beat the charge, so I jumped on it. Taking the deal brought about a feeling of resignation—I wasn't the kind of person people called "institutionalized", but I'd surely gotten accustomed to being locked up. I always assumed I'd get my shit together whenever I got out, but it never happened and would invariably find myself on the streets with the dirt and the scum.

I figured to have a little less than nine months left after everything was said and done. Sitting in jail knowing I wasn't hitting the streets anytime soon made prison sound appealing. It looked to be about a month until I got there but at least I was done with the cycle of court appearances and cavity searches when getting back to the jail. It's fair to say I took the sixteen months so I wouldn't have to deal with the stress anymore.

I was escorted back to my housing unit after getting my asshole checked and given the compensatory burritos, and then went to my rack knowing my next stop was prison. The next morning, however, my name was called for Wayside. I went through the long process of being moved from cell to cell in IRC until a crew of transport deputies came to take me and the other guys catching the chain to north L.A. County.

This time I was brought to Eastmax—another one of the many facilities at Pitchess Detention Center. Eastmax was a collection of old army-style barracks built in 1951 to be used as disciplinary units for inmates who received infractions at the honor farm. In 1957, it was designated as a maximum-security unit, the first of many in Los Angeles County. The buildings were old and run down, but the scenario was the same: a bunch of overzealous deputies watching and clashing with a jail population consisting of hoodlums and gangbangers.

Just like anywhere else in the jail system, the deputies conducted a cavity search and then brought us to our housing units. The barracks were packed with triple-rack bunks with a seating area in the front where we could watch TV, play cards and eat. Following jailhouse politics, Blacks had their side of the unit, Whites and Mexicans the other. Phones and workout areas were also segregated. The showers, toilets and bunks were the only areas in which race didn't matter. There was a deputy who sat at a desk on the other side of a cage from us in case it jumped off, but for the most part, each race kept their people, and the peace, in check.

The days were long and uneventful. We were only let out for yard once a week and that was for only two hours. I found myself so bored I even went to church when they called for it. It was as boring as I thought it would be, but I was able to steal a loaf of bread from the adjoining bakery, making the journey worthwhile. I also went to a twelve-step meeting that was called one day, remembering the feeling I got when I saw my old friend Cherokee at one in the King County Jail so long ago, but it was cut short because a riot kicked off in one of the dorms and we were sent back.

It took a little over a month for me to catch the chain. The deputies told me to roll it up after dinner, and I made it out to the first of many more holding cells I'd be sitting in over the next twenty-four hours. I was put on a bus with a large group of others going back to County and when we got there, I enviously eyed the ones separated from the group going to the release tank, while the rest of us were herded to the cells of IRC. As bad as sitting in a cell packed with men

155

going to prison would seem, time moved fairly well and it was devoid of tension because we were excited to be leaving the jail. Eight hours later, around four in the morning, we heard the chains being wheeled in on a cart.

The deputies shackled us together then marched us to the bus, and just like that we were on our way to Delano. Pulling up to the prison instilled the same sense of awe that it had my first time, but this time I was more focused on being able to use the bathroom after the long four-hour drive. The guy I was sitting next to hadn't been before and he wore his feigned bravado like a tattered garment, but I could tell he was scared. He kept asking me what he should do if someone tried making moves on him. I joked with him and told him to start wearing his boxers backwards, granting easy access to his butthole.

I was brought to D Yard again and this time my cellie was a hick from Missouri who carried the nervous demeanor of a man that was guilty. Of what I didn't know, I just hoped I wouldn't be passed a kite telling me I had to stab him or some shit. I didn't like him at all. Some guys find God in prison and end up hiding behind the bible, claiming they're exempt from politics because of their Christian beliefs, others just want to do their time and go home, then there are those who feel the need to be in the middle of everything. He was one of the latter.

There was a Swastika penciled on the wall and he'd sit in front of it praying for guidance. If it weren't so comical, I would've found it disturbing. Many of the Skinheads in prison put their faith in Norse mythology, incurring the powers of runes to assist them in acts pertaining to battle and race and whatever else. As much as I didn't agree with them, I could stomach them because they were at least passionate about their beliefs. My cellie was the type who was jumping into something he had no knowledge about. Through fear and intimidation, the Skinheads had converted him—much like the missionaries who converted indigenous tribes in third-world countries.

Fortunately, I wasn't celled with him for long. A couple of days after I'd gone through diagnostics, I was moved to C Yard. The building I was placed was rife with tension—it was extremely quiet when I walked in and everybody was on their toes anticipating violence. As I was making my bed, all the races started grouping in separate areas of the dorm. We were told to disperse and go back to our bunks by the building C.O. and when that didn't get any results,

156

he called for reinforcements. Within a minute, a legion of goons swarmed into the dayroom with pepper spray canisters armed and ready, giving us all cause to stand down without resorting to violence. A sergeant called out representatives from each race and when they came back the situation was squashed. Whatever it was that had everybody on edge was decidedly forgotten about.

The unease that was present when I rolled into the dorm lingered for a few days, but it wasn't long until things returned to normal. As the program relaxed, I passed my time playing pinochle, watching football and exercising. Each day was spent knowing I was another day closer to seeing my counselor, hitting the mainline and being released.

It can go from calm to crazy in the blink of an eye, however. The Southsiders and Blacks got into a verbal altercation over who had rights to the TV one day. It started because the Paisas, who the Southsiders were aligned with, had been disrespected when a black guy turned the channel to a soap opera—doing it in a manner that said he didn't give a fuck what the Paisas thought. After being informed that the guy who turned the channel needed to be regulated, the Blacks blatantly refused, thinking the Mexicans would back down.

We were told to keep our eyes open and to stay on our toes by our shot-caller. We were also told to stick together and that it wasn't our battle. The Southsiders did a masterful job of keeping their retaliation under wraps; they waited until after dinner was served and the dayroom had been opened again.

When they struck it took us all by surprise, but none more so than the Blacks. There was a guardrail separating the bunk area from the dayroom and on a signal, the Southsiders jumped over it, swarming the Black's section of the dayroom like locusts. Many of the Mexicans had the padlocks for their lockers inside socks and were swinging them like madmen, and when they connected blood would pour. The guys getting hit with locks had it bad but the ones who had it the worst were the ones getting rat-packed. I counted at least four different groups that were absolutely destroying any black man unfortunate enough to get caught alone when the shit went down.

As soon as it jumped, the C.O. on duty hit the alarm and yelled, "Get on the ground!" Guards stormed the unit, armed with pepper spray canisters and batons, dousing combatants who wouldn't get down. One of the Mexicans, a homie named Caveman from Riverside, was locked in a melee with one of the black soldiers and when the C.O.'s saw they weren't reacting to the pepper spray, they moved in with their batons, beating them into submission.

All of us not involved in the riot watched from prone positions, coughing and fighting back tears from the pepper spray. The guards moved in fast, using zip-ties to cuff anyone within the perimeter of the battleground. There were many involved in the melee that managed to get back to their bunk areas and there were also a few who hid when the shit went down. It was comical watching the ones who hid scurry out from under their bunks to the edges of the dayroom, trying to give the impression they were part of the action so they wouldn't be perceived as cowards.

Everyone involved in the riot was escorted to cages where they'd get the pepper spray washed off and then taken to the hole, and many of them were brought to the infirmary to be treated for injuries. We were all put on bunk status and watched as a group of inmate workers came in and mopped up the blood, then bagged up the property of everyone who was sent to the hole.

The next couple days were extraordinarily quiet but others were eventually brought in to take the places of those taken to the hole. Our program went back to normal after about a week and counselors returned to making their rounds. Mine came three weeks after the riot and I was told the same thing as last time—I was going to a CCF. I knew better than to get my hopes up this time, but took great satisfaction in knowing my half-time had officially kicked in and was one step closer to hitting the mainline.

My name was called to trans-pack three weeks later and when I went up to the podium with my property, I was told that I was going to California Men's Colony in San Luis Obispo. When I told everyone where I was going I got mixed reactions; some said it was Disneyland and others said it was a haven for rapists and child molesters. Regardless of how great or how fucked it was supposed to be, I was grateful to be moving on to the place I'd parole from. Going home was right around the corner.

CMC

The ride from Delano was made under the cover of darkness. We left R and R at three in the morning, so many of the occupants were sleeping, giving the C.O. behind the cage with the shotgun the silence he demanded. Our bus navigated numerous farm roads before connecting with the highway James Dean lost his life on fifty years earlier and then continued westward through canyons surrounded by hills covered with grapes and cattle.

San Luis Obispo is a quaint little college town and as we drove through it, I thought to myself that it was a hell of a strange place to put a bunch of convicted felons. The prison was built in 1954 and later expanded in 1961 to include the East Facility, a medium-security lockdown unit with a hospital and even a hospice. Rumor had it that the East Facility was a "no good" yard. That's not to say everyone there was bad, but it was common knowledge among prisoners that protective custody prisoners lived within its walls. East also had its share of celebrities. Ike Turner, "Hollywood" Henderson, Suge Knight, Timothy Leary, "Tex" Watson and the skateboarder Mark "Gator" Rogowski had all been there at one time or another.

Much to my satisfaction, I was going to the yard adjacent to there, the West Facility. West was a minimum/medium yard with a razor wire fenced perimeter and old guard towers dotting its landscape. The C.O.'s used the same precautions as the bus rolled into the sally port, checking the storage compartments and undercarriage for contraband and escapees, then marched us into an old building that looked like an army barrack. We were stripped of our paper suits, given a thorough search, then handed sets of state-issue CDC prison clothes. We waited in a packed little cell while the guards did our intakes and took our pictures and then were escorted to an area of the facility called Unit 1.

Unit 1 was a collection of dorms surrounding a baseball field and a spattering of administrative buildings. The dorm we were put in was an orientation unit, a place to be held until we were assigned a counselor, classified, then moved to the appropriate unit relative to our classification. Units 1 and 2 were standard yards, filled with prisoners

---

159

who worked and went to school; Unit 3 was a fire camp yard that handled local brush fires and fire prevention; and Unit 4 was designed for prisoners cleared for fire camp and for men with less than a year left in their sentence. All the units were on the same compound and separated by fences, but sharing an infirmary, visiting area, library and an assortment of other buildings used for schooling and work programs.

The dorm was made up of a long room with bunk beds lining its walls, two TV rooms separated by racial alignments (Blacks and Asians shared one, Whites and Mexicans the other), a restroom and an officer's station. As is typical within California's prison system, the dorm was crowded to the point of it being just one small incident away from a riot jumping off. Navigating tension in a dorm setting was a skill I'd mastered through my many years of living in such environments, but it still didn't make it any easier. Just because I was proficient at treading water didn't make me a good swimmer.

When we got there, the building C.O. facilitated an orientation group giving us a rundown of the place. This wasn't a prison worthy of a resume—it wasn't the kind of yard convicts made a name for themselves on. He didn't come out and say it, but we'd all heard there were convicted sex offenders on the yard. It was a place where prisoners minded their own business, did their time, and went home.

Despite the fact the guy sleeping next to you might be in prison because he had a thing for little boys, it was an easy place to do your time. It was right off the coast, so the weather was comfortable; the air coming in from the Pacific Ocean kept it cool and much more habitable than the extreme temperatures of the San Joaquin Valley. Small mountains surrounded the prison and I'd watch the ant-like hikers climb to their summits, wondering what they thought of us in the prison below.

Modern prison yards all share the same design, more or less: flat and even expanses of grass and/or dirt, littered with handball and basketball courts, a walking track and towering lights with enough wattage to illuminate even the darkest of nights. CMC was different, however. The yard was set on a slight grade and still had trees. In addition to handball and basketball courts, there was a softball field and tennis courts that were actually used when there were enough people to play. There was even a Bocce court we used in a manner that surely would've caused an Italian to roll over in his grave—we called it Caveman Bocce.

Just because the prison wasn't of the "modern" variety didn't mean shit didn't go down. You still had to be on your toes and keep your eyes open for potential violence, but it was nowhere near as tense as other prisons. The situations that did arise primarily came from races checking their own people for violations and such. Most prisoners had adopted routines that would be changed drastically with the onset of violence and did their best to steer clear of drama.

I was brought before a committee when I had two weeks in and told that I'd be transferred to Unit 4 that same day. I only had five months left in my sentence by then so it made sense, being that Unit 4 was used for prisoners leaving, either to fire camp or home. Knowing I'd be paroling from there, barring any unforeseen events, gave me the feeling I was turning a corner in my journey toward being released.

Unit 4 was significantly smaller than Unit 1—space was designated for dorms, an admin building and a cafeteria. The dorms were basically the same except they had an extra TV room to accommodate the Paisas. For some reason I never quite understood, Unit 4 had a large population of "border brothers" awaiting extradition to their country of origin.

The yard was just as relaxed as Unit 1 but there was an added bonus—there were no rapists or child molesters there. All prisoners had to see a CDC committee before relocation to any yard, which meant a counselor's access to your C-file, and because you had to be eligible for fire camp to go there, inmates with sex crimes on their jackets were prohibited from being housed on the unit.

I received a ducat at my four-month mark stating that I had to report to a program called "Arts in Corrections". I had no idea what it was but was pleasantly surprised when I showed up the next day. Arts in Corrections was a program created to open prisoner's eyes toward expressing themselves through writing, painting and music. There were two facilitators—one was a teacher who worked for the CDC and the other a prisoner who'd been down over ten years. The teacher didn't know shit but the one doing time was well versed in song structures and chord progressions. I'd sit with him whenever I went to the class, picking his brain for knowledge regarding music.

One of the guys in the dorm had a guitar loaned to him through AIC, and he'd lend it to me so I could practice. I'd been raised around musicians in Seattle but never really got around to playing myself. The time spent in rehearsal studios and garages when I was a kid made me proficient enough to sit in when a drummer or bass player was needed, and that was in a fashion that could be described as rudimentary at best. I knew which guitars were worthy of stealing and where I could sell them, but didn't know a damn thing about playing them. I never took the steps to learn how to play and further, lacked the vision necessary to see myself playing. I was a bona fide slacker—traits that most possess, such as drive, ambition and setting goals, weren't at my disposal.

I spent my nights practicing three basic chords—G, D and A. Hearing the notes coming out of the guitar made me feel good and after a while I started to believe I could learn to play if I stayed with it. Being as self-conscious as I was, I'd play in a spot on the yard where there wasn't much activity and would stop when others approached. It was only with discipline that I started to learn—it certainly wasn't because of hidden talent—and with time I did, piecing together rhythms and humming melodies.

The days were flying by with my new hobby and before I knew it, I had two months left. Right around that time, I received another ducat; this one for a pre-release class. It was mandatory and supposed to help steer prisoners in the right direction after they paroled, but with an 85% prisoner recidivism rate I don't how much stock could be taken in their value to society.

My counselor ducated me around this time as well, requesting that I report to her office. The CDC checks for warrants and holds as prisoner's release dates approach and I had a feeling it was the reason I was summoned. I feared the worst as I walked there but couldn't think of any charges I might have. I was scared something out of Seattle had popped up or that items I'd sold to pawnshops in L.A. had been reported stolen.

My fear turned out to be valid because I did indeed have a warrant, but not for anything I anticipated. Close to a month before getting arrested, I was stopped by a deputy on the Blue Line and given a ticket for fare evasion. Making a court appearance was the least of my concerns at the time and I promptly filed the ticket into a part of my brain that rarely got used and forgot about it.

The warrant hadn't been issued until after I made it to CMC and because it wasn't discovered until right before I was due to be released, I didn't have the time necessary to get it taken care of. The process used to squash the warrant would've involved notifying the court and letting them know I was being held in state prison. The warrant would've likely been dismissed if I'd taken the proper steps but because it would take at least ninety days for it to get dropped, I was screwed. Instead of paroling from CMC, I'd be picked up by the sheriff's department and transported to the county jail to be seen by the judge—all because I didn't pay my train fare.

My experiences with incarceration had taught me anything could happen when it came to being released—I'd been let out early, had charges dropped, gone to the hole, had friends post bail unexpectedly, been released by my parole agent and also dealt with charges popping up at the last minute before—but even with this knowledge it felt like I'd been slapped in the face. It was because of situations like these that you never celebrate your freedom until you walk out the gate. Fortunately, I had a routine to keep me busy and knew I'd be released as soon as I made it to court. It wasn't that big of a deal when it came down to it, and I even joked with the fellas about not having to buy a bus ticket to get back to Los Angeles.

Another issue arose when I had twelve days left that threatened to compromise my freedom even further. One of the Whites in another dorm had gotten into a fight with a Southsider and ended up getting rat-packed. If it had been one-on-one it might've been squashed but because he got jumped, it turned into an issue that had to be dealt with. All the Whites were told to stay on their toes and to stay together because it was going to kick off.

I'd met plenty of people over the years who lived for situations like these, but I wasn't one of them. I still had to deal with my warrant in L.A., but that was merely a minor hurdle. Getting caught up in a riot and a potential new charge could possibly jeopardize my release date, and I'd end up finishing my time in the hole. I was seriously contemplating wearing the mark of the coward and staying in the dorm for the whole ordeal, but I knew I'd have to live with the shame and cowardice, as well as the fear of getting jumped by my own people for not getting involved. The shame and cowardice I could live with, it wasn't like I lived a life of nobility, it was the constantly having to watch my back I didn't want to worry about.

I'd like to say it was pride and loyalty that swayed me, but in the end, it was self-preservation and ego that dictated my actions. I

163

didn't want to be perceived as a bitch, nor did I want to be jumped in the shower or TV room, so when plans were made to attack the Mexicans the following day, I followed suit.

It kicked off after breakfast, at the first yard unlock. All the Whites started grouping in the courtyard, catching the attention of both the Mexicans and the C.O.'s. The Southsiders began grouping on the other side of the courtyard in response but before there were enough fighters to effectively counter our attack, we were on them. A group of Skinheads led the charge, running headlong into the center of their congregation. The Mexicans fared well at first, but they were severely outnumbered. It wasn't long until I saw guys rolling on the ground trying to avoid an onslaught of Skinhead boots. That isn't to say they didn't inflict any damage—a group of Southsiders came flying out of the dorm that was closest to the action's side door and attacked the rear of a group of Whites, and there were other instances in which the Southsiders came out advantageous, but all in all they suffered a resounding defeat.

All of this happened in a span of about two minutes. The C.O.'s, when they saw us gathering, told us to disperse, but their warnings fell on deaf ears. They showed up in force, coming through the gate connecting to Unit 1, but by the time they got there the disturbance was in full swing. A phalanx of ten officers marched toward us with their "super soakers" (large pepper spray canisters) and batons at the ready, spraying anyone they came into contact with and yelling to get on the ground. About half the people involved followed their direction, rolling away from where the action was, but the others kept at it, delivering retribution until the pepper spray became too much to endure.

There were close to eighty bodies lying in prone positions on the dirt courtyard by the time the fighting stopped, some writhing in pain, most fighting off the effects of the pepper spray and all wondering what was next. But I wasn't one of them. My wits had come to me during the riot and instead of jumping into the middle of the fight, I maneuvered into a flanking position, preparing myself for an evasive route. I wasn't scared of getting my ass kicked; I was, however, scared of getting more time tacked to the end of my sentence. I figured I'd covered myself by being present when the shit kicked off, and I also justified jumping ship by the small amount of time I had left and because the Southsiders were getting beat.

164

Instead of dropping to the ground when the C.O.'s came marching up, I ran into the dorm bordering the action through the door the Mexicans ran out of. It was a foolish decision because I could've easily been attacked by anyone inside, but luckily didn't run into any opposition. Everyone inside the building was standing at the windows watching the riot come to a close, and I took it as a perfect opportunity to run through the dorm and out the back door. It was less than twenty feet to my dorm once I got outside but that didn't make it easy. C.O.'s were in the towers on the yard looking for any type of movement. I decided to make a dash and luck was with me because I made it back to my dorm without anyone seeing me go in.

I ditched my workout clothes and put on my state-blues, trying to alter my appearance in the event a guard saw me run inside, then joined the rest of the guys in the unit looking out the windows toward the action. Most of the Whites and Southsiders were out on the yard—the makeup of those present was overwhelmingly Christian. Nobody said anything as I joined their ranks and I hoped I wouldn't face any repercussions by anyone down the road thinking I was trying to avoid the conflict. C.O.'s were busy cuffing everyone on the yard with zip-ties and lining people up by race against the perimeter fence. We watched for no more than five minutes, until a small group of C.O.'s came in and ordered us to our bunks. They then checked our hands for cuts and scrapes, looking for anyone who might've slipped through the cracks and made it back to the dorm.

We weren't allowed out of our housing unit except for passes to the doctor and so forth, and those were done with escorts. We ate sack lunches that were brought to us and were not allowed to leave our bunk areas unless it was to go to the bathroom. It made the days stretch, but I really didn't mind because the chances of it jumping off while on lockdown were significantly lower. I was just happy to be leaving and that I wasn't sitting in the hole with everyone else.

We stayed on lockdown for the duration of my stay and on March of 2004, I was told to roll up my property for transfer. I was brought to the same cell I'd been put in when I first arrived to CMC and waited for the pigs to arrive. It was early in the afternoon by the time they did. The deputy who handcuffed me told me that it was a $200 ticket and seemed genuinely surprised that L.A. took the time to pick me up for something so small. He even joked with me, as I'd joked with others before, that at least I didn't have to buy a ticket to get back.

It was a long bus ride; we took Pacific Coast Highway all the way down, stopping at the Ventura County Jail to pick up two female inmates. There were eight of us on the bus when we arrived to Los Angeles—four guys from where the journey started in Santa Clara County, a mental patient we picked up at Atascadero State Hospital, the girls from Ventura and myself. Despite the way I arrived, I was excited to be back in L.A. and to the streets that were calling my name. I held no illusions about staying clean…there was a Mexican hanging out on Spring Street with a mouthful of balloons waiting for me.

The jail was as packed as always, but I was able to bypass the clusterfuck of prisoners in the first three intake cells because I was brought in as a transfer from prison. I had to go through a cavity search upon entry—prisoners coming in were notorious for smuggling drugs, tobacco and messages from shot-callers into jail. I was put in a cell brimming with miscreants who smelled like sewage, leading me to contemplate the contrast between coming to jail with a habit and coming in clean. My previous experiences in these cells were of me lying in a corner, curled up in a ball, with a peanut butter sandwich for a pillow and wanting to die.

I was stuck in that cell for at least six hours because a riot had kicked off on another floor and movement was restricted until they got everything back in order. Even so, I made it to a cell on the 3000 Floor in record time—less than twenty-four hours—and that can be solely attributed to not having any medical issues. There were many deterrents used by jail staff to keep inmates from reporting medical issues and time spent in the dreaded "cage" was but one of them.

Within an hour of arrival to my cell a trustee told me to report to the court line—effectively making the time spent on housing me a wasted effort. Not that I minded, of course. My only concern was making it to court and being released.

Tickets pertaining to the Metro Transit Authority's Blue Line were handled in the Compton Courthouse and the holding tank I was put in to await transport reflected the city's nefarious gangster roots. Outside of one other Wood, the cell was entirely Mexican. 90% of them had shaved heads with their sets blasted all over their bodies, necks and faces. Blacks were held in another cell, not just because of politics, but because many of them were sworn enemies on the streets. Some of the Southsiders were at war with each other also, and it was only through their shot-callers that a tentative peace was reached, a peace that teetered precariously and was only held within the confines of the system. Most were soldiers, ready to die for their neighborhood, street or set, and many of them knew they were never getting out. And my junkie ass had one thing in common with them—we were statistics in a society that was failing.

The two hours spent in that cell waiting for the transport deputies were tense. The other white guy and I stood against a wall trying to be invisible, getting looks from the homies here and there, beckoning us to challenge them or say something stupid. Responding in any manner deemed reactive would've guaranteed a severe beat-down and possibly worse. Situations like these were nothing new to me; I'd been through them before and knew we'd probably be okay. My companion, on the other hand, looked like he was going to shit his pants. I wanted to tell him to keep his cool, that they thrived on fear, but there wasn't anything I could tell this kid. It was something he'd have to learn himself.

The bus finally came and after loading us, we were on our way to the heralded city of Compton. The deputies separated us once we got there and put us in our own cell. While being much safer, it also made for an extremely long day because of the lack of activity and movement. It was just the two of us in a large and quiet cell, with nothing to do but pushups, talk shit and eat from the abundance of sack lunches the deputies threw our way.

A public defender came by in the afternoon to tell us what we already knew, that we were there because we didn't pay our tickets, and that we'd be released from the courthouse that same night. Neither of us even had to see the judge, we just had to sign a paper acknowledging our guilt and saying we'd pay a court cost of $200 at some point. To be extradited back to L.A. County for such a miniscule charge was ludicrous but I found it laughable after everything was said and done. It was a blatant example of wasting revenue to satisfy a false principle of justice.

My cellmate and I had gotten to know each other a little by that point. He knew I'd just paroled, had nowhere to go and wanted to get high, so he invited me to a riverbed camping spot a few of his meth buddies had commandeered. To most people, this would hardly be considered a great plan but to a junkie who wanted to get loaded it sounded like heaven. He was a tweaker and speed wasn't exactly my thing, but right then it would work just fine.

We were released, in the City of Compton, at eight in the evening. We had no money and our clothes were in the property room downtown, so we were given white jumpsuits to wear out. The whole situation had an *Escape from New York* feel to it. The local residents were surely used to seeing guys in jumpsuits walk out of the courthouse, but to anyone else we must've looked like we'd just made a break. Making it even more comical was the fact we were white. The words "white" and "Compton" haven't been used together since the "white flight" migration of the 1950's, when most of the Whites in the area moved to Orange County.

We didn't have time to appreciate the stares from the curious eyes because we ran straight to the train station where we fit right in with the crackheads and locals used to seeing people in our predicament. It was the same when we boarded the train—the nightlife onboard didn't bat an eye over our outward appearances. Once we were characterized as non-threatening, they went back to looking out for cops and rival gang members. And as is common on a train in any big city, the rest of the passengers stared at the ground, pretending they didn't see us.

Both of us were giddy with excitement from being released and the anticipation of getting high. His camp was only two stops from Compton by the Del Amo station and when we got off the train, we continued our running, not wanting to be noticed by any cops. The camp was in-between an old railway and Compton Creek, a trickle of water subsidiary of the L.A. River. We had to navigate a trail to get there, climbing over and around various barriers, but once we did, we were in the middle of a tweaker's paradise. Scrap piles that had long since been stripped of anything of value dotted the landscape, intermixed with camouflage tarps covering cooking and sleeping areas. It was a No-Man's Land taken over by nomadic meth-heads. The police turned a blind eye to their presence and lawlessness— sometimes hauling in a cashless meth addict isn't worth the time.

We encountered no one as we walked through the dwellings, but I could feel the eyes upon us. My buddy told me to wait while he went in to talk with one of the camp's inhabitants, leaving me alone in the tweaker jungle and feeling more vulnerable than I'd felt in the cell of gangsters earlier that morning. A long minute later he came back to tell me I was okay, then we went into a camp occupied by an old speed freak who looked like Santa Claus to smoke crystal meth. He continuously talked about pagan gods and runes, pausing only to stir a fire he had going in a pit and to put more meth in the pipe. I didn't mind at first, but the euphoria associated with speed only went so far with me and I began to feel like a hostage to his incessant and nonsensical banter.

By the time the sun started to rise I was out of my mind. I managed to break free from the safety/insanity of the encampment and on toward the relief awaiting me downtown, telling them I'd be back but knowing I was done there. I'd been through these early morning rituals before, spending hours shooting coke and looking for veins or smoking crack with burnt fingers until my last dollar was spent, but never with meth. The insanity was the same and I knew there was only one cure—a shot of dope.

Spun out of my mind and fully conscious that I was wearing a jumpsuit, I got on the train to the city. The contrast of the morning commuter crowd from the nightriders was glaring—I stuck out like a nasty cold sore and could feel the eyes of every single passenger on the train burning into me. I tried riding with my eyes closed but they twitched under their lids…I was a ball on nervous energy and on the verge of exploding.

Two hours of hell later, I walked into the L.A. County Jail and got my property, clothes and money. Being there felt comfortable in a sense, offering a subtle calm to my spinning mind. I was sheltered from the insanity of having to think and deal with a society I felt no part of. Coping with the monotony of the jail system seemed easy compared to the challenges life was comprised of. As crazy as it sounds, there was a part of me that wanted to be snatched up and thrown back in with the rats and the roaches. But as I went to the bathroom to change into my clothes, I came to my senses. There was a long-overdue dark and lovely kiss awaiting me.

DIRTY CITY STREETS

The cop had his gun drawn and pointed at my chest and was screaming at me to get on the ground. I was already on the ground, which made his command both redundant and comical, sitting in a secluded area of the park and had just finished drawing up a shot when he rudely invaded my space. I set the needle and cooker down at my feet and slowly reclined to a prone position, wishing I had the balls to do something that would instigate him to pull the trigger, sparing me of anymore painful and unnecessary breath.

I'd been out of prison just two months, quickly acquiring a full-blown habit and an abscess that was eating me up. It all happened so fast—my intent was to get high a few times but somehow didn't foresee the fall. You'd think I would've known better by then, but the junkie's mind is adept at self-deception. The day after I'd shown up at the jail to get my property, spun-out and needing a fix, I had gone to the welfare office in Compton to get benefits and a voucher for a dive hotel in Long Beach. The voucher was only good for two weeks and by the time I had to vacate, the general relief money and food stamps were long gone, and I was boosting to support my habit.

With nowhere to go, I naturally found myself back downtown, close to where the drugs were. I set up shop in a stairwell on 7th and Hope Street, staying there after the office workers left the area and leaving before they came back in the morning. If I wasn't out and about trying to make a buck, I'd either be between Broadway and Main Streets looking to score or in any of the alleys, parks and bathrooms doing the drugs.

The park I'd often hit was on 4th and Hill, nestled between the Angel's Flight Railway and Pershing Square. It was there that I found myself looking down the barrel of a gun with a shot of dope I was about to do at my feet. The cop cuffed me up, took my loaded syringe as evidence and brought me straight to the Glasshouse. The Glasshouse was a nickname for the Parker Center and had gotten its name because of its architectural design and for being technologically advanced at the time. It had been built in 1955 and was the headquarters for the LAPD, right down from the iconic L.A. City Hall building. It had graced the TV screen in shows such as Dragnet and as a site of civil unrest on many occasions, one of them being when the cops involved with beating Rodney King were let off the hook in '92.

The cop, who had the audacity to apologize for pulling his gun on me, put me in a cell and left me there while he did his paperwork. I was loaded from my breakfast intake of Xanax bars and heroin, and delirious from lack of food, sleep and a large abscess I had on my arm. The abscess had gotten to the point where it resembled a zit and I figured in my insanity that if I popped it, they'd take me to General Hospital where I could possibly get some opiates. The problem was, they'd already taken my property so I'd have to use my fingernails to do it. Because of how swollen it had become, the skin was thin enough that it was possible, so I dug my fingernails and twisted until it gave, sending a flood of blood and pus onto the floor.

It didn't hurt but it smelled something fierce and a good amount of the toxic fluid drenched my clothes. I yelled to the watch officer that I had a medical emergency, bringing two cops to my cell. After their initial display of disgust and listening to them bitch about having more work to do, I was told to get ready to be transported. I was given a paper suit to wear out and brought to General Hospital in East L.A., where I sat in an emergency room with other hapless unfortunate souls from all walks of life. Prisoners were generally brought to a jail ward on the 13th floor but for some reason it was decided I'd be seen on the main floor. The officers had me cuffed and stood with me the whole time, even when the nurse cleaned the wound and packed it with gauze. It seemed he was trying to hurt me while he packed it and I was fully kicking by then, so the pain was even more severe. As if that wasn't bad enough, I wasn't given any of the painkillers I fooled myself into thinking I'd get.

When the medical staff was done, I was brought directly to the county jail and then taken to the infirmary because of my wound. MRSA (staph infections) had become an issue within the jail and they didn't want me in GP because I could possibly spread an infection and was also susceptible of contracting one. My plan to get pain medication didn't work but I did manage to bypass the torturous booking process and the dreaded cage.

The nurses conducted a general checkup, then sent me to my housing unit on the 8000 Floor. I was put in a wing where most of the inmates were suspected of having MRSA and we were all kept isolated in single-man cells. They were spacious and had their own showers,

---

171

but the time moved agonizingly slow. I was only let out to use the phone and when the nurse pulled me out to change the gauze in my arm. I'd had many abscesses in the past, but I'd always had heroin to subdue the pain. With nothing to dull my nerves, and kicking dope on top of it, the pain was so intense I'd hyperventilate during the procedure, then go back to my cell like a dog beaten by a sadistic owner.

Ten days into my stay, with 1000 showers and buckets of tears under my belt, I was called to roll up my property. I thought I was being released but soon discovered my parole agent was taking me to a program. It was a letdown in a sense—I needed a fix—but I did find solace in knowing I was leaving the goddamn county jail.

Because I didn't have any clothes, just the paper suit I came in with, the deputies gave me some old throwaways people had left behind. My agent came in to get me personally, leading me out to his car in cuffs. I was a sorry sight—I still wasn't sleeping so my eyes were bugged-out, I hadn't shaved, my hair was disheveled, I was gaunt and to top it off, I was wearing tight acid-wash jeans and a bright orange sweater five times too big for me. If I had a mullet I would've looked like a white trash runway model.

I'd been assigned a new parole agent when I got out of prison, a young white guy who did everything by the book. We were a picture of sharp contrast: him with his Dockers and dress shirt, and I with my atrocious hand-me-downs…if you would've seen us together on the streets you'd have known something was amiss. We drove in silence for most of the ride and when we got to Hollywood he looked at me and told me he knew I'd end up fucking this up and if it was up to him he would've just left me in jail. I didn't really care what he thought but I told him not to worry—I was going to be a model prisoner.

The halfway house was called Hollywood Reentry, on the corner of Franklin and Vine, one block up from the Capitol Records building. Everybody there was on parole—most of the residents wore the time they'd done on their sleeves and acted like they were still in prison. Parole agents constantly stopped by to drop prisoners off and also bring them back into custody.

I didn't jive too well with the prison mentality of most of the guys there but liked the place after settling in. Once I got through a one-week lockdown orientation phase, I was able to leave on passes, working at Labor Ready during the day and hitting twelve-step meetings at night. Staying clean began to feel good.

I was going to meetings practically every day, and even though I'd heard warnings from those who'd been clean a while that it wasn't enough, I felt positive about the direction I was heading. When they said I should get a sponsor and start being of service to others and to the group, I discounted their suggestions as words from brainwashed kooks. But sure enough, as I was coming back from work one day, I got the calling. It came to me quick, first as an idea then later an obsession, but the end result was a stop in Pershing Square before going back to the halfway house. That one time led to a series of events that eventually led to the loss of my freedom.

I've never been one to "chip" successfully and it didn't take long for me to get a habit. Within two weeks I'd fallen back to my routine of mixing pills with the dope, which led to nodding out and spending considerable time locked in the bathroom. The staff promptly got hip to my ways and one morning I was called into an office that had three parole agents lying in wait, wasting no time in hemming me up and searching my pockets. I had a cigarette cellophane with about twenty Klonopin in my front pocket and when the agent searching me found them, I was taken back to the county jail.

I went through IRC in another blackout and came to a couple of days later on the 3000 Floor, wondering what the fuck happened. When I was told that I was in for a parole violation, my first reaction was one of incredulity, quickly followed by gratitude knowing I wasn't in for anything serious. It brought to mind a memory of the man in King County ten years earlier who'd committed a robbery in a blackout and had no idea why he was there. If it wasn't for the report I later read at my parole hearing, I wouldn't have had any knowledge of what went down.

I was given six months for the violation, doing four with good time, and did it all at Supermax. Half of that time was done in another of L.A. County's useless "training" programs…the sign shop. Like the print shop, it was put into place to satisfy the need for rehabilitation but in actuality was used for free labor. The certificates, issued by a local college, were practically worthless. The money saved on labor, on the other hand, was significant. All the signs in the L.A. County system—the jails, precincts, courthouses and wherever else—were fabricated there, and there was never a shortage of workers. The

173

biggest farce relative to "rehabilitation", however, was the fabric/sweatshop next to the sign shop. The entire crew was Latino and the majority of them were awaiting extradition back to their homeland. They'd sit at their sewing machines all day, sewing everything from boxers to the outfits worn by inmates on suicide watch.

As October came about my release date came with it and I was bussed downtown to MCJ. I went through a six-hour cell shuffle in IRC, then on to the release tanks. While sitting in the cell, waiting for our clothes to be wheeled to us, an OG homie was brought in and stood by the door. He looked around the crowded cell, trying to read people and if they might snitch, then asked one of the little homies to keep point for him. While the youngster was making sure the coast was clear, he went to the toilet and pulled out a package he had hidden between his ass cheeks. Bundled inside a tight roll of toilet paper were a plastic spork, a syringe and a balloon of heroin. He put the dope and water into the spork, stirred it with his finger and then drew it up with the syringe. His veins weren't cooperating and I watched him try to hit himself repeatedly until I couldn't take it anymore, asking him if he wanted me to hit him in the neck. I was sympathetic to his plight but what I really wanted was some of his dope.

The needle was a "binky"—a syringe cut down to half-size and easier to conceal—and it was ancient. The markings had long since rubbed off the outside of the syringe from all the times it had been used, exchanged hands, and been stuck in some hoodlum's ass, and the needle itself was barbed from countless injections. I had him stick his thumb in his mouth and blow, making the vein in his neck stick out, then jabbed the needle into his skin. It was a roller so I had to poke again to puncture the vein itself and when it did, blood filled the air pocket inside the syringe and I pushed the plunger in. His reaction was instantaneous—he mumbled something expressing his love for the drug and started scratching the spot on his neck where I shot him up. Within seconds, he was where I longed to be.

To assume he was going to reward me for hitting him was rather presumptuous. He did, but not in a manner that satisfied my needs. He left the rinse and cotton—it wasn't really a cotton; it was a small piece of fabric from his sock—for me to get what I could out of them. He also gave me the rig, forcing my hand in making another of many bad decisions. I'd shared needles plenty of times in the past but mostly when I was kicking and knowing the person I was sharing with—at least somewhat. I was neither dope sick nor knew the guy this time. My biggest concern, however, was reporting to my parole agent the next day, knowing he was going to pop a drug test on me.

The craziest thing about it all was that it wasn't even enough to get me high and I was still willing to jeopardize my health and freedom in the pursuit. That being said, I pounded the cotton, drew it up and muscled it into my ass. I thought I'd feel it at least a little because I hadn't done any in four months, but after looking at the fluid inside the syringe I knew it was unlikely—it only had a slight brown hue and could've just as easily been from the filth-tainted water pumping through the jail's pipes.

I gave the binky back to him when I was done and he passed it to one of the corridor trustees to bring back to general population so it could be recycled amongst the jailhouse dope fiends. I willed the dope to hit but after ten minutes it became evident I was chasing ghosts. I was going to have to wait until I was out.

A few hours later, I was released from the county jail without a dime to my name and the need to score. I slept in Union Station until the Red Line started running and when it did, I took it to a Labor Ready in Silverlake. They sent me to a driving range on Melrose and after helping replace the giant nets that prevented golf balls from flying through kitchen windows, I had enough money to pay for an evening's worth of drugs. But when the money was gone the need to keep getting loaded was still present. Boosting paid much better than spending all day at Labor Ready working for pennies, so it was only natural I jumped back to it.

Needless to say, I never reported to my parole agent and it only took a month for me to get busted again. It happened at the same Hollywood Video in Lakewood where I caught my first prison term. I was inside the store sticking DVD's down my pants when the cops came up on me. I got lucky because the store didn't press charges, but the pigs still brought me in and contacted my parole agent, who slapped a hold on me for coming into contact with the police and not reporting.

My agent had me dry out for a couple weeks. When I was released, I started hanging with a dope fiend I'd met in one of the punk rock bars in Long Beach, our mutual love for drugs drawing us together. His story was like so many other junkies I'd met over the years, a childhood filled with tragic tales of abuse and suffering, searching for a remedy to quiet a brain full of discomfort. He was a heroin addict like me and supplemented his habit by selling his ass. I'd hang out with him in Hollywood while he waited on tricks to pick him up and then meet with him to go score after. I'd known plenty of guys over the years who'd turned tricks to support their habits, but they were gay; my friend was not. He worked the streets out of necessity, opportunity, low self-worth, and because the sexual abuse he endured when he was young steered him that way.

We'd meet my connect after he did who knows what in a motel somewhere, his eyes blank and needing to be blanked even more, and he'd share his drugs with me. I used to think the reason he liked me around was because I had a good connection, and I'm sure that was part of it, but looking back I believe he needed companionship and felt safe around me.

In mid-December, out of our drug-addled minds, we decided it was safe to sleep in a park on Selma and Schrader in Hollywood. We camped out in a kid's jungle gym, putting up sheets and making it into a fort comparable to one a nine-year-old might make in his or her parent's living room. It's hard to imagine what we were thinking when we made it, but it certainly raised a red flag to the cop driving by in the morning. He walked up to us with his billy club in hand, saying something to the effect of, "Rise and shine, fellas", then prodded us toward the entrance of the park where his car was waiting.

While walking out of the park I remembered I had three balloons stashed in my cigarette pack and tried to fish them out without him seeing. I must've looked sketchy when I did because as soon as I pulled out my smokes, he came straight at me, grabbing my arms and pinning me to the ground. Within seconds, I had handcuffs on my wrists and he was pulling the dope out of its hiding spot. We were put into his squad car when his backup arrived and brought down to the Wilcox Substation, on the other side of Sunset Boulevard. The "Wilcox Hotel" was legendary, having first heard about it in a song by the punk band Fear. It was the main precinct for the Hollywood area, where stars would go when they got busted for drugs, drove drunk or beat up their girlfriends…and it was also the place where a torn-up street junkie such as myself found himself with a possession charge. They could post bail from the bondsman across the street. But me? I was at the mercy of the judge and his gavel downtown.

The setup was the same as many of the precincts I'd been in over the years, having an area where cops handled specific assignments and a separate location designated as a lockup. We had to sit on a bench while they did their paperwork and when they were done we had our mugshots taken, were fingerprinted, given jail ID bracelets and then escorted to different holding cells.

The cell I was put in had six bunks but only two occupants, an Armenian and a sleeping Mexican. The Armenian sized me up as I walked in and he must've pegged me for a dope fiend right away because he asked me if I wanted to get well. Not one to turn down free drugs, I took him up on his offer and snorted some of his dope with him, setting me straight for the next few hours. It was hell from there, though. I knew he was holding and waited for him to offer more, but the offer never came. When he did pull out another balloon he looked at me as if to say, "Sorry amigo", then went about his business.

Sleep was scarce that night and I knew it was just going to get worse. By the next day I was in full withdrawal and spent my time in a constant state of anxiety—the voice in my head longing for comfort coupled with the physical pain of my sickness had me longing for death, but all I could do was toss and turn on my bunk, regretting the actions that got me there and hating my life.

On the morning of my third day, I was transported by bus to the Criminal Courts Building downtown to see the judge. CCB is a massive courthouse that was built in 1972, across the street from City Hall. Richard Ramirez, O.J. Simpson, Phil Spector and countless others had traversed its numerous corridors in shackles at one time or another, then on to fight their cases in the many courtrooms within. The courthouse has been the sight of picket lines outside, fights between rival gangs awaiting trial inside, heard the cries of mothers seeing the faces of their children's killers for the first time as well as the elated cries of mothers seeing their children complete drug court and move forward with their lives. It's seen ruthless gangsters break down in tears after being sentenced to life in prison and it's also seen them jump for joy after they'd beat their cases.

The bus wheeled into a cavernous parking garage below the courthouse. There were ten of us in the back—including a now dope sick Armenian—and four others in the cages up front. The ones in the cages were transvestites who'd been picked up on Santa Monica Boulevard for turning tricks. There wasn't anything as sad as seeing

---

trannies after they'd been in jail for a couple of days—the makeup had long since been wiped away, their hair disheveled and ratty, and they were all coming down from meth. But the worst was the beard growth. I couldn't help but feel sorry for them as the masculinity they tried to conceal became apparent.

My partner in crime wasn't on the bus and I assumed he'd been released until I saw him in one of the holding tanks. He was impossible to miss in a cell full of Mexicans and after a quick little hug, I sat down with him to shoot the shit. He'd told the cops at the Wilcox Hotel that he was kicking dope and needed medical attention. Being that they didn't have medical staff at the precinct, he was brought to the Glasshouse so he could be observed. When the court line was called, his name was on the list and he was shuttled to CCB to see the judge with me. He was also terribly sick and regretted the idea of sleeping in the park as much as me.

Holding tanks in L.A. County courthouses are basically the same—they're painted in neutral colors with etchings from different gangs and people's names littering the walls. Dirty yellow/white light flickers from fluorescent bulbs, giving prisoners a sickly pasty pallor and you can feel stress emanating from just about everyone in the cell. Stainless-steel benches line the walls as well as stainless-steel toilets that are constantly being flushed. Some guys talk proudly about their cases and their neighborhoods and others sit with their heads hung in sorrow. Strung-out junkies lie in corners, too sick to move, while veteran convicts bust out quick little workouts. Besides a deputy coming in to break up a fight or letting us out to line up for sack lunches, the only time the door was opened was when inmates went out to see the judge or their counsel.

We sat there trying not to feel sick as people were called out for court and their turn in the barrel. My turn came late in the afternoon, but it was far from a "turn in the barrel". My friend, myself and three others were told the DA had rejected our cases. I couldn't believe it but was hesitant to get too excited because I was on parole. I was expecting I'd be called for the chain to MCJ with all the other guys and was pleasantly surprised when the cops pulled me out with the ones being released. That meant, for whatever reason, the cops hadn't notified my parole agent or that he didn't bother placing a hold.

They let us out in a group around eight o'clock and we walked to the county jail to pick up our property. I had just under $30 on my books and told my friend that I was buying. After what felt like an eternity in the jail lobby, I was finally given my wallet, belt and shoelaces, and off we went. We ended up scoring some dope in Skid Row and fixed in an alley right off Broadway. The anxiety of the past three days promptly subsided and was replaced by feelings of warmth and contentment…tomorrow's pain was a world away.

We had nowhere to go after we fixed so we decided to go back to the jail and check in to a shelter. We walked by a newspaper stand on the way, where I learned about a tsunami that destroyed the coast of Thailand. Hearing or reading news items rarely made an impression on me but for some reason this did. It seemed wrong that I was making a wreck of my life and those around me, while on the other side of the Pacific Ocean people were dying. The knowledge that I could change my life hit me like a bolt of lightning. All I had to do was quit doing drugs. It was a revelation to me and as we walked back to the jail, I did so with a new resolve.

There was a van at the jail that took people who'd just gotten out to a shelter upon release. We climbed aboard and were taken to a program on 6th and San Pedro, right in the heart of Skid Row. The sidewalks outside were packed with tents and cardboard condominiums—dilapidated habitats for broken souls to push their crack pipes, turn tricks, cop a nod or pass out drunk. The driver of the van walked us inside, leaving us at a desk where a morbidly obese black woman was (not) working. She logged our personal information into a computer with a pained expression on her face, gave each of us a sack lunch, then passed us off to a man who brought us to our sleeping area.

We were each given a ratty old wool blanket and told we'd have to find a spot on the floor. Besides a couple of old men who had long since lost their minds, we were the only white guys there and we definitely weren't welcome. About half the residents were sleeping and the other half eyed us cautiously, seeing what we were about. Nobody seemed willing to concede floor space and after finding a spot we had to spoon to fit in, we closed our eyes and tried to sleep.

The place reeked of bum piss, mildew and ass. I used my shoes as a pillow and tried to overlook the fact that my face was a mere six inches away from some of the nastiest feet I'd ever seen or smelled. Dirty yellow toenails poked out from the ends of his socks, taunting me in a fetid form of derision. Making matters worse, as if

179

feeling out of place, the stench and sleeping on concrete wasn't bad enough, there was a consistent barrage of sound coming from almost everyone there. Between the snoring, people talking to themselves and the constant arguing amongst each other, I found it difficult to get any sleep.

By six in the morning I'd had enough. I told my "road dog" about my desire to get clean and that I couldn't live like this anymore. He told me that his mom was going to wire him some money later that day, but it wasn't enough to sway me. I thought about it for a minute—another shot of dope still sounded good—but I was too burned out and tired of it all. In the end, we wished each other the best of luck and I left the mission feeling sorry for him, just as I'm sure he felt sorry for me.

A storm had hit Los Angeles that same morning, bringing with it a torrential downpour. I walked out to see a street that was now a lake and the rows of tents littering the sidewalks gone. In the middle of San Pedro Avenue was a smoldering garbage can that a few hours earlier would've had a host of drunks standing around it, huddling close to the fire and greedily drinking their bottles of Mad Dog, but was now just a relic of yesterday's crime. At its base was a drunk and quite possibly dead man, half-submerged in the rising water. Skid Row had always exuded a malignant charm—one mired in waste and scum, yet somehow regenerative. The empty flooded streets could've been perceived as apocalyptic in the sense that the street urchin living there were gone; but in reality, the storm was a tool used to wash the surface of a festering wound. A wound too deep to be cleaned.

By the time I got to the bus station on Pico and Grand, I was absolutely drenched—the rain had been coming down at a level comparable to a monsoon—and I could feel my toes starting to prune from all the puddles I had to walk through. I must've looked like hell to the bus driver because he didn't bat an eye when I told him I didn't have a fare. My plan was simple: go to my moms, tell her I was done and beg her to let me stay with her. It took thirty minutes to get to Culver City from downtown and I was deep in reflection during the entire ride. I was ready to change and hoped she was there to take me in.

When I knocked on her door, the combination of rain and tears, along with my broken disposition, surely evoked imagery of a sad dog lost in a storm. She took one look and let me in, telling me that she

---

180

couldn't stand to leave me on the streets and that she believed me when I said I was done. She nursed me back to health, having a faith in me only a mother could have, and we spent the time talking about our family history and her acting career.

I arrived at her place with an unprecedented desperation to stay clean, and with willpower alone I did…for five days. I went to Long Beach to pick up some clothes I'd left at a friend's—they were left on her porch, wet and mildewed, because she'd had it with my shit—and the longing to get high hit me again. I battled with it internally at first, remembering the promise I'd made, but finally said fuck it, telling myself I'd do it just once. I didn't have any money so I ended up boosting some DVD's and it was on. I made it back to my mom's that night, and when the morning came I was gone.

JOINT SUSPENSION

The DVD's I stole were second-rate, previously viewed movies sitting in a bargain bin at the front of the store. I knew I wouldn't get much for them, but I had enough to at least make the heist worthwhile. I'd gotten away clean and was sitting at a bus stop on 7th and Redondo in Long Beach when I was accosted by a crazy bum. He claimed that I didn't know what it was like to have fought in 'Nam, getting angry and waving his cane at me in a manner I interpreted as threatening. I responded by picking up my skateboard and telling him he'd better chill or I'd knock him the fuck out.

He calmed down after that and we both went back to waiting for the bus, warning each other with hostile looks. Not three minutes later, two squad cars rolled up with both cops jumping out, ordering me to put my hands on my head. I had two balloons in my mouth and I quickly swallowed them. They wanted to know why I was going to hit the old man with my skateboard. Apparently, someone driving by had called the police. After telling them what happened, the cops fucked with me for a couple minutes and were about to let me go when they saw the bag of DVD's. It was sitting by the bus stop bench next to my skateboard. When they looked at the DVD's they saw stickers indicating they came from a Hollywood Video only two blocks away, and that was enough for them to arrest me. One of the cops went to the store to confirm that they did indeed come from there and to see if there was any video footage of me stealing them, while the other cop took me to the city jail. The bus pulled up as we were driving off and I caught a glimpse of the crazy old vet snickering as he got on, giving me cause to wish he'd die a horrid death.

As it turned out, there wasn't enough evidence to book me for theft, but they did get me for possession of stolen property. I had no bail because I was on parole and after getting fingerprinted, I was brought to the felony tank, regretting my decision to threaten the old man and preparing myself for another bout of misery.

My first night wasn't too bad but by the next day I was in a world of shit. The dayroom was full as usual and my mind was focused on the balloons I swallowed, knowing I'd have to wait until I was back in my cell to get them. I had tried puking them up the day before, but

182

by the time I was in a cell with no cops around, it was too late. I was going to have to shit them out.

When the dayroom was finally closed that night, I was put in a cell with two Paisas. They were talking to each other in Spanish, so I just sat down on the toilet and told them I had some business to attend to, knowing there was a good chance they wouldn't understand a word I said. I was reluctant to handle my business in front of them, but necessity dictated my actions.

The code in jail when using the toilet is "drop one, flush one", and I didn't need to know Spanish to know they were getting angry when I didn't. I heard and understood one of them say, *"Agua!"* and the other, *"Puta Madre!"* but when they saw me get up from the toilet without even wiping my ass, then break the turd apart with my hands, frantically searching for the two balloons, they started chattering in a dialect a well-trained Spanish ear would've had trouble discerning. Fortunately for me, and for them, I found them both easily then was able to flush the toilet, wipe my ass, clean my hands and most importantly, clean the balloons.

If it had been any other race I was locked in the cell with, I would've had to contend with their anger over my actions and/or share my dope with them, but their rumblings soon ceased and I was able to sit on my rack and get well. I mixed the heroin with some water in a plastic spoon I'd kept from the evening's dinner tray and snorted it. The rational thing to do would've been to save one of the balloons for later but I opted to do them both, hoping to catch a buzz.

I was so sick by then I would've needed a needle to catch a nod, but I did get well enough to sleep. By the time the cell door popped open in the morning, however, I could feel the sickness creeping its way back into my bones. I was fucked, I knew it and with no more dope to do, the best I could hope for was to be released on my own recognizance by the judge.

It didn't happen. When I saw the judge later that day, he ordered I be kept in jail until my next hearing. I was in County by early evening, going through the dreary routine of moving cell to cell and getting yelled at by deputies. I withheld that I was kicking dope from the medical staff to expedite the housing process and sometime the next day I was placed in a large cell on the 2000 Floor nicknamed the "Whitehouse". Appropriately named, it was called the "Whitehouse" because all its occupants were white. It could've just as easily been

183

named the "Roach house" or "Rat house"—both names that would've stuck due to our nocturnal visitors.

I still wasn't sure what the court wanted to do with me, but knew they intended to prosecute. To muddy the already foul water even more, I was called down to booking one night and slapped with an add-charge—the DA had decided to file on me for the possession case I caught in Hollywood two months prior. That meant I now had court in CCB as well as Long Beach. I was guilty in both cases; I didn't have much of a defense and it looked like I was well on my way toward going back to prison.

It was a possession case so I knew I'd be eligible for Prop 36 (Proposition 36 was passed by California voters in November of 2000, giving drug offenders busted for possession the opportunity to go to treatment instead of doing time) but because of my other case in Long Beach, it wouldn't do any good to go through with it. But I did have an ace up my sleeve—the prosecutor in Long Beach seemed willing to go along with my public defender's suggestion that I be given a three-year "joint suspension". It was really my idea; my public defender told me not to do it. By agreeing to the terms, I'd be put on probation, on top of already being on parole, and any violation would put me at the mercy of the court and a three-year term in state prison.

I spent the next few weeks going back and forth between the courts and the jail, getting up early to walk the court line with the hope I'd soon be getting out. It took almost two months and in March of 2005, I pled "guilty" to a charge of petty-theft-with-a-prior, California penal code 666, to a term of three years joint suspended. My other public defender had been getting continuances for my drug case in CCB, and after my case in Long Beach was taken care of, we were ready to move forward with the proceedings.

My case in CCB was concluded a few weeks after I took my plea in Long Beach, and with some misgivings from my public defender, who wisely thought I'd bitten off more than I could chew, I was given Prop 36 by the judge. That meant I'd have to report to a Prop 36 assessment office upon release and they'd make a decision regarding the type and severity of treatment I was to attend, but I'd be let out that night. It also meant I was now on probation in two separate jurisdictions as well as parole with the state. To say I'd have to walk a fine line was a severe understatement. From a realist's perspective, binding myself to a program in which failure meant doing three years

184

would've been perceived as insane. But to me, the poster boy for one living in a fantasy world, the prospect of getting out of jail, coupled with my ignorance and denial, was cause for celebration.

I was let out of the courthouse in a white jumpsuit similar to the one I wore out of Compton a year prior, then beelined it back to the county jail to pick up my clothes and cash. And from there I went to Skid Row. During the whole process of scoring and doing the drugs, I battled with my obsession, knowing that getting high would jeopardize my freedom, but in the end the need to get loaded trumped any underlying thoughts of rational thinking.

I somehow managed to check in with my probation and parole officers, telling them both I was going into treatment, but it all went black from there. Within a few weeks, I was arrested in Long Beach, cooking up a shot of dope behind a dumpster. They had their cuffs on me before I ever knew what was happening—my affinity for benzo's had me on a wicked nod—and I was on my way back to jail. I went through the same tired booking process, was housed in the felony tank, but this time instead of going to court, I was released from the jail. The DA rejected the case, which wasn't too alarming because it was just a small amount, but what was strange was neither my parole or probation officers had put a hold on me. It appeared I'd slipped through the cracks.

There aren't many who deal with the law in such a manner, but it's safe to say that if they did, they'd probably summon the necessary resolve to steer clear of future entanglements. I was not one of those people. I was back on the streets doing what I did best and was subsequently back in lockup within two weeks. While sitting on the steps to the train station downtown, I was approached by two beat cops wanting to know what I was up to. I certainly looked suspicious enough being that I was on a nod, and the two black eyes I sustained when a thug tried robbing me three days earlier didn't help. Because I'd just gotten out of jail, I was certain I didn't have any warrants, so when I was told to put my hands behind my back, I was devastated.

Shortly after being released from the Long Beach Jail, a warrant had been issued by my probation officer stemming from the possession charge. He didn't care that the DA wasn't pursuing the case; from his perspective all that mattered was that I'd been arrested. They brought me to a precinct in the heart of Skid Row and then shuttled me over to the Glasshouse up the street.

I was put into an old rundown dorm, packed with bunks and an assortment of unsavory types. It seemed that half the prisoners were winos and the other half junkies…a collection of the bottom of the Skid Row barrel. The bathroom—really just a cluster of toilets along a wall at the front of the dorm—was constantly occupied. The stainless-steel receptacles bore witness to foulness straight from our vomiting guts or our diarrheic assholes. The mood in the dorm was somber and depressed. Very few made bail and if you were one of the unfortunate ones with a new case, the only way out was to see the judge. There was a constant flurry of inmates leaving for court in the mornings, with guys coming in during the afternoons and nights to replace them.

After sitting in there for three days, I went out with the court line then was separated from the rest of the group and put on a bus going to Long Beach. It was packed with guys coming from MCJ who were already housed in the jail and dressed in county blues, so I was put in one of the cages at the front of the bus. Knowing the cages were typically used to keep PC or gay inmates away from those in general population, I couldn't help but wonder what the guys in the back of the bus were thinking when they saw me sitting up there. Did they think I was a snitch or in for a sex crime? I knew I'd be mixed with them when we got to Long Beach, and if any of them thought I was "no good", I'd be smashed.

We pulled into the garage under the courthouse and I was put into a cell with the others, my fear of getting jumped being abated when nobody said anything about having been in the cage. I was called for my arraignment in the afternoon and told I had no bail and would see the judge in two weeks. Because the DA initially rejected the possession case, I'd been hoping that they'd lift the warrant for the probation violation, but when the judge told me I had no bail, I knew I was fucked and was in for another kick in hell.

Thirty-six hours later, exhausted from kicking dope, stress, lack of sleep, hunger and depression, I was housed on the 3000 Floor of MCJ. During my short time out on the streets, I'd gotten another abscess from muscling shots in my ass cheek. I'd noticed it had been getting worse, but it wasn't until one of my cellies started freaking out that I realized how bad it had gotten. The outbreak of MRSA cases in the last few years had been severe enough that the medical staff had posted fliers all throughout the jail, complete with information and

186

pictures relative to staph infections. While the info was great, it also led to drastic overreactions by inmates thinking that any red bump was staph and therefore contagious. My cellie's fear of getting infected, and the three others in the cell who also didn't want to get infected, prompted me to see a nurse when the med line was called the next morning.

I'd been under the spell of denial, hoping it would be one of those rare instances when the infection would go away without it needing to be lanced. When I saw the nurse, she told me what I already knew—that it was an abscess—and surprised me by saying I'd be taken to USC General to have it cut and drained. It was apparently worse than I thought because within an hour, I was put on a bus and driven to the hospital in East L.A., then brought up to the jail ward on the 13th floor.

The ward looked the part for an area designated to a 13th floor. Cracks lined the walls, fluorescent lights buzzed and empty spaces marked spots in the ceiling where tiles had once been. Gurneys were parked haphazardly in the corridors, some empty and others with inmates lying in them. Doctors and nurses walked the halls, checking on patients and looking at files, while a slew of deputies milled about, idly waiting to take whichever prisoners they were assigned back to County. This definitely wasn't the General Hospital they showed on the soap opera and it was hard to believe Marilyn Monroe had been born just a few floors below. But if someone had told me it was the hospital Miklo had been brought after getting shot in the movie *Blood In, Blood Out*, I would've wholeheartedly believed it. I later discovered that to be the case (somewhat, at least—it was only a movie and it was probably shot elsewhere), and that Stan Getz, the famous jazz musician, had been inside the same jail ward in the 1950's kicking a dope habit before being sent to Wayside.

The staff was gracious and a sharp contrast from the soulless nurses who worked at MCJ. I was seen quickly and when the doctor saw how bad it was, I was given a shot of morphine. Being a heroin addict I didn't feel the morphine much, but it did do a little to stave off some of my sickness. The abscess, once the size of a softball, had grown to the point that I had to keep the elastic from my boxers up above my waist to keep the pressure off. I was given numerous shots of a local anesthetic, bringing about intense pain each time the needle punctured the wound.

187

He then cut it with a scalpel, bursting the reservoir of blood and pus stored under my skin, the putrid mixture oozing out of the wound and down the inside of my thigh. When it was drained and cleaned with a saline solution, the doctor stuffed the cavity with gauze stripping. The pain was excruciating. While it was numb on the outside, the wound from within was sensitive to the poking and prodding essential to it being packed with gauze. I was given two Norco's after it was bandaged and even though I didn't feel them, I would've gladly gone through the procedure again for more drugs. Some might say I was a glutton for punishment, but I preferred to look at myself as one endlessly searching for relief.

All of this took place within an area partitioned off to create a makeshift surgical center and when the procedure was done, I was put into a room with ten other inmates to await transport back to County. The room was comfortable for jail standards—there was a view looking out over East L.A., we had hospital beds and the nurses even brought us dinners cooked in the hospital cafeteria…a pleasant reprieve from the concrete and steel waiting downtown.

It was, however, a short-lived recess because the deputies came and loaded us back onto the bus after we ate. We were then driven back to the jail and brought in through the medical wing, and after the staff registered our conditions, we were sent to our housing units. I now had a wound on my ass that was four inches in length. MCJ was a breeding ground for MRSA so they transferred me to a semi-sterile environment on the 8000 Floor. Being in a clean area wasn't the only reason I was housed there—I needed to have the gauze inside my wound changed and my cellies weren't about to play nurse.

The morning of the next day I was brought to the nurse's station, told to lie down on a gurney and she went to work. She pulled what must've been three feet of the pus and blood-soaked stripping out, every inch of it pulled causing me excruciating pain. A deputy stood behind me whistling something that resembled a circus tune while she changed the bandage, giving me cause to think she must've looked like a magician pulling a never-ending handkerchief out of a hat. It felt like a paper cut as it was being pulled out, but the real pain was when the new gauze was packed in. The end of the gauze stripping was held with surgical pliers and pushed in as far as it could go, while she packed the wound with more stripping using a pushrod. The pain was unbearable, amplified by kicking dope and having nothing to dull my nerves.

That was the main part of my daily routine for the next few weeks, dreading the moments before the gauze was changed and lying in pain after it was done. During this time, I started getting in good with the main deputy on the floor and became a trustee for the wing when the wound had healed enough for me to walk. My job was to pass out meals to the inmates and clean the halls, and as long as my duties were performed, I was free to do whatever I wanted, within the parameter of jailhouse rules, of course. Being locked in a cell for the entire day, excluding the time spent in the nurse's office or the rare occasions when I had someone to call, was hell on my mental state and I truly appreciated being able to walk around and talk with other people.

There were close to thirty inmates in the wing and most were there for MRSA. I had access to food and would slide them cookies and packages of meat under their doors, knowing how scarce food was. I'd have to pass it to them on the down low and would've been rolled up if caught—the cops didn't like seeing the trustees get too friendly with the ones in confinement.

While making my rounds, taking on my self-proclaimed title of jailhouse saint, I'd come across people I'd met previously in lockup or on the streets. One of them was a musician from Long Beach named Opie. He used to hang with all those Sublime guys in the '90s and played in a band called Long Beach Dub Allstars after Brad died. He was nice to me, but in a superficial way, like he thought I was an admiring follower or some shit. I didn't have it in me to tell him that I couldn't stand Sublime or any of the ska/punk/rap fusion bands he was in; I just slid him some meat and cookies, then moved on to the next cell.

I also saw a guy I'd met in CCB named Ian. We'd met in the court holding tank, waiting for our judges to make decisions relevant to our cases, and discovered we knew some of the same people in the skateboarding world. He told me that he used to ride for a company called Skull Skates out of Vancouver, B.C. People say all kinds of shit and tell countless stories when locked up, trying to portray an image of living a different life out on the streets, but I knew he was speaking true when he brought up Carlos and P.D.'s names—one a friend who rode for the company and the other the owner. As much as we shared

189

the same passion for skating and punk rock, however, our conversation always came back to what we loved most—drugs.

Both of us had gotten out shortly after that day in court and we both came back soon after. He came to the 8000 Floor by way of making up a story, telling a nurse he thought he had staph, and I later found he was trying to get out of a drug debt he couldn't pay. Ian and his girlfriend had broken up some time before and because he didn't have access to a phone, he gave me her number to call and tell her he was okay. He was only on the floor a few days and after the nurse saw him, he was sent back to the same housing location from which he came. When he was told he was going back, he was visibly shaken by the news and tried getting the deputy to assign him to another floor with no success.

His ex-girlfriend's name was Cherie, a sweet girl from Placerville in Northern California who came to Los Angeles because her musical aspirations were larger than anything Placerville could offer. When I told her that I was calling on behalf of Ian, she was quick to tell me they'd been broken up for quite some time, but not in a way that reflected resentment toward him. She was genuinely concerned about his wellbeing but knew he was a fuck-up and wasn't going to stay clean. Knowing Ian just a little, I'd expected Cherie to be some crazy tweaker, but she was far from that. She was easy to talk to and seemed interested in what was going on with my case, and what my plans were when I got out. It had been quite some time since I'd had a conversation with a woman who was doing anything positive with her life and I got off the phone feeling good about myself. And, to my delight, she told me to keep her posted on what happened with my case and that I was free to call her anytime.

During my time being housed on 8000, recovering from my wound and then working as a trustee, I'd been going back and forth from court, hoping to catch a break from the judge and his sentencing. When I took the deal a couple months prior, the judge had let it be known that any arrest would be cause for the suspension being revoked and I'd be sent to prison. From my perspective, because I was arrested for a drug charge, and one that was dropped, I should've been given another chance. I felt like a victim in a system set out to prosecute those gullible enough to take a deal that was too good to be true. I thought that if the judge could see things my way, and with my

---

190

assurance I'd complete a treatment program, I'd be given another chance.

It goes without saying the judge and I didn't see the world through the same pair of glasses. I'd walk into the courtroom with high hopes and after the prosecutor would tell me there was no deal on the table, I'd go back to the county jail disconsolate and broken. In my final attempt to sway the judge, a representative from a rehab showed up on my behalf and told the judge they were willing to take me, but he still wasn't having it. When it finally registered that the court wouldn't budge, I gave up and let the judge give it to me the way he saw fit. And the way he saw fit was to revoke my probation, sentencing me to a term of three years in state prison, forthwith.

THIRD TIME'S A CHARM

It took over a month to catch the chain and the only thing different, as far as the process was concerned, was the demeanor of those I caught the chain with. They represented various streets and neighborhoods of Los Angeles and they all shared one of two stories—a history of drug abuse and/or being from a gang. Two of the prisoners were sentenced to life and rode their charges like "G's", exuding a calm and cool that surely belied their true feelings of despair. I couldn't possibly gauge the mental state of a man being sent away for life but knew from seeing others doing time that it would take a few years for the sentence to fully sink in. The letters would start coming with less frequency and the visits would all but disappear, until the only ones coming to see them were their mothers, whose eyes ceased crying long ago, and their lawyers. Once the appeals process was exhausted, and the burden of concrete became too much to endure, there was nothing left but to die.

I was housed on D Yard again, with the only excitement coming from the rare occasions when we were let out for yard, the dayroom and the showers. My cellie was duller than a Skid Row junkie's needle and was also hard of hearing, making him either the best or worst cellie a man could ask for, depending on your perspective. The only conversation we had was right before chow when he'd tell me how hungry he was and when he'd ask questions relative to the amount of food served on the mainline. He wasn't a bad guy, just a little slow, but the lack of conversation was enough for me to almost miss the Nazi's I'd had as cellies during my previous terms.

Having him for a cellmate was somewhat comparable to doing time in solitary confinement, so when my name was called for transfer to C Yard, I felt like I was rolling it up for release. The scenario was the same as the other times I'd been there—prisoners wasting time in the dayroom, TV area and by their bunks, all stopping what they were doing to check out the new prisoner being brought in. A Wood came up and helped bring my belongings to my bedding assignment, all the while getting the scoop on where I was from and who I ran with.

I was bunked in a corner of the top tier with a guy from Santa Cruz. He grew up surfing and skating the area, listening to punk rock and spending time on the streets, so there was no shortage of subject matter to the stories we'd tell each other. Even though I'd never been before, I had quite a few friends from there and was able to keep up when he talked about the local venues, skateparks and big wave events.

The excitement of having someone to talk to who shared the same interests and having a similar background, while certainly significant, soon lost its allure, however, and it was back to the dull routine of doing whatever I could to pass the time. It was then that I learned how to make a contraption I'd heard much about over the years—the Fifi. It was basically a "pocket pussy", a sex toy used because masturbation could get boring. It was easy to make: all you need is a towel, latex glove and lotion. First, you fold the towel into a rectangle and then place the glove inside with the open end out. Holding the glove in place, you fold the towel around the glove, keeping it good and tight, then stretch the open end of the glove over the end part of the towel, creating a hand-held cylindrical shape with an opening to stick your dick into. Lubrication is essential, so a healthy dose of lotion, cocoa butter or whatever else you have on hand is needed, and once the lube is inserted the Fifi is ready to go and the evening's festivities can begin.

My love for the Fifi was short-lived. I suppose if I'd been in a cell I might've been a little more comfortable, but being in a dorm, never sure if anybody knew what you were doing, made things difficult. If I were the type who regularly indulged in pleasuring myself with a Fifi, word would've gotten around. Masturbation is common in prison but you still had to be discrete, and the last thing I wanted was to be known as the guy who kept a Fifi in his locker.

The unit I was transferred to had an abundance of pruno circulating the tiers. Just like on the streets and in bars, alcohol could make men crazy and there were a few fights that broke out during my first week there. They were all one-on-one scrapes and none of them ended up crossing the racial divide, so they weren't thought of as serious among the prisoners in the building. The same could not be said for the C.O.'s, however. One morning, the 1st watch C.O. noticed there were a few guys lumped up and walking sluggishly, which prompted him to run with his instincts and notify the investigative arm of the CDC—the Investigative Services Unit. Later that morning, a small platoon of officers in dark uniforms swarmed the unit, had us strip to our boxers, then marched us out to the yard.

193

While we were outside, the officers from ISU busied themselves by going through the building with a fine-toothed comb. I watched them carry out bags of apples, kicker, pruno and anything else they saw fit to dispose of. Besides the loss of pruno and having our property torn apart, it wasn't too big of a deal—most everyone on the yard seemed to take it in stride and the tension was relatively low. The calm which was prevalent during the first few hours of being outside began to dissipate with time, however, and it wasn't long until the yard was a powder keg looking for a spark.

The spark came in the form of a black youngster who'd disrespected a Southsider. We'd been on the yard about four hours and tempers were already starting to flare when the kid bumped into a homie. When he was confronted about it, the youngster said something along the lines of him not running a Southsider program and that he didn't need to apologize. They both walked away from each other and it looked like the incident was going to be swept under the rug, but as is often the case in prison, seemingly small events often become major storms. When the homie told his shot-caller what had happened, it was determined the youngster should be regulated by his people for his actions. The shot-caller for the Southsiders got together with the shot-caller for the Blacks and told them the kid needed to be disciplined for the shit to be squashed. The Blacks absolutely refused and in doing so, escalated the matter into a situation in which violence was inevitable.

Immediately following the two sides holding conference, an ominous silence gripped the yard and prisoners began grouping with whichever race they were aligned with—the Blacks in one corner of the yard and the Southsiders, Paisas and Whites in the others. The C.O.'s picked up on what was going down immediately and could've prevented any violence from erupting by ordering us to get on the ground, but instead chose to let it unravel. Their course of action was to record it all with video cameras, using the footage later to identify combatants for add-charges.

Even though the incident was between the Blacks and the Southsiders, it was decided the Whites and Paisas were to get in on the action as well. That meant the Blacks were outnumbered about three to one. We were told to form a line and be ready to attack when it was time. Everyone out there was standing and holding a position, anxiously waiting the moment when the yard would explode.

194

We didn't have to wait long. A group of close to fifty Mexicans and Skinheads ran headlong into the closest group of Blacks with fists and feet flying, looking to cause as much damage as possible. It reminded me of the scene at the end of the movie *Braveheart* when the Scots stormed the British ranks with a loud war cry and full of fury. The Blacks never had a chance and their line broke quickly, leaving most of them to fight from a defensive position, doing whatever they could to fend off blows from their attackers. There were a solid dozen of them who were holding their own and inflicting damage by themselves, however. These guys were one-man army's, obviously veterans of prison riots. I saw one of them single-handedly take on four Southsiders, fighting them off and sending them running.

Even with the heroics of those who could fight, they were overwhelmed and fortunately, the riot was over as quick as it had begun. C.O.'s on the catwalks began discharging tear gas canisters from rifles into the fray, conjuring a fog that made it difficult to see and breathe. They were yelling at us to get on the ground while their eyes and rifles scoured the battlefield, presumably looking for anyone wielding a shank. Another contingency of guards wielding batons and wearing gas masks stormed the yard after the canisters were shot, reminding me of the W.T.O. riots that'd happened just before I left Seattle.

I managed to avoid getting caught up in the riot by skirting the edges of the conflict. I wasn't trying to build a name for myself as a warrior on a prison yard. I was too focused on going home to waste my time on such bullshit. When the guys most heavily involved in the riot took heed of the guards' commands to get down, I was relieved because it gave me the green light to follow suit. Within two minutes of it jumping off, everybody on the yard was in a prone position. There was gas everywhere, reminiscent of a First World War battlefield.

Another wave of C.O.'s came to C Yard with zip-ties soon after. Because there were close to 120 of us on the yard, it took them quite some time to get the job done, but when we were all in restraints, we were herded to different areas by race and by how involved in the riot we were. The guys positively identified as combatants were taken to the hole, the Blacks to B Yard, and the Whites and Mexicans to D Yard. Everyone was put in restraints—even the guys confined to wheelchairs who weren't anywhere near the action. It was funny...the Christians were huddled together far from the violence and behind the handicapped prisoners, but there were at least two guys I'd played pinochle with sitting with them and I was fairly certain not one of them said a damn thing about rolling with the Christians. I guess they "saw the light" when all hell broke loose.

We were kept outside on D Yard until after the sun had set, then were escorted back to our dorm. While sitting out there, cuffed on the grass, the C.O.'s had reviewed their footage and found more guys from our assembly to bring to the hole, cutting the amount of men going back to the building to about fifty. The dorm was torn apart—the bedding had been ripped from our bunks and the property from our lockers strewn across the floor...it looked like a cyclone had ripped through the unit in our absence. Everybody in the dorm busied themselves with the arduous task of retrieving their ramens, honey buns, coffee jars and hygiene products from the floor, while C.O.'s watched us from the podium, keeping their eyes open for any strange behaviors.

With less than half of the inmates being in the unit, the mood was extremely calm and relaxed. We were happy to be back inside after spending over eight hours on the yard. To avoid hostilities, the C.O.'s had decided to move the Blacks to a different yard, but they never sent any workers in to collect their property. Because of this, a free-for-all ensued over the Blacks' belongings—people were tearing through anything of value left behind and even going so far as to ridicule their photos and personal items.

There was little movement in the week following the riot—the dayroom was closed and we were ordered to stay on our bunks—but the time came when new guys were brought in. The powers that be thought it would be a good idea to bring a black man in by himself to see how we reacted. You could've heard a pin drop when he entered the building. After the guard gave him his bed assignment, he cautiously walked toward his bunk, knowing he was the only black man there. I could feel the fear radiating from him from my vantage point on the other side of the dorm, and I also saw a small group of Southsiders huddled together, talking about what they were going to do. He must've seen them also, or quite possibly picked up on the vibe, because he abruptly turned and practically ran back to the officer's podium. I don't know what he said but whatever it was gave the C.O. cause to rehouse him, saving him from what would have likely been a beat-down.

196

The next day we were told new guys were being brought in and were also told by our shot-callers that the shit was squashed. There was a level of unease when they arrived, but it wasn't too much worse than what was normally the case, and within a few days the dorm was back to full capacity. None of the guys brought in were in the dorm prior to the riot, so the backlash that would've occurred after discovering their property had been rifled through wasn't an issue. We were more or less back to normal—close to 120 men living in close quarters, doing what we could to pass the time and getting one day closer to going home.

My counselor came to see me that same week and dropped a bomb on me, telling me I'd be going to a SAP yard. Even though my controlling case was a theft charge, the possession of heroin arrest in Hollywood was enough to warrant being "sapped" again. It never occurred to me that I might have to do my time on a program yard, so the news hit me hard. I had just over a year left and the thought of listening to a bunch of kooks tell me what they knew about a lifestyle in which they knew nothing about filled me with bile.

I was called to trans-pack three weeks later and told I was going to the Substance Abuse Treatment Facility at Corcoran. I'd heard all kinds of rumors about SATF during my previous terms and wasn't looking forward to discovering which were true and which were false. It was reputed that coffee wasn't sold in commissary and that we'd only get yard on weekends because of the non-stop barrage of classes being held. It looked to be a long year ahead of me.

Four days after trans-packing, I was awoken early in the morning to catch the chain, then brought to R and R and chained with other prisoners sharing a similar fate. The transport officers wore the same black uniforms and demanded the same silence once the bus started rolling. The bus ride, although relatively short, brought about the feelings a man accustomed to a life of depravity should feel—I was leaving one hell to go to another, the familiarity of it all wearing me down, and knowing I deserved more out of life but ignorant as to how I'd get it. I'd exerted myself to the point of exhaustion, much like a hamster on his cyclic track. I was going nowhere.

NEW CORCORAN

The long shadows cast from the mountains to the east began to shorten as the sun rose, bringing to light the familiar visage of farm acreage and cattle enclosures. Corcoran SATF sat across the street from Old Corcoran, where I did my first term, and had been built to keep up with the ever-increasing prison population. It opened in 1997 and had a total of seven yards, ranging from the dorm settings of Level 2's to cell-living units of Level 4's. Both prisons combined for a total of over 10,000 prisoners and just like Old Corcoran's list of famous inmates, New Corcoran had its share as well, with Robert Downey Jr. and Phil Spector being two of them (Robert Downey Jr. had paroled from there in August of 2000 and Phil Spector transferred there in 2009).

The transport officers stored their firearms in the guard tower overlooking the gated entrance before driving into No-Man's Land and on to the R and R building. Characteristically, the landscape was the same as Delano and the prison across the street; concrete buildings set on flat, rocky ground within a perimeter of chain-link fences topped with razor wire and guard towers. As we drove down one of the many service roads toward our destination, I could see prisoners peering out of their cell windows, looking our way with half-hearted interest to see the load of cargo being brought in.

We were all taken off the bus and unshackled, then put into a large holding cell while the C.O.'s handled the reception process. Five of the guys were placed in another cell—presumably to be taken to one of the more secure yards—and the rest of us waited for our escort. A few hours later, after having our photos taken and talking to medical staff, we were brought to a gym used to house inmates going to F and G Yards. Yards A-E were cell living and for prisoners with higher point levels or needing protective custody, while F and G were designated as dorm living for prisoners in the Substance Abuse Treatment Facility.

The gym was much like the one I'd been in during my first term, except it contained fewer bunks and there wasn't a catwalk with a gunner staring down at us. Men were constantly being transferred to

---

either of the SATF yards, so it was difficult to get a sense of stability due to the high turnover rate. The only time we went outside was when we walked to the chow hall and that only took about five minutes, which meant that the gym began to feel suffocative after time. The drudgery relative to sitting in therapeutic groups started to sound appealing.

Cherie and I had maintained contact after I'd left L.A. County and by the time I got to Corcoran, there was a steady rhythm of letters flowing between us. She'd taken an interest in me for some reason I couldn't understand, and her letters were the high point of many dark and lonely days. Her father and brother had also struggled with drug addiction, as well as many of her friends in Los Angeles, so her understanding of my plight seemed sincere and emphatic. There are many girls who take interest in convicts because they're more fucked-up than themselves, but Cherie didn't seem to fit into this category.

I'd taken an interest in her as well. Besides her being a musician, she also skated and the way she wrote sparked me. She had an animation to her being and a desire for wanting more out of life. I'd lived in the shadows for so long that her optimism and goals seemed foreign to me, and I latched on to her love for life with a restored longing to start living mine.

A long three weeks later, I was finally pulled out of the gym and assigned to G Yard. The design of the yard was similar to most of the other prisons I'd been to, with Blacks and Asians sharing one area of the yard, and Whites and Southsiders another. I also noticed that there were no Northerners. Some of the guys stopped what they were doing to look as I was being brought onto the yard, but most kept to themselves and whatever workout routine they busied themselves with.

The entire inmate population on G Yard was subjected to SAP programming, as opposed to Old Corcoran where it was just one building, making it so we were all equally fucked. I was placed in an orientation unit with a large carpeted dayroom and classrooms, having two tiers on one end where the dorms were located. The dorm I was put in was small, with seven other guys also trying to adjust to their new surroundings. Most of us had been to prison before but none of us had ever been to a place like SATF.

The CDC had decided to try and break the code of segregation by forcing prisoners to bunk with other races but had no success in doing so. Whites were under direct orders not to bunk with any Blacks, which created an underlying tension in the dorm. Not all Whites are down with the basic Skinhead beliefs, but we had to abide by the prison code or face repercussions. When it came down to it, everyone stuck to their race regardless, but the attempted installation of these changes, and our subsequent refusal to bunk with Blacks, helped to reinforce the rift between us.

Even with the drama everyone in the dorm got along well. We went on lockdown within a week of my arrival because someone had supposedly dropped a kite into a suggestion box threatening to stab correctional officers, and their response was to slam us down for two weeks. We weren't allowed out of our units except to go to chow and got to know each other because of it. After being forced into a sometimes-rocky co-existence, we bonded as a group and found humor in each of our shortcomings, misfortunes and our common dislike of the powers that be. We'd stay up late telling jokes and stories about what we'd seen, where we were from, how we were arrested, why we were fucked and when shit was better. It was like being in camp with a bunch of guys who had never been to camp and being in a cell instead of a cabin in the woods.

The officials at SATF would slam us down for anything—if a riot jumped off in another prison we'd be locked down because of it. When Stanley "Tookie" Williams, an OG Crip on death row for a murder-robbery, was put down by lethal injection we were locked down for fear of it jumping off; and if two guys of the same race were involved in a mutual combat, they'd lock us down for that as well. It didn't matter how big or small the incident was, we'd lose our program strictly for "precautionary" reasons. (It must be noted that the CDC would also collect "hazard pay" when working under such conditions.)

I was finally transferred to a program dorm to begin my indoctrination of all-day classes just after the 2006 calendar came into play. There were some days when we'd have half-days or no class at all due to staff training, but most days were spent enduring hour after hour of bullshit redundant teachings. The classes were held inside our building, so the morning fog, which was beneficial toward getting us out of SAP at Old Corcoran, did nothing for us. The days were dull and long, but there was also less tension on the yard. I told the guys I ran with that I would've much rather been at a prison with some action, but deep down I was grateful to be at a place where a full-scale riot was less likely.

Two months after my move to the programming dorm, I was assigned to the illustrious job of yard crew, earning nine cents an hour. 55% of my "paycheck" went toward paying restitution, leaving me with scraps, but I wasn't overly concerned about it. It wasn't like I was actually working; my job description entailed watering the grass and picking up cigarette butts—of which there weren't any because smoking had become illegal—and I rarely worked due to us being on lockdown or fog. It seemed wrong to be forced to pay restitution on top of court costs, but it did cut my hours from the SAP classes I had to attend.

As spring came about, SASCA held an extravaganza of sorts on the yard, complete with "Convict Olympics" and representatives of treatment centers coming from all over the state to sell us on their drug program upon release. During their visit, after the hot dogs were served and award ribbons given out to staff members and winners of events, Christopher Atkins—who starred with Brooke Shields in the movie *Blue Lagoon*...and nothing else—gave us a little talk about how sobriety changed his life, but his words were lost on me. I didn't care about his insignificant acting career nor did I feel a common bond between us through our drug addiction. He was an actor and couldn't possibly have endured the same hardships I had, so when he talked about being a slave to the bottle, I dismissed his proclamation as if it were lip service. The judgment and bias I held toward the well-to-do prevented me from opening my mind to the common peril we shared.

When he was done with his talk, two of the prison bands performed sets comprising of cover songs. The first band had a singer who called himself Johnny Rotten and the only song they got to do was the annoying pop punk tune "Bro Hymn" by Pennywise. A mini slam-pit kicked into gear during the song, with the Skinheads goose-stepping and *sieg heiling* in the middle of the pit. That was all it took for the C.O.'s to get them off the stage, much like a penitentiary version of the *Gong Show*, ending the "punk" show for guys accustomed to listening to bands like Korn and Sublime.

The next band to come on was one that did classic rock songs heard too many times, such as "Smoke on the Water" and "Hotel California". I don't know how many guys I'd heard over the years tell me that Hotel California was based on another prison by Chino called

Norco, and each time I'd have to bite my tongue or possibly incur the wrath of an angry Eagles fan. I personally never cared what the song does or doesn't mean; I couldn't stand the Eagles, nor could I stomach listening to a song I'd heard over a million times, but them playing that crap gave me the incentive to get a third SATF band started.

It took us a couple of months to get a time slot in the music room, but by the time we did, all the players were in place and we were ready to go. I was going to play drums, another guy from Long Beach was on lead guitar, and three other guys from the Inland Empire rounded out the rest of the band. I was the one who got everyone together and talked to the staff about getting us to play, so I naturally thought I'd be instrumental in the direction we'd take as far as sound was concerned. I wanted to play dirty rock and roll and to write our own songs about prison life. Everyone said they were down, but by the time we got together they insisted on playing Creed songs and some other shit I'd never heard of. It felt mutinous, but when it came down to it, the Whites in prison were mostly fans of radio shit and that Neu-Metal crap I abhorred. We didn't mesh musically—I sucked on the drums and they sucked in other ways, but I figured we'd be able to figure out a way to make it work. When they insisted on playing "Arms Wide Open", however, it was too much for me to take and I abandoned ship. Our little prison band had broken up before it even began, proving that, even in prison, musicians' egos were capable of creating insurmountable hurdles. I would not play Creed.

With the prospect of playing in the band behind me, I focused on my program of running, reading and writing Cherie. We submitted paperwork with the CDC administration clearing her to visit me, and by the beginning of summer she did. I fully expected the worst— thinking she'd back out and not come, that she wouldn't be anything like the girl I talked to and saw pictures of, or that the conversation would be dull and we'd end the visit in awkward silence.

She was already seated at a table when I was escorted in and after a brief hug I sat down across from her. I couldn't believe how beautiful she was...the pictures she'd sent didn't do her any justice. Her green eyes were clear and sharp, with dark brown hair that fell below her shoulders and a curvy athletic body to match her pretty face. She spoke in a welcoming high-pitched voice, her country upbringing coming out on occasion, giving it a musical quality. We both spoke freely and openly—we talked about our upbringings, how we got where we were, our love for music and anything else that came to mind. We were allowed a brief hug when the visit was over, and then I was escorted to a cell to go through a cavity search before being brought back to the yard.

She'd make the drive up to see me about once a month and I'd have butterflies in my stomach prior to each visit, then when it was over I'd walk back to my building wondering what she could've possibly seen in me and knowing each visit was my last. But each month she'd prove me wrong. At some point, she introduced the idea of staying with her when I got out and I jumped on the opportunity. My plan had been to go through a SASCA-funded treatment program and transition to a sober-living, but the last place I wanted to be after spending nineteen months locked up was a rehab. I truly felt that I could abstain from getting loaded due to the consequences I knew I'd endure if I did.

I made it through the rest of the summer without any major incidents coming to fruition on the yard—the C.O.'s had since loosened their grip with their overzealous lockdown procedures—and when I had sixty days left, I was ducated for pre-release. The classes were as boring and useless as the ones I went through when I was at CMC, but they got me out of attending the just as boring and useless SATF classes. On my first day there, the instructor told me that I was in a movie they showed. I didn't know what he was talking about— the only film work I'd done was through a casting agent my mom knew, and that was just audience participation work—but sure enough, he put in a videotape and there I was.

In 2003, during a stay at one of the rehabs I'd been in, I had gone to Santa Monica to be part of a drug awareness video, which I promptly forgot about. I'd gone as an extra but one of the cameramen kept his lens on me for some reason, giving me significant time in the film. It seemed obvious that it was just a video of a guy giving a lecture, with extras sitting in the audience to fill up seats. How anyone could think it was a movie was beyond me, but everyone in the class, the instructor included, wanted to know how much I got paid for being in it. I tried explaining that it was just something I did because of the treatment center I was in, but they weren't having it. I eventually gave up and let them keep their beliefs that I was a struggling actor who got caught up in the drug game, or whatever else it was they might've thought.

My S-Time ducat arrived toward the end of September, meaning I only had fifteen days left and no longer had to attend any of the ridiculous classes. I was starting to get anxious about my release date—I knew I didn't have any warrants or holds but I still lacked faith that Cherie would be there when I got out. She had told me repeatedly she'd be there no matter what, but I'd heard countless stories of girls leaving their men as their time approached, and even though we weren't in a relationship of that caliber, my insecurities put me right there with them. My head told me she was playing some type of game in which I'd be the ass end of a sick joke when I hit the gate and she'd be nowhere to be found. The fears I had were groundless and reflected a state of worthlessness I felt toward my being. Stress is common in prisoners as their release date approaches and everyone handles it differently. The only thing I could do to keep my sanity was to stay as busy as possible.

With October came my release date and a C.O. telling me to bring my property to the officer's station. After saying my goodbyes, I was escorted by an officer to the R and R building. I joined a group of ten others sitting in a large cell, waiting to be given their dress-outs, gate money and a ride to the Visitor Center. Half the guys were from the other SATF on F Yard, and the others from one of the many other yards at the prison.

Once we were given our standard issue of $200 and dress-outs, we signed papers acknowledging our release and were on our way. We boarded a bus that drove the gray and barren service roads of No-Man's Land, stopping at a gate where a guard confirmed our load while another checked the exterior of the bus for any potential escapee's, then drove out to the Visitor's Center on the outside.

Getting out of jail or prison gave me an elation that couldn't be matched, even though I was, by then, quite familiar with the process. It was one that became less sensational as I grew accustomed to being let out in the middle of the night from whichever city I was in or from whichever yard I was on, but the vividity and brilliance of the "free world" was always striking in its contrast from the dull gray of concrete and steel. The speed with which the world moved would invariably give me cause to wonder how I was going to adjust and I'd compare myself to others in a society I felt distant from. What was most compelling and striking though, was the fence I'd find myself straddling. No matter how fierce my resolve, I'd be mired in a purgatorial wash, weighing my desire to stay clean or get loaded. My track record reflected that I'd succumb to my predisposition to get high, but this time I felt I had solid ground on which I could begin anew.

As the bus came to a stop, I saw a throng of people sitting on benches and surveying our cargo, expectantly waiting for their loved ones to join them. I wasn't sure how long they'd been there, but it was safe to assume they'd been there since dawn. They looked like family members in a maternity ward, eagerly waiting to lay eyes on a newborn child for the first time. Some of them carried balloons and flowers, and a few were openly shedding tears. It's easy to disregard the feelings of those who love us through denial, justification, anger, self-pity and/or self-loathing, but when you see them standing in front of you with open arms, it hits you right between the eyes. I'd told myself on numerous occasions that my actions weren't hurting anyone, but if I truly and honestly looked inward, the lies I lived became apparent. My self-centeredness was laid out for all the world to see, yet somehow eluded me—I'd been living my life with my eyes closed and the only time I opened them was to look out for myself. By doing so, I'd been depriving myself of love and compassion, leaving me with an emptiness to endure.

When we were getting off the bus, the cluster of people on the benches rose to their feet and casually separated from each other, focusing their attention on whichever prisoner they were waiting for. My fear that Cherie wouldn't show was extinguished when I saw her stand and start walking toward me, but it still felt too good to be true. She gave me a hug and a pack of Camels and then we got on the road. I felt like I'd just been given a new shot at life and knew with every fiber of my being that I was done for good. I'd finally caught the break I felt the world owed me. Next stop, Los Angeles.

ODDJOB AND THE DING MOD

My eyes were heavy and tired from all the tears I'd shed; I wanted nothing more than to go back to my unit and lie down on my bunk, but I also didn't want to end the visit because I hadn't seen Cherie since I'd been arrested. It had been almost a year since we'd broken up but had somehow managed to stay friends, even though my contribution to that friendship was minimal at best. Yet here she was, sitting on the other side of a Plexiglas window, talking to me through a phone mounted on the wall of the visiting booth. She told me that she still loved me and would always be there for me, and I had no doubt her words were true…I just had a hard time accepting them.

Getting arrested again brought about a depression so severe that I felt compelled to plead with the jail psychiatrist to keep me in one of the mental health units in the Twin Towers. The units made up the largest mental health facility in the United States. Many of the inmates were suicidal, homicidal, schizophrenic and/or dealing with severe depression, and most were fed a steady diet of whatever the doctors saw fit to administer. During my stay, I had witnessed inmates bang their heads into walls attempting to quiet the voices within, spread shit all over of their cells, openly jack off in the middle of the dayroom and run around naked, screaming at the top of their lungs. The deputies usually just laughed and talked shit but when they did respond, they'd storm the unit and put the "ding" in restraints, then lock him in an observation cell wearing nothing but an anti-suicide smock (a tear-resistant garment used to curtail the making of a noose). You never knew what you'd see, and it made the 7th floor psych ward in the King County Jail look like a kid's menu.

* * * * *

I'd held it together when I first paroled and was cool up until the day I went to see a doctor for a bone I'd broken. It was only a slight fracture in my wrist, one I'd gotten from a fall a week prior to being released. I'd been out a couple of weeks and was still adamant about not using heroin, but figured I'd be able to work some pills and get a free buzz with no repercussions. My plan worked—he prescribed me Vicodin for the intense pain I told him I had, and I promptly took eight of them. I was pleasantly high, certainly not wasted, but Cherie could tell and she convinced me to flush the rest down the toilet. But by then it was too late.

Within a week, I was going downtown to score with whatever money I could put together and it didn't take long for me to get a habit. Cherie saw the direction I was heading and convinced me to check in to Stanton Detox. I reluctantly agreed and caught the Blue Line toward Orange County. When I got off the train in Long Beach, I snuck into a downtown bathroom to do the last of my dope and came out in a stupor. I nodded out sitting on my skateboard and when I came to, it was to a Long Beach cop bringing me to my feet and slamming me on the hood of his car. I'd done all my drugs but still had a needle and spoon on me, and being that I was on parole, I was booked into the City Jail on a paraphernalia charge.

Much to my surprise, I was released the following night and jumped the train back to Hollywood. I was given an ultimatum upon my arrival—go to rehab or move out. Cherie wasn't down with my bullshit and the following day I discovered my parole agent wasn't going to put up with it either. He told me that I had to get into treatment or be violated, so I made some calls.

I went in December of 2006—two months out of prison, and after a ninety-day commitment, I was ready for the world. My life came together quick with the drugs behind me and I stayed strong until the summer of 2008.

The skate team I was on—the Jak's—was holding our annual reunion in Austin that year and I decided to fly out and make it. We were all at a warehouse party, skating a ramp and having a blast, when I found myself with a keg cup in my hand. It obviously didn't magically appear—I tortured myself by obsessing, reminiscing and weighing the decision to drink until I finally said fuck it, telling myself that I wouldn't drink when I got back to Los Angeles.

207

The flame Cherie and I once had was extinguished by this time. We'd grown apart and wanted different things out of life—she had goals such as buying a house and furthering her career, while I just wanted to catch up on all the life I felt I'd missed out on. We broke up the day I got back from Texas. I loaded my Mustang that Fall and hit the road, travelling the country, seeing friends and partying, then drove to Seattle with the intention of settling down. I'd only been in town three days when I talked to a friend from Oakland who told me that he needed a guy on his crew to help sell merchandise at political rallies for the presidential election.

It was like touring with a band. We'd load up equipment (merch), travel to a venue (rally) and sell our wares to fans (overzealous patriots). We sold them anything they'd buy: stickers, buttons, hats, shirts, and we crashed both parties. The McCain rallies were the best largely in part to there being less competition amongst vendors, but mostly because of the fanaticism of his supporters. We sold buttons with photo-shopped pictures of Sarah Palin holding an AR-15 saying "Just Drill Baby", and the Republicans couldn't get enough of them. Another favorite of theirs was the "NOBAMA" bumper sticker. I heard the words "this is the WHITE house!" from many racist rednecks thinking I was one of them, and just smiled as they gave me their money.

We were on the road constantly, going state to state in a van loaded with Democrat and Republican merch, chasing rallies and the money from their supporters. I'd been on the trail with them a month and made several thousand dollars and had enough, so when we hit a rally in Henderson, Nevada, I jumped ship. I knew we'd end up going back to goddamn Ohio or Pennsylvania from there, and because I was only five hours from L.A., I figured Las Vegas was as good a spot as any to call it quits. I was tired of the crowds of people wearing pins of presidential hopefuls, the "OBAMA" and "NOBAMA" chants and driving across the eastern seaboard with little or no sleep.

I had enough money saved to get my own place once I got back to Seattle, but I wanted to get good and loaded in Los Angeles first. The old desire had come crashing back when we were at an Obama rally in Indianapolis, after seeing a vendor from another crew with the familiar heroin-pinned eyes of the dope fiend. I jumped on a Greyhound from Vegas, went directly to Skid Row and it was on from there. Shortly after arriving, I hooked up with a girl of questionable integrity, forging a relationship based on her pill supply and my fat wallet. Our drug-fueled "romance" lasted somewhere around two weeks, up until the day I got busted cooking up a shot of dope.

We'd been shopping in the Garment District and gotten into a fight, leading me to leave her there. I went directly to 6th and San Pedro to score, then to a spot on San Julian Street and threw my dope in a spoon. It was only a block from the precinct but that never stopped me or anyone else from doing drugs right there on the street. It may be hard for most to imagine, but the police typically didn't get involved in drug activities east of Spring Street. What I didn't know was that the city was in the process of refurbishing the area, clearing the way for the lofts, galleries and hipsters there today. Cops who might've driven past if they'd seen me fixing behind a dumpster a few years back were now more than willing to hem me up and bring me in.

And that's exactly what they did. Two pigs on the beat materialized out of thin air, surprising me and some black guys smoking crack, putting us up against a wall with our hands behind our backs. They ended up letting the smokers go after smashing their pipes, then cuffed me up and walked me to the precinct, telling me I was going to jail because I still had a chance to get my shit together. According to the cops, the other guys were too shot-out to be saved.

From a different perspective, their words could've been perceived as insightful and complimentary, but I was livid. I figured that I should've been given a break. When my pleas to be set free were met with laughter, I told the cops they were worthless and were only working because I paid my taxes. It was all rather humorous—I was thirty-six years old and had about two total years of employment under my belt. Having the audacity to make such a statement revealed my narcissistic traits and just how fucked up I was, and I'm pretty sure the absurdity of it all saved me from a beating.

They booked me for possession of a controlled substance and brought me to the Glasshouse, setting me up for another kick in the county jail. I'd only been on a two-week run, but that didn't make it any easier. The same restlessness, unease and suicidal thoughts were weighing me down, making every second of the day an agonizing chore. I was once again in a cesspool of downtown swine, listening to the endless banter of demise, smelling other men's shit, watching people get jumped, eating horrid meals and getting yelled at by angry cops. All I could do was hope the DA rejected my case and I knew my chances were slim.

I was brought to CCB three sleepless days later and called in to see the judge in the afternoon, effectively smashing any hope for a DA reject. As the deputies were taking us out of the cell and on to the bus, one of them scanned my wristband then asked if I was "K-11". I knew K-11 was a designation used for gay inmates and brushed it off as a disparaging comment trying to get me upset, but about twelve hours later, the length of time it took to be transported, unshackled, searched and classified, I was scanned by another deputy who told me queers weren't allowed in General Population. I was separated and put on a bench designated for K-11's and "softies", then told to take off my blue pants and put on a pair of yellow ones. I told the deputy that they'd made a mistake and he told me to shut my faggot ass up and take it like a man.

I was then escorted from the bench, bypassing the showers and cage, straight to the podium overlooking the main holding area for inmates waiting to be seen by medical staff. Along the base of the podium were an assortment of other K-11 designated men sitting on benches—some had breasts, most had feminine features and they all looked extremely tired. I was told to grab a seat and given a new wristband with the letter "G" in front of my booking number.

The "G" stood for gay and as I sat with the throng of protective-custody inmates, trying to hide my face from the GP inmates circulating about, I reflected on my misfortune. My regret was misdirected, however. Where most would've conceded that doing drugs was the problem, I found myself wishing I'd chosen another spot to do them and thinking that if I hadn't gotten into a fight with my girlfriend, I wouldn't have gotten busted. While this was certainly true, I neglected to address my drug addiction as the issue. My grasp on reality was tentative at best—the narrow scope of my mind's eye was ill-fitted for anything beyond that which impacted my present state.

I eventually gave up trying to hide from the rest of the jail population and found solace in knowing it would all get straightened out one way or another. I sat on the same bench for over twenty-four hours, feeling like a character in some sick tragedy, then was escorted to the Twin Towers for a medical evaluation. The Towers were mostly used for housing inmates with psychiatric issues or serious medical conditions, but if you came in going through withdrawals, the medical staff would keep you there until you were evaluated. The ACLU had sued L.A. County over the deplorable conditions inmates with medical issues had to endure, ending the days of sitting in the cage for days at a time.

I was kept in a medical unit with other guys waiting to be seen by a doctor, and after two days of kicking on a plastic mat, waiting to get my blood pressure taken and being prescribed shit that didn't help with the kick, I was brought to MCJ. They put me in another dorm, one with men trying to get in to the gay modules. Most of them were truly gay but there were some who were either hiding from enemies, didn't want to pay their drug debts or were just plain scared. To circumvent the issue of having men who weren't gay in the modules, the deputies surveyed each man, asking questions about where they were from, what they did for work and even gave a test relevant to gay history. If they passed the deputies "gaydar" they were housed in one of the K-11 modules on the 5000 Floor, and if they didn't they were sent to GP.

I watched everyone in the dorm with half-interested curiosity—the guys gossiping while they prettied themselves as much as they could with what they had, the gay trustees coming in to crush and snort antidepressants and offer advice on passing the test, and the ones who were trying to hide eagerly absorbing that advice—and after two days I was finally interviewed, telling the deputies that I wasn't gay and had no idea how I'd been classified as such. They laughed about my set of circumstances, then one of them went on to tell me it happened a lot; the cops had done it to fuck with me.

I was then brought down to the 2000 Floor and put into a housing unit with small cells lining one side of the unit and a row of bunks in the hallway on the other. On the tier above us were twelve cells that held PC inmates who were constantly yelling to each other and obscenities down to us, trying to get us to shout back at them. They'd scream throughout the day and most of the night, venting their pent-up tension our way and stealing the possibility of any calm.

I'd been there a few days when I noticed the inmates on the upper tier hanging sheets on the fronts of their cells. They hung them in unison. I was wondering what was happening when one of the guys on my floor shouted that we needed to move our bunks under the tier quickly. Still puzzled as to what was going on, I helped with the

---

211

process and not a minute too soon because a steady flow of dirty toilet water began spilling out from the cells above to where our bunks had been. I didn't know it then, but about once a month they'd stuff sheets, towels and whatever else they could get their hands on to clog their toilets, in solidarity with each other over whatever it was they felt to be unjust.

Our only recourse was to stay under the overhang of the tier and wait for the toilet water to stop flooding out. The deputies would impose their own form of justice against such actions when it affected them, but for our predicament they sent in a crew of trustees with mops and left us with extra blankets to soak it up. We enacted our own revenge later by filling milk cartons with piss, then throwing the cartons into their cells after they'd taken down their sheets, perpetuating a grotesque cycle of revenge upon each other.

I went back to court the following week and was released on Prop 36. By seven o'clock of that evening, I was out on the streets. I knew from the last time I was on Prop 36 that I had a few days to report to the assessment center and I had plenty of money in my bank account, so I took it as an excuse to fill my spoon.

It wasn't long until I was strung out again and the money made on the campaign trail gone. I stretched my court dates and filled the judge with lies until she was sick of my bullshit, and finally checked into a rehab in North Hollywood. It took three months from when I was released to get there, during which time I had OD'd, been locked up in a psych unit, been fired from a job, gone to detox, and gotten on methadone. It was the necessary push I needed toward living a life without drugs.

Within two weeks, however, I was kicked out for not filing disability paperwork with the billing department. I was collecting unemployment at the time and filing with disability would've cut it off, which I was willing to do, but I wanted to collect one last check before doing so. Greed was certainly at play when it came to my decision, but I felt entitled to it because Prop 36 was already paying for my bed. When it came down to it, they were even greedier than I was. On top of Prop 36, they would've collected all the disability awarded me, so I think they could've waited the week it took for my check to arrive, but I was instead told to vacate the premises and to do so immediately.

212

I left the rehab with a healthy resentment and the feeling that I was destined for a life of shit. My anger kept me clean for a week but the temptation to use became too strong to withstand, and I soon had a full-blown habit again. I was staying at my mom's in West L.A. and when it became evident to her I'd been using, she told me that I had to find another place to stay. With nowhere to go, I went back to the streets and continued my downward spiral into the world I knew best.

On an evening in March of 2009, desperate and tired, I went into the Disney Store on Hollywood Boulevard. I knew my run was coming to an end—all the music and video stores from the Valley to Long Beach were hip to me and it was common to see workers tailing me as soon as I entered—but I somehow talked myself into believing I could get away with stealing from a goddamn kid's store.

I didn't fit the bill of a Disney shopper and they were on to me the moment I walked inside. Sadly, I was too out of it to notice due to my intake of benzo's. I took three DVD's, removed the alarm sensors—taking an eternity in doing so—and then stuffed them down my pants and walked out the door. Some Asian dude who looked like Oddjob from the James Bond movie *Goldfinger* immediately grabbed me. My reaction, as has always been the case when incarceration looms ahead, was to make a break. He read it all the way and when I tried to bolt, he used some judo shit on my ass, twisting my arm behind my back and putting me in a headlock. No matter how hard I tried, I couldn't break free and once I realized this, I switched tactics, promising that I'd never come back if he let me go. My pleas were met with disdainful laughter and angry words telling me to shut the fuck up and quit crying.

Two officers patrolling the Red Line station on the other side of Hollywood Boulevard saw the commotion and ran over with their billy clubs in hand, ready to subdue me if need be. I knew then that I was going back to County. As they drove me to the Wilcox Hotel, the regret of getting kicked out of rehab began to sink in, as did the knowledge that this arrest would almost certainly send me back to prison. Getting arrested had always brought about feelings of hopelessness and despair, but staying out for a couple years made the shock of going back unbearable. I'd managed to shake the shackles of parole, which seemed impossible at one point, and put together a semblance of a normal life, but it was all for naught. I was back in the system again.

213

* * * * *

Our visit came to an end after thirty minutes and I reluctantly hung up the phone, knowing it would be a long time before I saw her again. We took one last look at each other through the visiting glass, then I dried the tears from my eyes the best I could and went back to my dorm. Getting the visit had reenergized me, at least for the time being. Cherie and I were never getting back together, we'd moved on in that sense, but we would always be friends. When she told me that she loved me, regardless of whatever bad decisions I made in my life, I knew she was speaking truth. It was the first time since getting arrested that I felt optimistic about the future and that everything was going to be all right.

I'd been in the mental ward close to a month and still wasn't sure how much time I'd end up doing. They were trying to get me for strong-armed robbery because Oddjob claimed I'd elbowed him as I tried to escape. He stated at my preliminary hearing that he might've been wrong about me throwing the elbow, but it was still enough to get me bound over for trial. I knew a jury would never convict me for robbery, that the prosecution was working a scare tactic so I'd take a plea bargain for a lesser charge, but I still found it absurd. Robbery was a violent crime and it reflected the guile and cunning used to prosecute.

Ideally, the scales of justice represent an impartiality in which the wrongs of society are measured and the correct punishment delivered. But somewhere along the way, prosecutors began collecting convictions like notches on a bedpost, hoping to gain favor with District Attorneys and voters to further their political ambitions. Elected officials control the court system and the best way to gain favor with the voters is to have a high conviction rate. The best way to get a high conviction rate is to throw plea deals on the table, which also effectively eliminates court costs. It works out great for everyone involved, except the judicial system, which is supposed to be the pinnacle of moral reasoning, becomes tainted by the lengths it will go to get convictions.

It didn't take long for them to offer me a deal and by the time they did, I was ready to jump on it. On the morning of my next hearing, making the move from the Twin Towers to the court line, a group of deputies walked alongside us, screaming that we belonged in an insane asylum and other such obscenities. I wasn't too bothered by it personally, but I was worried one of the guys with serious psychiatric issues might take the bait and end up on the receiving end of a deputy boot party. The most vocal of the deputies was a giant cornfed man with a bespectacled fat face of a little boy who undoubtedly got the wrong kind of attention growing up. He was screaming at an inmate with severe issues and a catatonic gait. I wondered how a cop like him could be admitted to a force whose motto was dignity and integrity.

I was brought to CCB and saw my public defender in the afternoon, and he told me they were offering two years, that I wouldn't get a strike because they were lowering it to a lesser charge and that I wouldn't be on Prop 36 when I paroled. I was going to take the deal regardless, the thought of going back and forth between the jail and the courthouse sounded hellish, but it felt like he was trying to sell me on it. His intent seemed to be of a man trying to lighten his caseload than that of a man willing to fight a case. But realistically, who could blame him? I was a three-time loser, a junkie and obviously guilty. In a system hell-bent on using shortcuts and offering plea bargains, to find true representation without having the money to pay for it would've contradicted the efficiency they were shooting for. I pled "guilty" to a charge of grand theft—it should've been an even lesser charge of petty-theft-with-a-prior because the merchandise totaled $120, but grand theft looked better on the prosecutor's resume—and was given two years in state prison.

In one of the cells I had to wait in before being processed back into MCJ and the cavity search, I saw a guy I'd been in Supermax with a few years earlier. He recognized me right away and appeared shocked that I was wearing a yellow shirt (inmates designated with mental health issues were required to wear them). When he asked me why I was in the ding dorm, I found myself struggling to give him a straight answer. I came in suffering from severe depression and then found myself comfortable there because I didn't have to deal with the entanglement of jailhouse politics. I didn't have any real psychiatric issues, so if I was to honestly break it down, I was hiding. I couldn't tell him that, of course, and ended up saying I was there to get my head back on straight.

He knew what I was doing and seemed to dismiss me when he sat back down on the bench, as if to say I wasn't worth talking to. The time spent in the psych ward was safe in a sense, but the other inmates ostracized me when I had to leave my shell to make court appearances. In all my previous court dates, I'd been content with playing the role but seeing someone I'd done time with before, a man who knew I had the mental competency to be in General Population, brought up feelings of guilt and shame. He didn't so much as look at me when we were called out to get cavity searched, driving the feelings of spinelessness even deeper into my heart.

Being the coward that I was, I shook off my emotional state of disgrace and settled back into the comfort of seclusion found within the Twin Towers. My unrealistic sense of honor stated that I should've been doing my time in GP, but the separation from the politics was enough to keep my pride in check. Staying consistent with jail procedure, however, I was transferred to MCJ one week after I was sentenced, effectively negating any feelings I'd held about hiding out. My concern now was getting back into a workout routine and doing what I could to avoid any violence. My mind was filled with a false bravado over going to GP, but in my heart I was full of fear. I knew the day would come and that I'd adapt, but I wasn't exactly excited about hearing the daily workout cadences, nightly roll calls and the nonstop chatter of angry voices on the tier.

I was moved to a four-man cell on 4000 Floor and it was every bit as chaotic as I remembered. Each cell had its own dynamic, dictated by the various personalities of its occupants, yet each cell mirrored the others. Some had soldiers who were vigilant in their routine of staying ready for the inevitable moment when it jumped, and others fat, lazy slobs who did the bare minimum.

I knew that any and everything happened in these cells. I'd once heard a shot-caller denounce his set in a pruno-infused rant and heard the sounds of the same guy getting beaten into submission when his people got back at him; I've seen men yelling into phones and punching walls, and others crying, begging for forgiveness; I've been in cells where each of us were spun out of our minds from speed and others where we were on a nod; I've seen guys make shanks full of fear and others make "spreads" full of love; I've walked down the tier and seen a youngster hogtied in his cell, looking at me with fear in his eyes as his captors glared at me, daring me to say something, and I've seen guys holding hands and praying together. Love and evil thrive in jail, just like in the "free world", and are in a constant battle for supremacy. The expressions of each may differ, with the whirlwind or calm setting the tone for chaos or peace.

The days on 4000 crawled by like the rats that came out on the tier in the middle of the night looking for scraps, then after two weeks of lying around and doing nothing, I was called for transfer to Wayside. I went through the standard ordeal of waiting in concrete hallways and sitting in cells, then loaded onto a bus with close to forty inmates. You never knew exactly where you were going until the transport deputies arrived and started calling names off their list, at which point you were shackled and taken away. I'd been through this process countless times and the efficiency with which the deputies handled it never ceased to amaze me. Men's Central Jail was essentially a bus depot for criminals, with busses arriving and departing all throughout the day, covering 4000 square miles. They were responsible for getting inmates to court on time, taking them to one of the many lockup facilities within the county when court was done, picking up inmates in other counties who had warrants in L.A. and dropping men off in prison after they'd been sentenced. The fine-tuning it took to coordinate all these movements within the most populated jail in the United States was astonishing.

I was thrilled to be leaving MCJ and even more so when I discovered I was going to Medium South. The south facility was a medium-security compound where all the inmates stayed in tents comparable to the Farm in Orange County. Some of the tents were designated for veterans, a drug program run by the court system and for schooling, but the rest were for workers. It opened in 1971 and had gone through many changes over the years, but in the summer of 2009, there were ten tents, each holding close to 100 men, lining one side of a large exercise yard. If you weren't assigned to one of the aforementioned programs, you worked in one of the many job details that were handed out. Besides the typical kitchen and laundry workers, Medium South also had crews that cleared brush from areas prone to fires, cleaned cop cars and busses, handled waste management and even groomed dogs.

The tents lacked the tension so prevalent in MCJ—most inmates were only doing county time and waiting to go home. Everyone wore yellow uniforms and lined up in a caged enclosure after breakfast, where we'd wait for our work detail to pick us up. The men who worked on the laundry crew packed into a bus and the rest of us jumped into the back of a truck with whichever crew we were assigned. I was in a group with five other men and our job, basically, was to drive around the facility and remove anything that could contribute to wildfires and then bring the shit to the Pitchess dump.

Wayside covered over 2500 acres and we'd travel much of it, but still nowhere close to its total in area. The deputies had gun ranges, a seemingly endless trail system, nurseries and who knows what else, all paid for with taxes and having the cheapest workforce on the market in charge of its upkeep. By navigating political alliances and using fear to manipulate the public, the sheriff's department had created a powerful monster—one which leached tax dollars and was free of scrutiny from the public eye.

The landscape of Castaic was magnificent, a land sunburnt and rocky, with dried and dying trees dotting its mountains. We'd strip excess brush along roadways from the entrance of Wayside to within, circling Medium North and South, Eastmax and Supermax. While making our rounds, we'd occasionally drop by the jail's laundry facility to get coffee. The building was massive. Giant receptacles were brought in from all over the county containing the filthiest laundry you could imagine—blankets soaked with piss, men's and women's underwear, bloody uniforms and all kinds of trash mixed in with it—each article of clothing part of one person's nightmare. The laundry came in bundles and was dumped onto a conveyor belt to be sorted through by a crew of inmates wearing gloves and masks, and then assorted and loaded into the largest washing machines I'd ever seen. Just like the sewing shop at Super Max, the workers were almost entirely made up of Paisas from south of the border.

I'd been working the same program for a few weeks when a Southsider from East L.A. hit the facility, moving into my tent. Racial tension was non-existent at the time, most everyone was low security and content with their program, but all of that changed practically overnight. Because of the ongoing war between the Blacks and Mexicans, and because the deputies didn't want to disrupt their

218

workforce, neither Blacks nor anyone affiliated with prison gangs were housed there. Occasionally, however, a man would slip through the cracks. The man in question had come down from a prison upstate with orders that Whites were to pay taxes to the Southsiders. Anyone ordering commissary from store was to pay 15% of their total spent to the Southsiders because, in their words, the Whites needed Mexican protection.

After their shot-caller's right-hand man gave us the order, we held court on the yard and discussed how we were going to handle the matter. What they wanted to do was basically extortion. To concede to their demands would reflect a position of cowardice and a refusal to pay would almost certainly lead to a full-scale riot. Between the Southsiders and Paisas, who were joined at the hip in matters such as this, we were outnumbered about four to one. Having no Blacks on the yard had created a vacuum and the overzealous Southsiders, in their quest for control, took it upon themselves to make a move.

Our shot-caller and a few of the other Whites were comfortable with paying the tax to avoid confrontation. I had a suspicion they were in league with the Mexicans so they could keep their tobacco hustle solid, but the rest of the Whites absolutely refused. This difference in opinion threatened the unity of our group and had many of us wondering if we were going to have to jump him and his right-hand man out, but in the end the decision was made to stand together in the matter and not pay the tax.

With our little meeting on the yard over, I went back to the tent somewhat shaken by the lack of unanimity and expecting the Mexicans to respond with violence. It felt like it could jump at any time and everyone was on edge. We were told to stay on our toes, to stay in groups of at least two and to take turns keeping lookout through the night. When the lights went out, it was so quiet the only sounds you could hear were whispering and the occasional flushing of a toilet. People were sitting up in their bunks, keeping their eyes open and planning a course of action for when it jumped. We were on a "one up, one down" regimen—meaning that if you slept, your bunkie stayed up, and vice versa, but I don't think anyone in the unit shut their eyes.

The morning of the next day arrived with a welcoming embrace and we all lined up for chow and then work, but with the knowledge a riot was brewing and that it would probably jump after the Southsiders spread the word. The crew I was on was made up of three Mexicans and another White, and we spent the day working in silence. There were no hard stares exchanged and we'd talk to each other if our work called for it, but a blind man would've been able to see something was amiss.

The deputies picked up on it and when we were done with our shift, we were put on bunk status when we got back to our housing unit. It was calmer than the night before and I wasn't sure if it was because the Southsiders hadn't organized a coordinated reprisal yet or if they were bluffing and weren't going to attack. We kept with our defensive posture, however, keeping watch and sticking together, doing our best to portray an image of a disciplined attack force.

If it ever jumped I'll never know, for after dinner was served, a deputy came in to read the transfer list and I was on it. I was spared the potential destruction of an oncoming train by the call of the prison line. I rolled up my property and gave my commissary to my bunkie, then was escorted to a fenced enclosure used for holding inmates going back to County. My gratitude for having made it out of the brewing cauldron of conflict outweighed the fear I had toward the change of environment and the unknown that came with it. In the enclosure were a couple other Whites, a few Mexicans, and a scattering of black dudes who looked on with disinterest to a situation that didn't affect them. We left the conflict behind us, like a turd you'd see in an alley, hoping someone else would pick it up. Any hostilities over us not paying their ridiculous taxes were now a distant memory.

LANCASTER AND DESERT VIEW

The bus taking us downtown rolled up around eight o'clock and we were on our way. It was practically full, mostly with guys being released and a sprinkling of others going to different counties— the rest of us were going to prison. The demeanor of the ones going home was that of electricity and excitement, while those of us catching the chain were somber and reserved. None of us going upstate had much time to do as far as prison sentences went, and it would've been fair to say we were all at least somewhat excited about moving on from L.A. County, but since we were going to prison, we had a machismo obligation to carry ourselves in a manner reflecting how badass we thought we were.

We arrived at MCJ an hour later and were separated once our chains were removed—the ones going home brought to the pre-release cells and everyone else to IRC. I was placed in a cell with the letters "LAN" written on the window and filled with close to twenty men. The cell was small and its occupants weren't thrilled they had to include another person, but they successfully accommodated me by manipulating body parts and packing together.

We were going to CSP-Los Angeles, nestled within Antelope Valley in the now thriving city of Lancaster. I had assumed I'd go to Delano because it was where L.A. County prisoners were generally sent, so I actually felt a subtle tug of excitement upon discovering I was going there. Excitement was the wrong word, but there was a certain level of mystique in going to a place I'd never been before. With the "excitement" came regret, however. I soon discovered that I could've brought my food with me if I wanted to. Unlike Delano, where the CDC didn't allow food brought in from the county jail, Lancaster permitted inmates to bring their commissary with them— except for certain spicy chips that could be used to make a crude pepper spray. Knowing I could've curtailed some of the intense hunger I'd have down the road was a bit of a letdown, but my biggest regret came from the stash of coffee I'd given away.

The night passed without incident, my nostrils polluted by the odor of men's bodies and the fragrance of shit, and I heard the familiar clanging of chains approaching the cell in the early hours of the morning. The deputies pulled us out one by one, scanning our wristbands and looking at our booking photos in the process. When they got to my mugshot they both started laughing. In my picture you could see tears in my eyes and utter despair written all over my face, knowing I was on my way back to the county jail to kick once again. One of them tried making me feel better by saying that I must've been wasted when I was arrested, but I was so preoccupied by what my cellmates would think if they saw the photo his comment did little good.

Nobody noticed, or quite possibly didn't care, and after boarding the bus we were on our way, winding through dirty Chinatown streets toward the northbound lanes of I-5. The bus rolled north through Burbank and the San Fernando Valley, then cut east on Highway 14. We stayed on the highway for two hours before coming upon the small city of Lancaster. It sat in the high-desert region of the Antelope Valley, at the westernmost point of the Mojave Desert. It looked to be a land of expansion for L.A. residents wanting out of the congested city landscape—an abundance of prefab houses and strip malls dotted the roads on the way to the prison, furnishing me with the fuel for my thoughts and urban analysis.

The prison bore resemblance to practically all the state institutions I'd been in the past, but different in the sense that whole communities of people lived right across the street. It had opened in 1993, before many of the houses in the area were built, and the contrast between the prison and the community surrounding it was striking. On the same square-mile tract of land the prison sat were also the Mira Loma Detention Center, which was used at the time to hold Immigration Customs Enforcement detainees, and a juvenile probation center, holding youth that hadn't yet graduated to the gavel of the superior court system. I could only imagine how tense the local townhall meetings were when they got together to discuss issues relative to their community.

The terrain at Lancaster was similar to Corcoran and Delano—ugly and uninviting. The desert climate contributed to the barren setting, but the main reason originated from the penitentiary's layout. The buildings were set on level ground and spaced in a manner that the officers working the prison would have a clear line of sight, devoid of obstacles such as trees that could block vision. Just as in any other prison I'd been, I could see shapes moving behind cell windows and knew them to be prisoners peering our way, doing anything they could to change the dull monotony of life in a prison cell, even something as mundane as watching a bus drive through No-Man's Land.

We pulled up to R and R, then were taken inside to have our chains removed. Unlike Delano, which had an entire building designated to handle the procedure, Lancaster conducted the booking process in the dayroom of one of the housing units. I could see prisoners looking out the windows of their cell doors trying to get a look at us as we stripped, went through a cavity search and then placed in a holding pen. I understood why convicts would want to see who was being brought in, but as I was standing there with my butt cheeks spread apart and coughing for a C.O. standing behind me, I couldn't help but question their motives.

The cage enclosure I was kept in was filled with the other occupants of the bus, sitting in boxers they'd outfitted us with after being strip-searched. A large black female officer was sitting at a podium directly across from the cage, calling out names on occasion and watching for guys who might pull something out of their asses while using the toilet. She had an evil eye and I didn't want it staring at me, so I decided to bide my time until I was put into my own cell and had a little privacy. It was the same process as Delano, essentially—prison photos were taken, I was given a new CDC number, a C.O. asked info pertaining to gang ties and if I had any known enemies, etc.—and by the time dinner was served, I was in the comfort of my new home.

I was celled with a guy who paced nonstop, mumbling to himself in an indecipherable language. He didn't appear threatening in any way, but his manner was curious enough to legitimize concern for my wellbeing, leading to an evening of sleeping with one eye open. Early in the morning, after breakfast was served, a unit of C.O.'s appeared at the door and screamed through the food tray slot for me to get on my bunk, and for him to kneel on the concrete. We both followed their instructions, me quietly and him repeatedly telling them that he didn't do anything wrong, after which three guards came in, cuffed him up and took him away.

I never discovered what he did to warrant such a response, but after he was surreptitiously lifted from the cell and deposited to wherever he was taken, I had the cell to myself and slept the sleep of champions. Much of the diagnostics tests new prisoners had to undergo upon intake were conducted inside the building and within a few days I was transferred to another unit. The building was the same as far as design was concerned, but where the dayroom in the R and R unit had been littered with desks and filing systems, the dayroom in my new unit was filled with bunks. I was put in a cell on the top tier with a view of the overcrowding below and felt fortunate that I didn't have to bunk down there with them.

Prison cells follow a standard design, more or less—a small desk sitting beneath a narrow window with a view of No-Man's Land, bunk beds protruding from a wall, a heavy steel door with a small window and food tray slot built into it and a stainless-steel sink/toilet unit sitting in the corner. It changes when you hit the mainline, but in reception the only time you're let out is for the walk to the chow hall, when it's your cell's turn to shower, the two times a week when yard is called and when prison staff call you out to go to medical or see your counselor. If a lockdown occurs, the only time you're let out is for showers and it's only for five minutes. Acclimation can be a struggle but it's a necessity. If you can't adapt, or refuse to, you'll be labeled a "program failure" by CDC officials and placed in a unit that fits your needs, such as the Segregated Housing Unit, until you're deemed compliant.

My cellie was a "J-cat" (a guy with mental issues) who had a penchant for collecting old newspapers and magazines, to the point that they were spilling out from underneath his bunk. He was from a town called Needles just south of Las Vegas and had done more than a fair share of methamphetamines in his life, which surely contributed to his mental demise. Besides his uncleanliness and rambling at times, he was actually a decent guy and it was fortunate he trans-packed to another prison shortly after I arrived, thwarting any violence over the words we would've inevitably had over his filthy habits.

My next cellie was an old-school convict who'd been extradited back to California from Phoenix for a parole violation. He arrived at Lancaster by way of Chino and had to be relocated because of a riot that had kicked off on the West Yard, during which buildings were burned and subsequently razed. He told me crazy stories about the Maricopa County Jail, where the infamous sheriff Joe Arpaio had ruled with impunity...how inmates were forced to wear pink underwear, about food so bad he would've been reluctant to feed it to his dog, how the sheriff had inmates earn TV privileges by pedaling on stationary bicycles and many other tales of insanity bordering hilarity. I knew better, but he made L.A. County sound like a destination for the elite.

We got along most of the time. Being locked in a cell with a man over any length of time can make it so you focus on his mannerisms, enough that those behaviors will fully negate a man's good qualities if you let them. Fortunately, the negative characteristics he displayed—or rather, what I perceived as negative—were insubstantial. My greatest annoyance was that he'd stand in front of the cell door, looking out the window to the dayroom in deep contemplation for hours at a time. The stress over his girlfriend, their living situation and knowing he was going to put his freedom in jeopardy when he went back to her after he got out was consuming him.

But the flipside to his stressed-out and lovesick demeanor was a man who possessed a boisterous personality with one of the heartiest laughs I'd ever heard. We'd stay up late playing two-hand pinochle, talking about rock and roll and sharing stories about our tragedies, mishaps and adventures. His welcoming nature made it extremely difficult to watch him sink into his depression, but I also found satisfaction when I could draw him out of it and make him laugh. The contrast between his personalities was significant but I did my best to keep in mind we all dealt with stress differently, and that I wasn't exempt from displaying mannerisms he also found bothersome.

Lancaster had opened in 1993 and was the only prison in L.A. County, even though about 40% of California's prisoners were from L.A. By the time I arrived, many of the yards were reputed to be PC, as well as two of the buildings on the reception yard—they were separated by a fence and we were never allowed out of the unit when they were on the yard. Almost all the prisoners in reception were from Los Angeles, as opposed to Delano, Wasco, Donovan and Chino, which handled receiving for inmates from all over Southern California.

I'd been there about a month when a riot between the Blacks and Mexicans kicked off in one of the other buildings, affording me the opportunity to get a job working in the kitchen. Both races were slammed down after it jumped, so the prison staff filled their positions with Whites, Native Americans and Asians. The job gave me a break

225

from the mind-numbing dullness of being stuck in a cell as well as time away from my cellie—much needed assistance toward maintaining at least a touch of sanity.

My counselor came to my unit when I had close to sixty days in and told me I'd be transferring to a CCF, the same thing I'd heard every other time I'd been in reception. Being that I'd never been sent to where a counselor said I was going, I had little basis to believe her, so I discounted her words and assumed I'd be sent to some shitty yard in the far-flung reaches of the San Joaquin Valley. And even that sounded fine as long as I didn't have to do my time on another drug treatment yard. As if I hadn't known it before, being on one of those yards was utterly pointless, unless you planned on using the resources allocated by the state for rehabilitation upon release, and I had no desire to take that route.

A mere week after my counselor dropped by my housing unit, I was called down to the officer's station and ordered to trans-pack. The C.O. told me I was indeed going to a CCF, one called Desert View near Victorville. I couldn't believe what I was hearing. Because my controlling case was for theft, I didn't think I'd be sent to a SAP yard, but still wouldn't have been surprised if I had due to the CDC's tendency to place prisoners wherever they saw fit.

Community Correctional Facilities were privatized lockups used by the state of California to hold prisoners who weren't considered an imminent threat to the communities outside. Besides the thirty-three state prisons in California, there were also twelve CCF's in operation, most of them located in the Bakersfield area. The idea was, because of the prisoner's lower security levels, the state would save money by hiring guards who worked for far less than the union-paid CDC guards.

A few days after I'd trans-packed, I was awoken early in the morning and put into a cell in R and R with five other guys who were going to the same place, then waited for the transport vehicle to arrive. It was approaching noon by the time they showed, and my displeasure with being held in one of many more holding cells I knew were waiting for me was beginning to surface. I was in yet another of an endless number of holding tanks filled with countless blank faces, each a part of the passing parade that was my life. I was hit with the realization right then that if I kept getting loaded, I'd live to grow old in more cells just like the one I was in. I knew from experience that a personal pledge to stay clean was futile and told myself that I was willing to die rather than live the nightmare I was in.

We were shackled and put on a bus, then driven east toward the heart of the Mojave Desert. The roads and highways we took were littered with decrepit one-story houses, trailer parks and the occasional cluster of prefab shopping centers various entrepreneurs with one-time visions of grandeur had built and failed miserably. Aside from the Joshua Trees shooting their broken and battered trunks from the ground, the landscape was nothing but dirt and rock for miles. It was a suitable habitat for the destitute, those who lived the lives of desert hermits and very little else.

Desert View was located in the small city of Adelanto, just northwest of Victorville off highway 395. We navigated the town's desolate roads and rolled up to the facility in the middle of the afternoon, parking the bus inside a gated entrance with access to the building. A tall chain-link fence surrounded the perimeter of the prison, but with none of the guard towers I was accustomed to seeing.

A crew of correctional officers was there to receive us and promptly put us in a cell while they did our intake paperwork and whatever else it was they needed to do to accommodate us. To call the staff working in the facility "correctional officers" is a bit misleading. The majority of the ones I saw walking the halls were extremely out of shape as opposed to the CDC guards who were predominantly well-trained ex-soldiers. They all wore polo shirts with the word "GEO" embroidered on the breast—a sharp contrast from the militaristic jumpsuits the CDC wore. They carried themselves in a manner reflecting at least some degree of discipline and I knew they'd likely work cohesively in arresting minor situations—but I also knew they'd be fucked if a riot kicked off.

We underwent a brief medical evaluation by a doctor who made the medical staff working in the prison system look like brain surgeons. After the "exam" was conducted we were escorted back to R and R, then split into groups to be brought to our housing units. Desert View had two separate buildings with four dorms in each, a separate cafeteria where we ate, a small yard outside for each of the buildings, a library and a few other areas designated for visiting, counseling, ad seg, medical and whatever else. At full capacity it held 700 prisoners, a number that was far less than anywhere I'd been. It was basically a warehouse used for storing bodies and I had a good idea tension would be high at times due to the number of people living in close proximity of each other.

I was escorted to my unit by one of the GEO staff and walked in, taking note that none of the other Whites acknowledged me when I entered. In every prison I'd been, excluding CMC, others within my race would want to know where I was from and who I ran with. My initial thought was that maybe prison politics were nonexistent, but quickly pushed it aside when a youngster approached and asked to see my paperwork. He came at me respectfully enough but I still found it bizarre. Anybody convicted of a crime that warranted an "R" suffix being put on their jacket wouldn't be eligible to do their time at a CCF, so I thought it was laughable that someone would want to see my paperwork—especially some kid trying to come across as a convict.

Being that I'd just gotten there and didn't want to raise a ruckus, I went into my bag of property and brought it out for him to see, and then surprised him when I asked to see his. The old convicts I'd met over the years had told me that if anyone ever asked for paperwork, I had a right to see theirs also. Two men checking each other's paperwork at a goddamn CCF was comical really, but it felt good to show this little shit from the Inland Empire that I wasn't an ignorant first-termer. I wasn't exactly trying to bill myself as a hardened criminal—when it came down to it, I was in prison for shoplifting three DVD's—but I did feel entitled to a little respect due to it being my fourth term.

With the formalities out of the way, I made my bed and settled in to my new home. Bunk beds filled the majority of floor space, with a healthy dose of plastic cots some genius with a blatant disregard for overcrowding had put into place, filling practically any open spot in the dorm. Despite how crowded it was, tension was relatively low, due in part to a riot that had taken place a few months earlier between the Whites and Southsiders. Riots tended to calm things down, at least for a little while.

The only jobs at Desert View were in the kitchen, working as a clerk or cutting hair as a barber, and they all took a long time to get. The yard was just a dirt lot with a basketball court in the middle and a couple sets of pull-up bars thrown in. It got so crowded it would often be a chore due to the lines of people competing with one another over their turns on the bars.

The company that ran the CCF, the GEO Group, was contracted by the state of California for the sole purpose of saving money. I had no idea how much or how little training they were subjected to before becoming certified correctional guards, but they didn't come close to matching the CDC's standards and were severely undermanned as well. GEO Group, Inc. was the second largest private-corrections company in the country and their reach was worldwide. Much of their business came from government contracts in which they presided over illegal aliens before being deported, county lockups, juvenile facilities and even holds in other countries. Their actions within these facilities had brought on a litany of lawsuits against them and externally as well—they were a public company on the NYSE and had numerous class action complaints filed against them for allegedly misleading shareholders and many other deceitful acts.

Because they were a company doing the minimum as far as training and manpower were concerned, they were easily manipulated, and we'd use their naiveté, or the fact they just didn't care, against them. There were no guard towers and only two 12' fences surrounding the perimeter of the yard, making it easily accessible to relations on the outside. Inmates inside Desert View would call their people and have them throw packages over the fences, right into the waiting arms of an inmate on the yard.

The timing of the drops had to be precise and were coordinated by cell phones sent over in previous packages. They'd have to be conducted when we were all out on the yard and usually happened in the morning when there was only one officer working. A car would drive up to the corner of the building, just out of sight of the yard and, more importantly, the peripheral vision of the guard, then an occupant of the car would jump out to lob a package over the fence. Just before the car pulled up, a few guys would create a scene on the opposite side of the yard from where the goods flew in from, and a bundle would come flying over.

There were always comedic elements involved when watching these events go down: the inmates creating the scene to draw the guard's attention would yell at each other in an over-exaggerated expression of bad acting; the man with the assignment of grabbing the package would run to it, then look around nonchalantly before picking it up, much like a guy finding a wallet on the ground with every intention of keeping it; anyone on the yard who knew the drop was taking place would shift their attention between whatever it was they were doing to watching for the package, even though they were under direct orders to mind their own business; and the driver of the car would often do a burnout in a panic as they made their getaway.

And things didn't always go according to plan, either. On one occasion the parcel got caught in the razor wire at the top of the fence; on another, the person throwing the package didn't put enough muscle into it and drove off before seeing it didn't make it over; and there were other times when the guard or the one working on the yard adjacent to ours saw the car, the throw or the pick-up, effectively stopping the goods from making it in.

With the abundance of contraband coming in came the inevitable drama associated with drug debt and envy. Whites were under strict orders to not buy anything from other races unless we had the means to purchase the goods then and there. Debts incurred in prison, and the debtor's inability to pay them back in a timely manner, were heavy contributors to riots and issues arising, giving us ample reason to stay away from potential train wrecks. We still had incidents within our own race, but they usually stemmed from guys not coming through after promises had been made and were resolved after the one making the promise got a beat-down.

The instances in which drops were made brought flavor to a dull existence at the CCF but they were only a slight break from the monotony. The lack of program was excruciating at times—I was fortunate because I had a radio and liked to read, and if not for that, my time would've been spent under a TV set or at a card table. I was well accustomed to days dragging by…my familiarity didn't make it easier or make the time move faster, though. There were times when it seemed the clock stood still, but as is always the case, the days accumulated and my release date drew near.

January of 2010 came around with a trip to the hole. I'd gotten into the habit of smoking weed, going halves on pinners with a surfer from San Diego who'd blown his mind fucking with meth. The joints were small but they served their purpose, and I found getting stoned a solid alternative to the intrusive habit that came with heroin. Getting stoned made doing time much easier and he was the one who did all the work—all I had to do was pay my half with the commissary I had in my locker and we'd sit on my bunk, smoking weed like a couple of hippies.

This relationship lasted close to two months and ended with me paying for my share of the weed, waiting for him to come through and him not paying up. Unbeknownst to me, he never scored, and when I went up to him in the TV room, asking when we were going to smoke, he started getting lippy with me. I was cool about it, telling him to talk to me with respect and that he owed me my share. Instead of responding to my request sanely and rationally, he got in my face and started flexing, feeding me the impression that he was trying to punk me. That was all it took for me to react the way I was taught, which was to crack him in his jaw. He backed down when I hit him and right after I did, a group of officers stormed into the dorm, put us in cuffs and escorted us to administrative segregation.

While all of this was taking place, he was yelling to the guards that I'd tried to jack him for his CD player and shouldn't have to go to the hole because he was the victim. His yelling like a bitch didn't do him any favor with the rest of the inmates in the dorm and it's fair to say he was marked from that point on. The strangest thing about it all was that he had less than a month until he paroled. I wondered if he wanted to get sent to ad seg to get out of a larger drug debt or some other bullshit. Whether he planned it or just decided to nut up on me, we were both going to the hole and he'd be labeled as a snitch when he got out.

The hole was a row of ten cells in a wing adjacent to R and R at the front of the entrance to the facility. It wasn't much different from the ad seg units I'd been in the past—a one-man cell with a sink and a toilet—but it was a little cleaner and the food was better. The staff had taken my property upon intake, stripping me of my radio and books, but besides that I was quite content. I spent my time doing set after set of pushups and running in place, and there was a white trustee who looked out for me by giving me extra food when he could. He also sent a kite I'd written to the guy who ripped me off, telling him not to say anything when the guards asked him what happened and that we'd have serious issues if he did. I'd never considered myself capable of excessive violence for the sole purpose of retribution, so it was hard to imagine doing anything crazy if he did talk, but my little stay in the hole had the strange effect of making me tougher than I really was. There was a direct correlation between my environment and the sub-societal prison mentality prevalent in that environment, shaping my decisions and thought process.

Five days into my reprieve from general population, I was brought to an office to talk to the lieutenant about my infraction. He was a dead ringer for Stacy Keach, with his pristine mustache and over-dramatic cop mannerisms. I thought about the scene from the movie *Up in Smoke* when Cheech pissed on Sgt. Stedenko's leg in the bathroom, so it was hard to take him serious. He asked about my involvement in the melee and when I told him we never hit each other, he gave me a look that said he knew better, then wrote something in his logbook and told me that I'd be moved back to GP as soon as the bed move went through. He also went on to tell me that the other "combatant" was being transferred to another facility. Some of the staff had apparently heard rumors about violence being directed his way over him yelling to the guards as we were being escorted to the hole. He wouldn't be safe at Desert View and because they weren't equipped to handle PC inmates, he had to go. I felt somewhat bad for the guy initially but discarded those feelings when I remembered he still owed me five bucks and was going home in a few weeks.

I was brought back to General Population the next day and put in a dorm next to the one I was in prior to going to the hole. Within a week of my arrival, I received a letter from a girl in Chicago named Sarah who'd heard I was in prison and wanted to get to know me. She stated that we had mutual friends and had heard about my being incarcerated when she'd visited Seattle a few months before. I didn't know what the fuck she was talking about, but later found that she'd stayed with my friends Ronny and Michelle while she was there. I'd sent Ronny an elaborate prison letter when I arrived at Desert View, joking about the conditions and strongly hinting at my need for a pen pal, preferably a female, and he responded by hooking me up with Sarah.

Our letters started with a degree of cordiality, but it didn't take long for them to become as sexually explicit as a Penthouse Forum piece. The institution didn't allow nude photos to be sent in, but she got around the rule by sending pictures of her breasts with her nipples covered up. She wasn't the type who would've minded, and I certainly didn't care, so I showed off my trophies to the guys I hung out with, fooling them into thinking I was some kind of player with a pair of tits I'd never before laid eyes upon. I wasn't sure if I'd ever really see them, but we flirted nonetheless and made plans to hook up when I paroled, regardless of the distance and circumstances.

March of 2010 arrived without any further incidents and my parole date along with it. I made my obligatory farewell rounds but having said goodbye to so many people in different facilities over the years, I felt like I was just going through the motions. It wasn't like I didn't care, it was more like reality had begun to set in, and with it came the knowledge that I'd never see any of them again unless it was on the streets, in rehab or at another prison. They were irrelevant to my future, another cluster of faceless people, forgotten as soon as I hit the gate.

CHICAGO AND THE LAM

The only memory I had of O'Hare was when I flew to New York City as a kid and it was a vague recollection of being stuck at the airport for a long layover. This time, however, I was in shackles and had two California Department of Correction's officers escorting me through the airport's busy concourse. Their job was to pick up parolees who had absconded and bring them back to California to face the parole board. It seemed a little over the top if you asked me, but my perspective was biased—I was the one on the run.

We sidestepped the long lines of the TSA checkpoints with a flashing of their badges and then walked the airport's long corridors amid stares of travelers overcome with curiosity as to why I was in restraints. The wide eyes and whispers amongst the onlookers gave me a sense of importance, like I was John Dillinger or Al Capone. I certainly looked important enough—I wore a hoodie and sweatpants a little too irregular for a civilian to wear in public, with handcuffs on my wrists and two C.O.'s walking beside me, doing their best to look inconspicuous but coming across as accessories to my outfit. I couldn't help but wonder what they would've thought had they known my controlling case was for shoplifting three DVD's from the Disney Store, and that my extradition to fulfill the "interests of justice" was nothing but a ruse, perpetuated by fear, misinformation and a multi-billion-dollar-a-year industry.

They had picked me up from the Cook County Jail, bringing two years of life on the run to an end. My hope that California wouldn't bother to get me was dashed when a Cook County Correctional Officer woke me early in the morning and told me to roll it up for transfer, then escorted me to booking where I was dressed out and placed in CDC custody. As we approached the airport, I began to come to terms with the fact that I was going back to California, leaving the cold winds of Chicago behind me.

Our flight was cancelled, so my escorts found a terminal that was sparsely populated and close to where we were catching our new flight. After getting me a Big Mac and a cup of coffee from McDonald's, we settled in for a six-hour inconvenience for them and a six-hour break of people watching for me. So much had happened since being released from prison that it gave me cause to reflect upon my potential. It wasn't that I'd accomplished any great feats or tackled insurmountable odds to emerge as a champion of life, but I'd gained a fair amount of courage and confidence with my experience. By going to a metropolis of Chicago's stature, far from anything the West Coast had to offer, I felt I was capable of anything. As long as I stayed clean.

* * * * *

A GEO correctional officer drove me to the Victorville Greyhound Station from Desert View, dropping me off with $200 gate money and wishing me luck before driving back to the facility. The bus arrived at noon, saving me from the blistering Inland Empire heat and taking me to downtown Los Angeles, where I made a quick walk to Skid Row and scored. I had my wits about me this time and waited to do my drugs until after I'd reported to my parole agent. The parole office was on 24th and Alameda and even though it wasn't too far from Skid Row, my longing to get high made the journey comparable to a trek across the Himalayas, but after dropping a urine analysis for him, I was free to do as I pleased. What I really wanted to do was party, so I kept my drug use to a minimum that night and instead spent much of my gate money drinking at the Burgundy Room in Hollywood.

By the end of the night I was riding a wave of self-pity and pain, compounded further by a decision to sleep outside so I wouldn't have to spend the rest of my money on a hotel room. Waking up in the bushes on the side of the Rock and Roll Ralphs on Sunset Boulevard had me feeding from the trough of tragedy I knew so well. I became convinced that night my life wasn't worth living and getting clean a chore too cumbersome to endure. There wasn't an inkling of desire within me to make a commitment toward enriching my life with positivity—it was too much work for a man accustomed to wallowing in self-defeat—so I turned the dagger inward, deciding to get loaded and hopefully die before getting arrested again.

I jumped on the Red Line in the morning, trying to shake off the misery of the night before, and rolled downtown to score. After copping a couple of balloons on San Julian, I fixed in one of the self-cleaning bathrooms nearby and contemplated my situation. My money was fading fast and with it my drive—life on the hustle was too much work as was getting clean. It suddenly became apparent the solution to my problem was to take the final step in a life I wanted out of.

My answer came in the form of a pocket full of pills. I decided I'd take all of them with my breakfast shot the following morning after I crawled out of whichever hole I slept in that night. The "hole" I slept in was the courtyard of the Midnight Mission and when I woke, I followed through with my plan by scoring four balloons and then went to a cafe on 7th and Figueroa to finish the task. I took all the pills on the walk there, went into the bathroom, locked the door and fixed my shot. The thought of taking my own life had entered my mind in the past but self-preservation had always gotten in the way of following through. This time, however, the longing to live was nonexistent—my desperation and solid resolution carried me into a realm in which suicide looked attractive. As I pushed the plunger in, I didn't feel like I was bidding farewell to a rotten existence, but rather, that I was embracing a justified end. I sat on the cold bathroom floor, calmly waiting to die, and then everything faded to black.

* * * * *

I could tell I was in a hospital by the angry fluorescent lights glaring at me when I opened my eyes, and if I still had any doubts as to where I was, the IV hooked up to a vein in my arm and the fact I was lying on a gurney put them to rest. As I was slowly gathering my thoughts, trying to figure out why I was there, a nurse came into view and told me that it had taken two shots of Narcan to revive me. My memory came flooding back and it only took an instant to surmise

236

what had occurred—as I was turning blue on the bathroom floor, an employee or customer tried to get in, got the key when there was no response, then called the paramedics when they saw my lifeless body on the floor. I had no recollection of being brought back to life and can only imagine how the customers in the café would've reacted when they saw the paramedics wheel me out to the ambulance. It was yet another example of how my actions impacted others, pulling the shroud of lies I'd woven to legitimize my self-centeredness, contradicting the belief that my drug use didn't affect others.

With the realization of what happened becoming clearer and feeling like shit from the Narcan, it came to me that I needed to get out of the hospital immediately. I wasn't handcuffed to the gurney, nor was there an officer standing over me, prompting me to pull the IV out and head straight for the exit. A nurse made a half-assed attempt at getting me to stay by telling me that I needed to speak with a doctor, but I kept moving and hit the exit in stride, then on to downtown L.A.'s stagnant air and dirty city streets.

I copped a balloon by shortchanging a dealer, then begged my mom to let me come over. She reluctantly obliged and while there, I gave Sarah a call, not telling her about my failed suicide attempt. She wanted me to come to Chicago, telling me that she was willing to buy me a ticket and could stay at her place. With absolutely nothing working out in my life and not ready to try killing myself again, Chicago sounded quite attractive, but I was reluctant to roll the dice and take my chances. As adventurous as it would be, leaving L.A. as a parolee at large would result in me being back in a cell at some point. The excitement and allure of splitting town did pull me out of the pervasive darkness eating away at my heart by giving me something to shoot for, however, so I took it as a conciliatory prize and stored her invitation away to potentially be used at a later date.

I tried my hand at staying clean while I was under my mom's roof but would still get high when she wasn't around—my fear of getting arrested keeping me in check for the time being. She said that I could stay there as long as I didn't use, so I kept my drug use to a minimum, supplementing my occasional excursions to Skid Row by getting on General Relief and food stamps. I managed my sporadic drug use for a few weeks, all the while knowing I was treading shark-infested waters in regards to my parole agent and the UA's I was subject to. He knew what I was doing and wanted me in a program, and I knew the time would come when his heavy hand descended upon me, putting me somewhere I didn't want to be.

True to form, he dropped by my mom's unannounced to tell me that I couldn't stay with her because it violated her rental agreement. He went on to tell me that he knew I'd been using—it didn't take a genius to come to that conclusion; my face was marred from a long evening of picking while under the influence of cocaine the night before—and that he was going to place me in a treatment center if I didn't straighten up my act.

His ultimatum scared me enough to get me out of my mom's and move into the Panama Hotel on Skid Row, but not enough for me to stay clean. Living in an environment in which every other resident lived by the spoon and crack pipe, combined with my own personal lust for getting high, made the transition of using every couple days to a daily ritual seamless, and I acquired a habit immediately. Being that there was plenty of crack in the area, I naturally gravitated toward smoking it, leading to the need for more cash and taking up my profession as a thief once again. I stayed away from pills this time around, knowing the inevitable outcome would put me back in handcuffs, and started hitting music stores in West Hollywood and the Valley. A couple of close calls later, I decided to get back on the methadone program at the BAART clinic in MacArthur Park.

It was around this time that I spoke with my parole agent and was told he had a bed set up for me at the Royal Palms, just a few blocks from the methadone clinic. He wasn't enthused when I'd told him I was residing at the Panama, and he took it upon himself to put me in a place where he could keep tabs on me. The Royal Palms was a county-run treatment facility I knew little about, except that most of its residents were on parole and was reputed to be a haven for people still getting loaded. Going to rehab sounded bad enough but going to a place filled with parolees sounded like a hell I wanted no part of, and I used it as ammunition to solidify my reason not to go.

I'd been talking to Sarah regularly and after each of our talks, I'd romanticize the idea of splitting town for Chicago. I had no desire to deal with the attitudes and prison politics I knew were in store for me at the Royal Palms, nor did I want to be subjected to their rules and mandatory meetings implemented by staff. I decided to put on my running shoes.

He wanted me to report to the parole office the following day. I knew he'd come get me if I didn't, so I packed my belongings into a duffel bag and checked out. With my mom's place out of the picture, I went to Hollywood and ran into my friend Katie, convincing her to let me stay at her apartment until Sarah came through with my ticket. She had a habit she was trying to kick and I had a good Klonopin connection, bringing about a symbiotic relationship we were each able to leech upon.

I was certain to have a warrant after skipping out on my parole agent, making it extremely stressful when I was out on the streets scoring and trying to make a buck. True to her word, however, Sarah came through, and not a minute too soon—I'd taken up boosting again and nearly gotten busted stealing a guitar from a store in West Hollywood, which I pawned to Katie with the promise of buying it back when I got my shit together. Benzo's were once again a large part of my diet, giving me a volatile disposition and reckless mannerisms, attributes sure to land me back in prison.

The ticket Sarah bought was for a bus instead of a plane, which meant a day-and-a-half ride through the heartland of the country. I was excited to leave and didn't mind at all—I actually felt safer on the bus because I didn't have to worry about my PAL warrant popping up on a TSA screening. After hooking Katie up with a handful of the little white benzo's, I packed my bags, loaded my mouth with balloons, then went downtown to the Greyhound station and jumped on the bus to Chicago with a new life in my sights.

My plan was to stretch my drugs for the duration of the trip but ran out by the time I got to Denver. I brought ten balloons with me, which was certainly enough to carry me through on paper, but I failed to account that I'd slam an issue whenever we pulled into a station. When the bus made its stop in Omaha, Nebraska, a group of police were waiting at the depot, giving me cause to think they were there for me. We transferred busses and as we did, the cops used a K-9 unit to sniff for drugs and pulled a Mexican passenger aside to search. One of the cops kept looking toward me as they searched him, knowing something was amiss, and I was certain they were going to get me next. But as our departure time drew near, the cops went back to doing whatever it was they did in a small town, leaving me be for another round in the ring.

I was fully dope sick by the time the bus pulled in to Chicago. Sarah was there waiting for me, which threw a wrench into my plan of trying to score when I got off the bus, and I found myself in the precarious position of acting like I was happy to see her, but really just wanting to get well. I truly was excited to be there, but that excitement was restrained by an itch that needed to be scratched, and the only way I'd be able to get at it was with a needle and spoon.

She had a place in an area called Lakeview and we drove there with different expectations—she anticipated a sordid love affair with a bad-boy convict from California. I, on the other hand, was there because an opportunity had presented itself that I was able to use as a tool for my self-preservation. I felt at the time that getting out of Los Angeles was the answer; that the city's dark underbelly had somehow influenced my drug use, depression and recidivism. Even though I was leaving L.A. on the run, there was an absurd notion present in my mind that stated being in Chicago would somehow make my problems disappear.

My first few weeks with Sarah went better than I expected but it quickly turned foul. She had a steady supply of Xanax prescribed by her doctor and a never-ending thirst for Bud Light, which I was able to use to somewhat stave off the discomfort associated with kicking dope. Instead of playing games with her in regards to my sickness, I came out and told her I'd started using again. She was surprisingly cool with it and even made the mistake of driving me to the Cabrini-Green projects and to some of the neighborhoods on the Westside to score. I'd always been adept at finding drugs and it would've only been a matter of time before I found a methadone clinic, strip club, shelter or just sniffed out some junkie on the street, but once she showed me where the goods were at, it was on.

It's been said that Chicago has the largest open-air drug market in the United States. The Westside is a concrete jungle and stretches for miles, with different gangs vying with each other over drug sales and power. Latin Kings and Gangster Disciples set up shop on corners and buildings selling rock and "blows" (heroin) to people driving up in cars, the local street crowd and people such as myself coming in on the train. Unlike L.A., where rival gangs didn't go near enemy territory unless they were committing acts of war, some of the gangs on the Westside would sell drugs across the street from each other in truces they'd made.

240

The only time I could convince her to take me to score was after we'd been out drinking, and she'd do so with great reluctance. She didn't share my passion for crack and heroin, leaving me with a desire that needed to be filled but without the means to support it. She must have never received the memo about not trusting junkies because she'd send me to the store with her ATM card to pick up beer, which I took as an opportunity to tap her account. I'd only take $20 after each run—I didn't want to jeopardize my cash supply, nor did I want to get caught and kicked to the curb—and then would catch the train to the 'hood the next morning while she was sleeping off the effects of the benzo's and beer.

We got along great when I had drugs but that was only two or three times a week. I'd spend my time locked up in her room, always at least a touch nervous about the warrant I had. By going to Chicago, I knew I'd have to deal with a host of problems from being on the run and that it would only be a matter of time before I was caught, but I'd read this dilemma from the perspective of a man who was looking at his situation from afar. The glasses I saw the world through were slowly becoming clearer. All these thoughts began to crash down upon me whenever I wasn't loaded and were accentuated by the feeling of being confined with a woman I ultimately didn't like.

My expectations going there weren't exactly stellar—though I'd spent the majority of my life basically in a fantasy world, I had enough vision to know that sooner or later my little house of cards would come tumbling down. We'd met, after all, because my friends had left one of my letters seeking correspondence on their coffee table. There appeared to be a feeling of control she got from having me penned in her room, like I was her personal "boy toy" whose sole occupation was to satisfy her unrealistic need to gain a foothold within my circle of friends and to fulfill her sexual desires. On the rare occasions I was able to spend with my Chicago friends, she would get insanely jealous and irate, leading to heated arguments in the early hours of the morning with her often threatening to call my parole agent and the cops.

Her threats helped shatter an already fragile relationship, leading to a fight of epic proportions. It started with me coming back to her place late, bringing about threats to call the police, and ended with me leaving in the middle of the night. I was out on the streets with nowhere to go, a position I was well accustomed to, except the streets

---

241

I now found myself on were far from my familiar stomping grounds on the West Coast. It appeared that my plan of splitting town had caught up with me a mere two months after leaving Los Angeles.

On a whim, I called my friend Rob and he told me that I was welcome to crash on his couch. His words were a blessing to my ears because I'd begun contemplating going back to California and doing the time they were sure to slap me with, but with a place to stay I quickly scrapped that idea. The only requirements he had were that I stay away from Sarah and to not do any drugs in his apartment, and I was willing to follow suit. Sarah had pissed me off to the point that I'd be being quite content if I never saw her again, and the endless pursuit of drugs had taken its toll on me.

There was a brief period in which Sarah called me nonstop, threatening to have me beaten and arrested. She stopped harassing me after about two weeks, and did it after delivering a *coup de grace* which was vindictive to the core—she put an ad up on Craigslist, complete with my pictures and phone number, in the men-seeking-men section. Her action led to me receiving phone calls from horny gay men all over Chicago wanting to know if I was still looking to hook up, to the point I'd often be reluctant to pick up my phone.

After her anger started to subside, I settled in at Rob's and got acclimated with Chicago's nightlife. We'd go out practically every night in the pursuit of girls and fun, hitting anything and everything in the city. I was picking up jobs in the Pilsen area working as a laborer, giving me enough money to buy beer and cigarettes, and I always had food to eat. I was comfortable in my minimalist existence, and as long as I had beer and some skirts to chase, I was content with staying in that world.

Close to six months had gone by without doing any heroin, but in December of 2010 my old familiar friend woke from his rest. I'd been drinking at a bar called the Liar's Club with a guy I'd recently met and as we were driving back to Rob's, he told me he had a stop to make on the Westside. Even though he didn't look high, I'd recognized his mannerisms as those of a dope fiend, and with a 6th sense junkies share, he surely detected I was as well. When he identified my reaction to his proposed stop as one of elation, his excitement was evident—he'd found one of his kind and we were soon feeding off each other's energy in our pursuit of drugs.

It was one of those rare nights in the city when there wasn't anyone out. Our quest for drugs had us driving all over the Westside on the prowl—my mind was in turmoil, bouncing between feelings of nervousness, apprehension and anticipation, until we finally connected through an old junkie who got in the van and took us to his spot. With drugs in hand, we raced back to Pilsen, fixed in a rehearsal studio on Western and it all went black from there. When I came to I was on Rob's floor, needle and spoon lying next to me, and his girlfriend screaming that I had to leave.

My days of staying on his couch were over and I spent the next couple months crashing on my friend Reid's floor until I wore out my welcome. In February of 2011, just after Chicago had been hit with one of its worst snowstorms in history, I decided Seattle would be my next destination and jumped on the Greyhound. I was on a nod for much of the ride, coming to when we pulled into depots in the towns along the way, where I'd do more dope and refurbish my dreamlike state. There was absolutely nothing to see during the ride—blinding white snow and frozen tundra commanded the landscape—so in that respect it was great I was on a nod. In one of the rare moments my eyes were open long enough to take in the view of nothing, I happened to catch a glimpse of guard towers and prison walls rising out of the whiteness. I conjured a vision of convicts braving the sub-zero North Dakota climate and trying to make a break like in the movie *Runaway Train*, then fell back into my slumber knowing they wouldn't stand a chance in hell.

The drugs had all but dwindled by the time the bus rolled into Butte, Montana, bringing about the knowledge I was soon going to be sick. To make matters worse, the bus had engine problems and wouldn't start, causing us to wait twelve hours for another travel-worthy bus. The tail end of the ride would be another dope sick journey on the back of another bus, heading to another destination too far away.

My brother picked me up from the bus depot in Seattle driving my old Mustang—I'd left it there in 2008 and never made it back due to my "legal entanglements"—and drove me to my friends Ronny and Michelle Bopo's in Crown Hill, an area I'd lived as a teenager. They were excited to see me and laughed when I told them of my adventures in Chicago, which came about as a result of the letter I'd sent them a year and a half earlier. Ronny was first mate on a cargo ship and setting

243

sail the next day, but before he did it was decided that I could stay in their extra bedroom and told me that I was welcome to stay as long as I wanted.

I stormed through my kick by drinking prodigious amounts of Budweiser and Fireball Whiskey. I'd been struck grateful by a dose of fortune. Just a few days prior, I'd been destitute, staying in a city cold enough to kill and was now back in Seattle, a city I dearly missed, living in a house in a beautiful part of town. I still had my warrant to worry about, but I felt my chances were good that I wouldn't get arrested—as long as I stayed away from heroin. That was the only rule Ronny and Michelle had. They weren't even concerned about rent. If I did any dope, however, I was out.

The love from my friends was a shot to the heart. I'd only been back to Seattle twice since moving from there in 2000, and although I wasn't thrilled with how much the city had changed, the time I was able to spend with them was priceless. A friend got me a job at an oyster bar on one of the piers downtown, giving me the opportunity to contribute to the welfare of the household and cause to feel like an asset as opposed to a leach. I was drinking a lot, but felt that if I stayed away from the hard shit I'd be able to hold it together.

I was also able to spend time with my father. We had grown distant, for obvious reasons. Whenever he responded to the letters I'd sent him when I was locked up, he'd tell me how much he loved me and that he'd always be there, but I can only imagine how tiresome and painful the ritual became. It had been years since we'd had a meaningful relationship and we both cherished the time we now had for each other. My life had taken a beautiful turn.

If I would've looked at my past experiences with drinking as a barometer, gauging my propensity to start shooting dope by the beers I raised to my lips, I would've foreseen the storm barreling toward me, but I couldn't gather the common sense and self-preservation necessary for such insight. It started with a small line of speed one of the line-cooks gave me at work, and within a week I was going downtown to score, bringing about another unraveling of my life. I lost my job, the girl I was seeing and my room at Ronny's in rapid succession, leaving me with a habit and one last check to support it. With nowhere to go and wondering how much worse it could get, I slept in some bushes downtown and was woken from my slumber by sprinklers set at some ungodly hour, driving home just how fucked I was. I drifted down to one of the missions in Pioneer Square, enduring a sermon from a preacher vilifying Satan and a bunch of other bullshit, then ate a wholesome breakfast of "shit on a shingle", reflecting on how good I had it before I'd gotten loaded. I knew if I didn't do something soon, I was sure to get picked up by the cops or kill myself in another bout of hopelessness.

I'd reestablished contact with some of my friends in Chicago prior to losing my job, calling them and letting them know how I'd gotten my shit together. They somehow bought into my bullshit and told me that I was always welcome in Chicago and had places to stay if I ever decided to come back. At the time, I discounted our talk as drunken banter but stored the invitation into the recesses of my mind the way a gossip columnist might collect information on a celebrity or politician to be used at a later date. When I found myself in a situation in which the wheels were falling off, my desperate and resourceful mind reached for the glaring answer to my predicament—I bought a ticket to Chicago.

Before leaving Seattle, I bought enough dope to get me through the trip and hit the road, excited for new adventures…I almost got busted in Spokane by some bums who took insult with me using the bathroom in the depot to fix in—the only thing that saved me was their incompetence in finding the proper authorities to apprehend me; in Butte, I fixed in the same bathroom I'd done the last of my dope in when I was on my way to Seattle, telling myself I'd never run out of drugs in Butte, Montana again; I nodded through a conversation with an oil man at a diner in North Dakota who tried convincing me that I could make a ton of money working the oil fields; and, true to form, I did the last of my dope in a Minneapolis bathroom, ensuring that I'd be sick by the time I reached my destination.

My friend Tim was there to pick me up in Chicago, and after we hit an Italian beef joint on Taylor Street, we went back to his apartment in Pilsen. I'd invested the extra money I had on Methadone and Suboxone, preparing myself as much as I could for the pain I knew to be coming my way, and started taking the Methadone right as the bus pulled into the city. My plan was to stretch the Methadone for a week, decreasing the dose with each passing day and then do the same with the Suboxone. It was an excellent plan in theory, but I neglected to weigh my desire to get fucked up and ended up taking all the Methadone my first day back.

Using the Suboxone to kick worked out well—it didn't get me high, unlike the Methadone that gave me a decent buzz if I took enough of it. The problem was, I ran out. With nothing left to calm the receptors in my brain telling me that I needed opiates, I was left with a mind full of insane thoughts and a need to get loaded. We'd stay up late, drinking and smoking weed, with people coming over almost every night, but when the alcohol ran dry and everyone went home, I was left with myself and my thinking, worried that Sarah was going to call the cops—she'd started threatening me again when she'd heard I was back in "her city"—and knowing a shot of dope would make everything alright.

As has always been the case in my life, the longing to fulfill my needs, blatantly disregarding the toes I stepped on, exceeded what I perceived to be right or wrong. I ended up taking a small stack of Tim's records to a store on the Northside and then went straight to the Westside to score. The $120 the store gave me was enough to shut my head up for a couple days, but when I ran out of drugs I found myself in a world of shit. We'd drink beer together when he got home from work and guilt would consume every fiber of my being. I felt like a fraud—like the story of the tweaker stealing his friend's wallet and then helping him look for it. My self-worth was at an all-time low and I also had to kick again, just after having gone through the worst of another round of withdrawals. And I knew it was just a matter of time before he noticed his records were missing, leaving me to wonder what would happen when that day came.

It took about a month for him to realize they were gone and when he did, I had to leave. His reaction was rather mild, all things considered; after asking me if I knew where they were, and hearing me reply that I didn't, he told me I'd have to start looking for another place to stay. I maintained my innocence, stating that I'd never steal from a friend and that there had to be a reason they disappeared. I had no idea what that reason might be, only that it could've been one of the many people we partied with. To think he'd buy into my concocted can of bullshit was pathetic—Tim wasn't stupid and, looking back, he surely must've struggled with not throwing me out, or cracking me in the jaw, right then.

I jumped around on a few different couches until getting an invitation to watch my friend Reid's apartment after he was hospitalized with a stomach issue. I got a job at a restaurant in the

246

North Loop just as I moved into Reid's, which was both a blessing and a curse; the steady income was a means with which I was able to buy more drugs. On any given day, you could find me pedaling deep into the 'hood, regardless of the weather or time of day.

I rode his bike to Pulaski and Lake on the Westside one night in February and never made it back. If I'd been one to read the signs, I would've seen I picked the wrong night to score. Chicago has long viaducts connecting and separating different parts of the city, creating traffic underpasses under the city's extensive railway system, somewhat comparable to the abundance of freeway underpasses in Los Angeles, and I noticed a few squad cars posted as sentries in various locations. When I got to the Westside, it felt like I'd entered a ghost town—the corners and buildings that usually had dealers loitering about were empty and there was a heavy police presence patrolling the streets.

My need to score outweighed my self-preservation and I rode from spot to spot in search of my fix. I spent close to three hours on my mission and finally gave up, opting instead for a consolation prize of whiskey when I got back to Pilsen. But as I shot down Pulaski from Madison Street a cruiser rolled up on me. Two cops jumped out, wanting to know what I was up to. I told them that I was riding home from a friend's, but they weren't buying it—they knew the only reason a white boy would be in the neighborhood was to cop dope.

They gave me the obligatory pat down, then started going through my pockets, taking my ID out of my wallet as they did so. I rarely came to the 'hood with it on me, but I'd been out drinking earlier and forgot to drop it off at the pad before leaving. When one of the cops jumped in his car to run my name I knew I was fucked, and within two minutes I was told to put my hands behind my back. They put me in the backseat of the cruiser and told me what I already knew—that I had a PAL warrant out of California. My usual tactic when being detained was to beg and plead with my captors, throwing a Hail Mary and hoping they'd see things my way. This time though, I took up the role of a hardened convict, calling them bitches and rookies, and that they wouldn't have stood a chance in hell of making it as a cop in L.A. I knew I was pissing them off and I'm certain the only reason I didn't get my ass beat was because they were rookies. If it had been two veteran cops, I surely would've been pulled out of their car broken and bleeding.

247

My first stop was a precinct on the Westside where they confirmed my warrant, then conducted a strip search and went through my property. From there I was brought to precinct on 18th and State, right down the street from a venue called Reggie's where I'd seen many of my friends perform. I went through a combination of different cells filled with primarily black and Latino gang members, everyone in their own world in regards to their predicament. I'd started to enter the initial stages of another kick and wasn't able to comprehend the dynamic of Chicago gang culture, and I really didn't care because I knew I was going back to L.A. I was kept there until the next day, trying to get comfortable while curled up in a ball on the concrete, then put on a bus and brought to the Cook County Jail.

The jail was just west of Pilsen and I'd driven by it on many occasions, offering a mini-salute to the inmates locked up inside, knowing the chances were good I'd be with them some day. It had been built in 1929 with separate "divisions" being added as the jail population increased, and it matched Chicago's gothic landscape—watchtowers, high brick walls and fences laden with razor wire adorned its perimeter. It was a foreboding appearance set within a residential area, making me think of the London that Charles Dickens wrote about in the 19th century. The jail was magnificent in both appearance and legend...I'd heard stories of the brutality taking place within long before I ever set foot on Chicago soil, and also remember seeing B.B. King's *Live at the Cook County Jail* album as a kid, back when my only knowledge of jail came from it being the place the town drunk on the *Andy Griffith Show* went after having one too many.

My cohorts and I were taken off the bus and brought in to an area affectionately referred to as "the cages". The booking area was basically a warehouse with chain-link fences separating each holding pen, with benches inside each enclosure and officer's podiums on the outside. The system they had in place was archaic compared to the jails on the West Coast; it seemed like I could easily have been lost in the shuffle, but they somehow made it work. An officer wrote my booking number on my arm and a mugshot was taken, then I was left to wallow in agony.

There were even less Whites in Cook County than L.A. County—the others I saw were going through the same shit as me. Everything about the jail was foreign to me; it was almost like I was doing time in another country. The lingo the Blacks used was basically the same, except they said "Folk" and "People" instead of "Cuzz" and "Blood", but the Latinos threw me for a loop. Most of them were Puerto Rican as opposed to Mexican, and they spoke in a rapid yet clipped dialect, contrasting sharply from the more drawn out and deliberate Spanglish of California. The other races basically ignored me, which wasn't too strange, but there were no Whites asking me where I was from and who I ran with.

At some point during my sojourn into the underbelly of Cook County, I was put into a machine comparable to ones used at airports to search for contraband. The correctional officers didn't conduct cavity searches like in L.A. County, opting instead for a more progressive and less degrading technique. They didn't make the move because they were more humane in Chicago; they did it because the Department of Justice had found that inmates 8th amendment rights were being violated. There were also class action lawsuits in which inmates were awarded damages because they were forced to sleep on the floor due to overcrowding and having to endure mandatory and painful STD checks, among other things.

After getting checked by "medical staff" and lying on the concrete for a length of time beyond my reckoning, I was escorted in a line of prisoners to a housing unit in Division 5 (the "Divisions" in Cook County were used to house inmates relative to their classification score. For example, Division 5 was medium and intake; Division 10 was maximum security, etc.). While walking its old and dimly lit corridors, I thought about a book I'd read a year prior and how the character in the book, a Latin King, talked about "neutrons". Neutrons were inmates who weren't in gangs and were basically considered to be punks by the "Folks" and "People" in the system. I wondered if I'd be thought of as a neutron by the Chicago gangsters, if I'd have to resort to violence to prove I wasn't a punk and if I'd be treated different because I was from California.

I was placed in an ancient two-man cell with a young black man, a kid really, and his only concern was making bail—that and keeping rats out of our cell—he called them mice's and used a storage container to try and block them from coming under the door. He was a Gangster Disciple and didn't talk much about his set, adhering to a code of secrecy I knew little about, but he was very knowledgeable for his age and told me a few stories about the Cook County Jail. I didn't believe it then, but he told me prisoners condemned to death had at one time been executed by electric chair in the jail (I later found this to be true. Apparently, the chair was used 67 times in the jail, the last time being when they fried James Duke on August 24th, 1962). He had a keen interest in Los Angeles gangs, particularly Crips, and I told him what I'd picked up from the streets and prison, encouraging him to read an autobiography written by a Crip named Monster.

I spent a couple days with him, then was transferred to a more modern unit in Division 11. There I was housed with another youngster, a Disciple, but this one was loud and cocky as opposed to my calm and cool cellie in Division 5. Although he didn't say it outright, I could tell he expected full reign of the cell because I wasn't in a gang. I'm pretty sure the only reason he didn't try any shit was because he knew I was in for a parole hold. Having been to prison gave me at least a little street cred.

Division 11 was arranged in a manner similar to the newer prisons I'd been to—a two-tier system that allowed inmates from each tier out at different times. The dayroom consisted of the same stainless-steel tables and benches used throughout the institutional world, with a TV mounted high and out of reach of the population, blasting the all-too-familiar daytime talk shows and soap operas. We were let out for two hours a day and when chow was served. The food was just as shitty as L.A. County's, just a different brand of shit. As disgusting as it was, it was also the only real thing I had to look forward to. The days of eating deep-dish pizza and hot Italian beef sandwiches were distant memories.

The days stretched on like they always did, with feelings of remorse and self-pity because of my actions, full of depression from yet another kick and wishing I could get another chance to do things different. I'd heard somewhere that the CDC had thirty days to pick up inmates from wherever it was they got busted and was hoping California wouldn't get me within that time frame so I'd have to be released. If that was true I almost made it, because it took them twenty-six days to get my ass.

* * * * *

We boarded the plane long before anyone else to avoid raising alarm with the other passengers. The captain, usually one to be jovial with his cargo, gave me a contemptuous look as I turned down the aisle, but the stewardesses looked at me with curiosity and what I perceived to be fascination that there was a convicted felon onboard. As we took our seats in the very last row, I thought that if given the opportunity I'd have a chance with either of them but knew I was just lying to myself. There would be no "mile-high club" activities with any of these pretty young ladies. Not for me, at least.

I was given a window seat with both of my escorts buffering me from the activity of the aisle and watched people as the plane slowly began to fill. Just after we'd taken our seats, a pair of TSA agents walked up, briefly checking me out before focusing their attention on the CDC guards. The TSA agents flew around the country, taking on a precautionary role, and their interaction with my escorts led me to believe there was a lack of respect between the two agencies. It seemed as if they were sizing each other up when they exchanged their feigned pleasantries, and after they walked off I heard one of the CDC officers mumble to his partner that the TSA hired fuckin' retards.

I still had my handcuffs on, but with my hands inside the front pocket of my sweatshirt so none of the passengers would notice. Not that it mattered now, but as the plane started rolling down the tarmac, I wondered what CDC protocol was when it came to prisoners who refused to fly. Would they have tranquilized me? Or if I started a fight, how would they subdue me? I knew they carried firearms, but did they also carry Tasers? And they surely wouldn't use the pepper spray the CDC was so fond of with all these people aboard. I decided to tell them that I needed a Xanax and a shot of whiskey to calm my nerves, knowing full well what the answer would be. Without saying a word, the officer sitting next to me leaned over and tightened my seatbelt, as if to show me who was boss, then leaned back in his seat and told me to enjoy my flight.

———

251

HITTIN' THE STREETS

I could almost feel the warmth of the sun from the moment we entered Southern California's airspace. My window faced the south, granting me a clear view of the ports of Los Angeles and Long Beach as we began our descent. The other occupants began to stir and many looked out the windows facing the north, trying to catch a glimpse of the Santa Monica pier, the Hollywood sign or Grauman's goddamn Chinese Theatre, all of them restless after the five-hour flight. I let myself imagine for a moment what it would be like to wear their shoes and worry about things like hotel reservations, car rentals, what I was going to have for dinner or if I packed my beach trunks. With these thoughts came a shroud of self-pity, enveloping me and taking me down a dark road that led to question my desire to stay clean and if I'd be able to assimilate with the squares of the world.

The time spent in Chicago, and the time spent reflecting while sitting in the Cook County Jail, brought about a sincere desire to face my inner demons. It seemed that I'd spent my life living in a dream, touching on brief glimpses of what I could've been and knowing I was selling myself short, but ultimately riding a never-ending wave of nightmares. Besides the short-lived time I had on the straight and narrow while living with Cherie, my life consisted of getting loaded and in the pursuit of getting loaded. I'd told myself I was done countless times only to chase my firm resolutions with a flurry of self-defeating actions—and the first of those actions always came with deciding to score.

Even though I knew I'd be going straight to the county jail from the airport, I caught some of the excitement from the other passengers, taking in Southern California's welcoming embrace as the plane touched down. After negotiating LAX's busy runways, we pulled up to the terminal where I saw a group of close to a dozen airport police waiting for us to dock. I had expected a welcoming committee but certainly not an army. While I understood the need for public safety and the desire a bored airport cop might have for being present when a captured "fugitive" was being brought in, it also exemplified a blatant waste of tax dollars.

My guards and I sat in the back of the plane while the other passengers gathered their belongings and filed out, leaving us to make an exit that was unhindered by gawking civilians. The captain didn't acknowledge us and wore a pained expression on his face as we walked by—it was easy to see he wasn't fond of his felonious cargo, nor did I think he appreciated the guns on his plane. I didn't really give a shit what he thought, but I took great satisfaction in seeing a man who was held in high esteem and often revered by the public flustered by my presence.

I tried to get a smile from the stewardesses but they weren't biting; the ire of the captain was apparently keeping them from making even the subtlest of flirtatious gestures—or so I'd like to believe. There was a mobile staircase connected to the jetway and at its base stood the regiment of cops I saw from the window, waiting for the transference of their long-travelled prize to occur. After being brought down the stairs, the CDC officers handed me over to a couple of LASD deputies, effectively washing their hands from the likes of me, then were off to another city to bring fugitives to justice.

I was put in the back seat of a squad car that was parked on the tarmac and we made our way downtown, leaving the other cops to do whatever it was they did. We went up La Brea on the way in, then cut east along Adams. My mom lived on Fairfax, just west of there, and I let myself imagine what I would've done had they dropped me off at her place. Could I possibly stay clean without a solid support system in place? How long would I last before my anger and resentments toward her, my parole agent, the courts or anything else drove me back out again? I was mad at the world, it seemed, and when my anger wasn't directed toward a specific entity or institution, I internalized it, redirecting it toward myself.

These thoughts made me grateful I wasn't going to be let loose in a world I hated, but also spawned a multitude of other concerns— Where was I going to stay when I got out? What was I going to do different? Had my friends lost faith in me? How much time was I going to do in County? Was it all worth it? I didn't know the answers and knew an immense change in perception had to occur in order for me to progress. The desire to move forward was present but when it came down to it, I lacked the skills and fortitude necessary for dealing with the most rudimentary of tasks. Setting goals, dealing with rejection, patience, persistence…problems most took as hurdles to overcome, I perceived to be failures waiting to happen and were to be avoided at all costs.

All I knew was that I never wanted to sit in the backseat of a cop car again, nor did I want to wear a noose around my neck. As we drove up Vignes toward the entrance to the Twin Towers, I clung to the hope that if I played my cards right I'd never have to come back. At that moment, my optimism outweighed the ever-present thoughts of hopelessness in my mind—but I still had to contend with the negative forces within the county jail system.

I was brought in through a side door, next to a long line of sorry souls who were making it to the jail from whichever courthouse they were in earlier that day. Some of the guys mean-mugged me, probably thinking I was a PC inmate or something to that effect, but most simply shuffled in their lace-less shoes, eager to get their shackles removed and to begin the process of getting housed. I knew that I'd be mixed with them soon enough—I was just happy I got to bypass the first three intake cells and the gauntlet of deputies on a mission to demoralize and degrade their prisoners.

There were five cops standing around in my cell, finishing up paperwork on inmates they'd brought in earlier. They barely seemed to notice me but when they overheard I'd been brought from Chicago, they all took a keen interest in my being there, only to lose it when it was discovered that I was only in for a parole violation. Apparently, the police were just as mesmerized by notoriety—and dulled by the absence of it—as the inmates.

I sat there over an hour, listening to bad jokes and "us versus them" cop banter, before being put with the rest of the guys being booked in. I was placed in a cell I'd been in many times before, with a view of new inmates being stripped and searched by angry deputies screaming at them to "Bend over!" and to "Spread your legs wider!" The domineering pomposity they displayed while barking their orders prompted my imagination to kick into gear, lending imagery of what went down on a BDSM porn set.

The inmates having gone through the hellish process eventually started to file into the cell I was waiting in. They were tired, hungry, demoralized and hanging from the end of a long and tattered piss-soaked rope. We went through the intake process together; being moved from cell to cell and enduring an indoctrination by the LASD that I was quite familiar with. The deputies used fear to control their subjects—brute force, strength in numbers and administrative segregation were the primary methods used to achieve compliance. And if you were a good prisoner you were rewarded with a peanut butter and jelly sandwich, then moved to the next cell.

I'd been booked into jail countless times but only a handful without a habit. Going through the process with open eyes made me feel both gratitude and sorrow. Gratitude because I wasn't the guy in the corner shaking, getting up every so often to puke, and sorrow because I felt that I deserved so much more. I was able to see the revolving door at work—new bookings were being brought in daily and on the other side of the jail they were being released at the same rate. A small amount would never come back but most would return to their neighborhoods and the lifestyle they knew best and were comfortable with, making a return to jail or prison inevitable.

The disparity between the resources spent on rehabilitating inmates and warehousing them was alarming; the programs within the jail system were a joke and the ones in prison weren't much better. The CDC was now the CDCR—the "R" stood for rehabilitation—but it was only a word put into place to justify their mountainous budget and to satisfy the liberal constituents who thought that something needed to be done. The truth of the matter was that the Substance Abuse and Prison Industry training programs were being cut across the board, making way for their new mandate—locking men away to satisfy a society gone mad.

I spent years numb to my surroundings, in a sense. While I certainly never found doing time to be comfortable, it did, however, become routine and acceptable. Sitting in that last cell, after having gone through an endless cycle of being scanned into systems, getting classified, moving to new cells, eating sack lunches, sitting too close to men I didn't know and being stripped naked, I was engulfed by a black cloud of despair. I could swear vehemently and with conviction that I'd never be back, but when faced with my history I knew I was making an empty pledge. Being packed into a cell, touching elbows with men just as fucked as me, the feel of cold stainless-steel against my bare ass, odors of crack, alcohol, dope sickness and shit polluting my nostrils, tainting my vision with a mirage of toxic fumes rising from filthy bodies...all of that wasn't enough to keep me clean. The optimism I felt earlier was a lifetime ago, leaving me to question my desire to live and feeling any attempt to do so was futile.

The smell and discomfort of that last cell would break the will of one unaccustomed to such low standards, but I buckled in for the ride. After what seemed an eternity, the door opened and we walked out through a phalanx of deputies and on to the showers. I did my best to wash away my misery, but three minutes of hard water and a bar of county soap could only do so much.

I spent the next twelve hours sitting in the customary "nuts to butts" position on steel benches, going through the tedious rituals of talking to quack psychologists, half-ass medical exams and waiting to be moved. The process wasn't nearly as painful and agonizing compared to if I'd been kicking dope, but it was still grueling because of the setting. The lines to endure and attitudes from the jail staff were 1000-times worse than any other county facility—the jail made the DMV and welfare office seem like leisure spas. Irate deputies besieged the inmates with evil glares and barked orders to shut the fuck up; men who'd lost their minds rocked back and forth, stroking their beards and mumbling to themselves; gang members from different sets eyed each other, ready to attack if provoked; dope sick ghouls wearing pain-stricken expressions on their faces sweated it out, waiting for a relief that would never come. The cyclic nature of the beast—a judicial system striving for convictions and a penal system hungry for prisoners—ensured that a steady flow of new commitments would take our place once we'd moved on.

The K-11 inmates were still kept at the base of the podium, waiting to be moved to the gay module, but the cage holding inmates with medical issues was vacant. I remembered writhing in pain inside the cage on numerous occasions and the time I was labeled as gay by the cops, sitting at the podium with my face in my hands, attempting to hide my identity from the other inmates. It was gratifying to bypass those areas, both of which had a strong degree of misery attached to them, and I once again thought how fortunate I was. Despite my head and the self-pity brimming within, I knew it could be much worse.

My name was finally called to make the trek from IRC to the jail and I was housed in a dayroom on the 3000 Floor. The dayroom was the same as all the others I'd been in before—filled with bodies living in too-cramped quarters, doing the best they could with a fucked-up environment.

A public defender came by the jail to discuss my parole violation soon after my arrival. He told me that the parole revocation board was offering me four months. The federal government had declared California's prison system to be in shambles due to a disproportionately high recidivism rate and severe overcrowding. California's budget was also crippling state expenditure, so the state responded by passing Assembly Bill 109. It was implemented October 1st, 2011, during my time on the run, and relaxed the guidelines the CDC used when sentencing parole violators. Prior to AB 109 being passed, I could've been sent back to prison for a year, so when I was told I'd only do a few months, I felt like a punk in a penis patch. In a sense, it seemed that going on the run had worked toward my benefit.

The following week, I was called out by a deputy and given a pass for my hearing. I walked down the escalator by myself to an area adjacent to the court line cells and was put into a dayroom with twenty other inmates who were anxiously awaiting their fate. Rumors were flying around the cell that parolees were being released due to overcrowding and parole revisions, but I didn't bite—I knew there was too much money and politics involved for the state to release prisoners in one fell swoop.

We sat in the cell and waited. Some of us engaged in conversation, and others kept to themselves. After an hour a door popped open, signaling they were ready. I was the first to be called out and stepped into a corridor to be escorted to the hearing. Two burly deputies wrapped a chain around my waist, then cuffed me up and connected my handcuffs to the chain. They then walked me to a room and sat me down in a chair across from a desk, standing directly behind me, as a representative from the CDC read from my violation report. She looked at me from time to time as she read the details of my charge, but she looked without seeing me. I was only a number to her and it was evident she wanted to finish with my case so she could move on to the others.

When she was done reading the report, which basically said I'd been absconding for two years, she asked me how I pled. I never had any intention of pleading my innocence—there was no getting around absconding—so I told her I was guilty. She accepted my plea, gave me four months and with a flick of the pen, I was done and brought back to the cell.

It took a solid three hours for the other prisoners to be seen and after they had, we were sent back to our housing units. I'd started calculating how much time I had left the moment I was sentenced, but it wasn't until I made it back to the unit that my head slowed down enough for me to internalize it. A four-month sentence meant I'd only do eighty days with my "good time" and was brought down even further with the time I'd already served. I had a release date of just under two months.

Knowing this brought forth the elation normally associated with an impending release date, but it also brought about a fear that was new to me. Being released sounded appealing enough, but I knew I'd end up coming back. The gutters lined with needles, broken crack pipes and used condoms; the bodies of drunken bums, sprawled out on sidewalks littered with broken glass; the spent whores turning tricks in alleys and cars; the Brothers on 5th and San Pedro with mouths filled with crack and the Mexicans on 6th and San Julian with mouths filled with balloons; the throngs of men and women beat down so thoroughly they'd rather reside in a desolate wasteland than live in a fixed society and abide by its broken rules…the insanity existing on the streets still held an allure that was compelling despite its dark underbelly. The price I had to pay to remain lost, however, was too much to endure.

It wasn't like I'd been enlightened by the knowledge I was fucked—I had carried it around with me for years, ready to be used as an excuse to rip my life to shreds. My perception had been shaped by it and I took it on like a beaten dog, driven to a shameful existence scouring for scraps. I'd taken on a role in which life had no meaning. My goals had been limited and solely based around getting well and making it through the day without getting arrested.

The worst part of it all was that I knew I was selling myself short. When I was in the 6th grade, my teacher had pulled me aside to tell me what he saw, comparing me to another kid at my school. The kid's name was Heath and we were both at the head of our class. Heath never got into trouble and made honors, and I was in the vice-principal's office and skipping class. With ominous insight, he predicted that Heath would likely go to medical school and on to a successful career, while I was heading toward a life of selling drugs and being locked away in a prison cell. His words didn't come across as malicious or condescending—they came from many years of watching students waste their potential and their lives. At the time, I took his warning as an award, like I was being recognized for an act of valor. With time, however, his words began to take on new meaning. It took a great many years to realize just how distorted my perception had been and I was now beginning to accept the fact that I needed to approach life from a different angle.

The question was how? Changing my thought process wasn't anything close to the simplicity of changing my socks. I wasn't one to throw myself at the mercy of some fictitious deity, buying in to a notion that God would somehow save me from myself. Subjecting myself to rituals when I lacked faith was absurd and tantamount to self-deception. The "God factor" had been a huge stumbling block when it came to my brief experiences with twelve-step programs in the past. While the concept of choosing your own God might sound novel to some, to me it was just regurgitated drivel aimed at subtlety directing me toward a religious dogma. I couldn't begin to tell you how many times people had approached me at meetings to explain their unsolicited concepts of God, claiming they were once just as lost as me and telling me that all I needed was to "let go and let God".

That was a lot to swallow for a man who'd always considered himself an atheist and I also found their approach rather arrogant. Whenever I heard someone talk about "living in the sunlight of the spirit", "being rocketed into the fourth dimension" or "thanking their lord and savior Jesus Christ for another day sober", I seriously had to fight back urges to bolt and run. I'd been in many arguments with God zealots contesting my absence of faith and they usually began with "who was I to say God didn't exist?" Well…who were you to say he did? The lack of adherence to a principle that was rudimentary to most might very well block me from the "sunlight of the spirit", but I couldn't "fake it 'til I make it" in regard to matters spiritual.

Many would view my stance as close-minded or quite possibly ignorant, but their views toward my outlook hardly mattered. They were my personal beliefs, after all. My intolerance to their spiritual posturing had always kept me from fully buying in to the program. However, there were many I'd met over the years who neither preached nor told me that my views were wrong. The open-mindedness exemplified through their demeanors held me in check, lending the belief that the program could work for me, thereby giving me an out, so to speak, when it came to my non-belief in God. I'd seen these guys climb from the gutters to find peace, but what was just as important was that they didn't shove their opinions down my throat.

There's something to be said for desperation and I used it as a basis toward giving the program another shot when I got out. Considering I'd have nowhere to go upon release, I really had nothing to lose. I knew I'd have to employ an unprecedented open-mindedness if I was to stick around, but I was willing to try.

I was transferred to Wayside shortly after my hearing and spent the last of my sentence as a trustee in Supermax. My job description was to serve food and clean up after maximum-security inmates, and to stay under the radar of deputies who got a kick out of rolling up trustees. The prisoners would often try and get us to pass kites to the other cells, right under the watchful eyes of the cops, sometimes going so far as threatening us with violence if we didn't comply. The rest of the time on the job was spent trying to put a dent in our endless supply of jail sandwiches and shooting hoops with a flat basketball in the rec area.

One night, after eating a course of lima beans and "eraser tips" (little pieces of processed meat resembling their namesake), my name was called to roll up my property. Being called out early usually meant they were going to book you for an add-charge, and because my release date wasn't until the following week, the announcement naturally had me stressed. I asked the deputy why I was going downtown and was told that I was being released, giving me cause to think they were making a mistake. I thought about telling them because I didn't want any issues when I got to MCJ, but instead decided to keep my mouth shut. I wanted out.

After bidding farewell to my running partners, I made my way out of the unit and was brought to a holding tank. I counted close to ten other inmates, and while most were going downtown to catch the prison chain, there were two others who were just as bewildered as me over the county's decision to let us out early. It wasn't uncommon for early releases to occur among the misdemeanor population—many did as little as 10% of their time in L.A. County—but I couldn't recall felons ever receiving the same grace.

We were left in there for an hour, then called out one by one, forming a line and walking to the massive octagon-shaped holding tank used for prisoners leaving Supermax. I'd always been struck by the contrast whenever I'd been mixed in with the rest of the population of L.A. County. If you were white, there was a good chance you'd be placed in a trustee unit, away from most of the insanity taking place within the jail and making it easy to forget how much of a minority we truly were.

The other races eyed us, sizing us up as we walked in, surely knowing they could stomp us out. Blacks lined one side of the tank and Southsiders the other, with a small group of Whites standing by themselves along a far wall. The Mexicans and Blacks were unified within their races, setting aside gang rivalries while in jail to make their contingencies stronger for what was essentially a race war. The Blacks were loud, the Southsiders quiet, but they were both on their toes, ready to throw down at any given moment. I walked the concrete patch separating the groups, joining the small cluster of Whites in the back, and waited for the chains to arrive.

My subjection to such scenarios over the course of my adult life made me well accustomed to the animosity present in jail, and although there had always been an element of fear involved, I adapted and learned to fit in like a chameleon. Every situation I encountered became an adventure and I felt that if I could only make it through the process one more time, I wouldn't be coming back. When I'd left the trustee unit and began walking toward the holding tank earlier, I felt with each step I took that it was my last—that each step was one closer to hitting the streets. I knew every portal and doorway I walked through could be slammed shut if it jumped in any of the units, giving me a sense of victory with my progress.

With freedom within reach, the longing to make it out heightened my desire to survive. The feel within the octagon was tense, as was usually the case when prisoners from different sets holding a variety of beliefs were thrown in together. The two hours spent in that tank were some of the longest and most tension-filled hours of my life, but the transport deputies finally arrived to take us downtown. You could always hear them before you saw them—the tragic yet somehow comforting sound of chains being wheeled on a cart told of their coming—and within thirty minutes we were shackled in groups of four, shuffling down the corridor toward the bus.

Boarding the bus evoked a feeling of conquest knowing I'd made it out of Supermax, and it grew stronger with each passing moment—the engine coming to life, driving out the sally port, passing through the Pitchess compound gates, getting on the freeway...freedom fast approached, hand in hand with a desire to live a life that wasn't controlled by drugs. As we passed Magic Mountain,

———

261

I eyed the park's magnificent rides with the knowledge that I could ride them if I wanted to. Approaching downtown, I could see lights illuminating a game in progress at Dodger Stadium and wasn't envious of the fans enjoying themselves, but rather, felt inspired to go to a game when I got out.

This transformation of perspective took years to occur and was by no means complete. I knew that I had the temperament of a man teetering on the edge of a treacherous truth—my optimism could plummet to despair at any given moment. Overcoming such fluctuations and inconsistencies to my mental state would be a struggle and I knew I couldn't do it alone.

The sun had long since dropped from the horizon by the time we pulled up to the Twin Towers and were marched inside by the deputies. We walked in a line toward IRC, where the two others being released and I were separated from the rest of the group. I had heard some of them talking about the prison chain and the time they had to do once they got there—"You gotta do your time, don't let it do you", "I'm gonna come out ripped", "Bitches love convicts"…the psychology of each reflected a state of mind that said life was going to be great when they got out. But I knew better. Besides being overwhelmed with loneliness, thinking about how much time you had left, waiting on mail that rarely came and wondering what you were going to do when you got out, you were also confronted with a system wanting nothing more than to send you back. California's recidivism rate was the highest in the nation and the programs set up to assist prisoners who wanted and needed help were being cut, both inside and outside the walls.

When I heard them talk about doing time like it was just a passing phase, I thought about Hoss, the vato I'd met at Corcoran during my first term, and the pain, sorrow and regret I read in his eyes knowing he'd never get out. There was also the Crip with the life sentence I'd caught the chain with my third time in, looking me in the eye and telling me he had no idea what was going to happen next. Or the man coming out of a Klonopin blackout in the King County Jail to the realization he'd committed an armed robbery, shell-shocked and knowing he'd be going down for a long stretch. I'd met countless others in passing, hiding behind an apathetic shell, swearing allegiance to a twisted creed and seeking validation from others who were just as lost. The light in their eyes was fiery, brought about by self-imposed

262

deceit and the longing to adhere to the "prison code", but I knew the fire would die when the years and the hidden tears became too much to bear, leaving behind a cold gray husk in a concrete tomb.

My experiences within the prison system were wide-ranged and certainly telling, but they were also limited—they came from the perspective of a man who'd never had more than three years over his head. I'd obviously never been on Death Row, nor had I been a foot soldier for any of the numerous prison gangs, so my observations, though keen, were those of an outsider in many ways. I did, however, understand the machinery of the institutional structure and the sociological implications on the groups within. And I also understood society's desire to lock criminals away, even though that desire was often misguided and fueled by fear, misinformation, politics and monetary implications.

Knowing my insignificance, to both the bureaucrats of the CDC gathering statistics externally and to those doing time internally, was gratifying in a sense, but it also made me feel like I was just another number in a game that was fixed. My life had boiled down to placing bets on a table in which the dealer always won. Payoff came in the form of $200 in gate money when I paroled—a sliver of life to be washed away by reckless abandon.

I nodded to a couple of the guys I'd developed a passing acquaintance with as they were led away, knowing the envy they surely felt. It was a feeling I knew all too well…there were many times I'd worn their shoes, wishing I was the one heading for the exit. It was all part of the cycle and you had to do your best to remember that your turn would come.

* * * * *

It was close to two in the morning by the time I made it out to the street. Thick Los Angeles air hit my lungs, giving me my first taste of the city and driving home the fact that I was still downtown. The same sad cabs filled the parking spots directly in front of the jail, their drivers on hand to compromise the needy and desperate, ready to take advantage of any woman or man being released.

I made my way past them, ignoring their parasitic inquiries, and walked to the corner of Vignes and Cesar Chavez. One block west, Cesar Chavez turns into Sunset Boulevard and begins its path through Echo Park, Silverlake, Hollywood, and on to Pacific Palisades. Down here, however, it was just another squalid road, home to rats, roaches and street life looking for scraps. During the day, the corner is lined with commuters impatiently waiting for busses to take them into East L.A. and the lands beyond, but when darkness fell it's taken over by the downtrodden and diseased, waiting for the next misery to come crashing down in an avalanche of pain. Any wisp of hope had long since dissipated with these people, leaving them to choke on the pestilential fumes of a decrepit society's waste. It was the perfect setting for a jail.

I took a seat on some steps leading to Union Station and began putting the laces back in my shoes. The others who'd been released with me beelined it up the stairs and on to the train station, on a mission to see their loved ones, score dope and who knew what else. I finished lacing up as they ran by, grateful that I didn't feel like getting loaded and looking forward to my new life. It wasn't going to be easy, but I knew I could do it if I remained vigilant.

I still hadn't had a cigarette and saw a man smoking in a bus shelter, prompting me to walk up and ask him for one. He fished one out of his pack, then gazed at me with dead black eyes and said, "Welcome to the free world." He gave me the smoke with a look that said he was a veteran of the streets; a look that sized me up, demanded respect and said not to fuck with him. I thought about asking him how he knew I'd just gotten out but thought better of it when I realized how obvious it must've been, and instead thanked him for the smoke and sat back down on the steps to enjoy it.

Not long after lighting it up, a man appeared from around the corner and walked up to the dude who'd given me the cigarette. He looked rundown and had a touch of desperation on his face, and that's when it clicked—he was there to cop some dope. They simultaneously conducted perfunctory glances around them, looking for anything out of the ordinary, and when it was determined that there were no cops staking them out, they exchanged money and product. The junkie stepped out of the shelter, unaware my curious and hungry eyes had seen the transaction occur, popping some balloons into his mouth as he rushed past me. He then disappeared around the corner from which he came, leaving me to process what had just taken place.

The man sitting at the bus stop was still counting his cash as I got to my feet. I felt drawn to him, like he was a savior in a land of locusts, brought to this very place for the sole purpose of lending his salvation. At that very moment, the promises I'd told myself, the longing to move on from the permanent shit-cycle I was mired in, the knowledge I'd be screwed if I opened the door, were just hindrances plaguing yesterday's thoughts. My lust for the divine beckoned, supplanting rational thought with desire, pulling me to him and the love he supplied. I knew I was fucked.

Epilogue:

IN THE GRAVEYARD

I looked down at the paper in front of me and wondered if I could do it. Words crept from my consciousness, ready to fill the page, only to be smothered by self-doubt and the feeling that no one would bother reading them. The fluorescent overhead flickered its pale white glare, daring me to make my move. I took a pull from the cup of coffee in front of me and winced. It tasted foul but would do the trick, and I chugged it knowing that I needed all the help I could get.

The sound of footsteps pulled me from my thoughts. My body tensed and my mind instinctively went to survival mode. There was a brief moment when I thought about lunging for a knife, but if anyone was coming for me, they'd be here before I got to it. Instead, I sat back with a calm that was new to me and waited.

"Hey, you got a minute? I can't sleep."

It wasn't a killer making his move, but rather, a kid named Ryan. He'd recently arrived to the house and was still kicking dope. "Of course, homie, grab a seat. What's up?"

He was from Chicago and used to score in the same neighborhood I'd pick up from. When I told him about my Westside junkie adventures and being locked in the Cook County Jail, he listened intently. The fact that we'd been on the same streets seemed important to him. That he identified with my tales of woe wasn't striking—many coming in could relate at least somewhat. The thing about Ryan was that he appeared to hang on to my words when I told him it would get better.

We talked for close to an hour and our conversation ended with him asking what the secret to staying clean was. A good question, and one I couldn't answer. Did I dare tell him that he had to lose everything? That his promises and sincerity wouldn't amount to shit? I'd heard many tell me over the years that I needed to find God or I

266

was fucked. Maybe they're right but I'm skeptical. I suppose that if I could've turned my will and life over to the care of "Him", I would've quit long ago. Not wanting to feed him some bullshit, I told him what I know and what's worked for me thus far.

"Shit moves downstream so don't stay stuck in it for long. And even more important? Help someone else."

He went back to his bedroom to toss and turn and I brewed a pot of coffee for the guys who'd soon be getting up. One of them being a spoiled little punk who was certain to bitch about his X-Box still being locked up in the office. Working graveyard was great in the sense that I rarely had to deal with those little shits; their entitled asses stayed in bed, waiting for the world to be brought to them on a platter. I picked up my pen and looked down at my notebook. "Where to start?" I asked myself. And then it came to me and I started writing. *By the amount of time we'd been on the plane, my guess was we were over Kansas or Nebraska...*

ACKNOWLEDGEMENTS

I'd like to begin by mentioning the many in this book who are no longer with us, and although I only touch on them briefly, they are certainly not insignificant. That being said, I feel it would be criminal not to mention their names: Jesse, Lisa, Spanky, Jimbo, Slim, Kurt, Trish, Gabby and Katie. Rest well.

Now to the living. This book began after I'd posted some of my experiences on social media. After one such post, my friend Bruce suggested that I start writing them down. I was working graveyard then and had plenty of downtime, so I followed his suggestion. I told my friend Jack about my plans while having coffee one morning, and he responded by saying that he liked the "institutional tour guide" approach. Both of these men were instrumental in following through with this endeavor by giving a slacker like me a subtle push.

I wrote it all in four notebooks and it took close to three years. Finally, in August of 2017, I announced over social media that I was finished. Little did I know how wrong I was. Being that I'd never written a book before, I was about to discover the pains of editing. I'm fortunate to have friends who were there to help during this process. A huge "thank you" to Jack Grisham, Iris Berry, Nadia Bruce-Rawlings, Punk Hostage Press, Trez Jak, Matt Locke, Court Finney, Jak Bruce, Vanessa Jean, Tom Hansen, Melissa Evans, and Donna Hargis for advice and taking the time to read a not-yet-finished manuscript, and to Michelle Don Vito and Scott Aicher for their artistic expertise. Your input and work was beyond measure. And another "thank you" to those who had said they'd read it, then weren't heard from again. I naturally assumed that what I'd sent was crap and it lit a fire under my ass to come up with a solid, finished product.

I suppose I could also extend my gratitude to our broken and maladjusted court system, as well as the police, jails and prisons, for without them I might've ended up writing a book about pottery or some shit, but I will not. While doing time saved me from myself, I can't ignore the fact that the system is broken and there are many who don't escape, nor have I been welcomed back. I paid my debt to society, coming from a legal standpoint, and I hold a belief that to truly repay society I have to do it altruistically. However, to use the lyrics from a Merle Haggard song, I am a branded man. I don't carry myself as such, but there are many who will forever perceive me as one.

Thanks to the following for their love, support or because they're in the book: Celeste Winslow, Jamie McCarroll, Frances Bean, Josh Schubach, Scotty Hansen, Ronny and Michelle Bopo, Tim Hayes, April O'Brien, Timmi Harrop, Joe Burns, Sacheen Wright, Cherie, Sharon Rose, Laura, Adam Byrd, Johnny Perez, Danny Metz, Ian Frahm, P.D. Skull, Carlos Longo, Ricky Long, Rob Villanueva, Reid Schmidt, Tim Gash, Nick 43, John and Joe Toutonghi, Todd Anderson, Susan Hayden, Eric Vandennoort, Joe Hanson, Joel Wilson, Sammy McBride, James "Sy" Cowie, Jak's Skate Team, Bopo Boys, Team Schmidt, my mom Jennifer Mims, my dad Jim Hayes, my sister Rebecca and my brothers Chris and Michael.

Last but certainly not least, my beautiful girlfriend Jenna— your patience and tolerance with me while I was writing this is beyond praiseworthy. I love you and thank you.

William S. Hayes was born in Texas and moved around the Southwest before settling in Seattle at the age of seven. He grew up in the middle of a burgeoning Northwest skateboard and music scene before drugs took their toll. After doing time in various institutions around the country, Hayes got clean, and moved to Long Beach, California, and is currently working on his next book.

MORE PUNK HOSTAGE PRESS BOOKS

FRACTURED (2012) by Danny Baker

BETTER THAN A GUN IN A KNIFE FIGHT
(2012) by A. Razor
DRAWN BLOOD: COLLECTED WORKS FROM D.B.P.LTD.,
1985-1995 (2012) by A. Razor
BEATEN UP BEATEN DOWN (2012) by A. Razor
SMALL CATASTROPHES IN A BIG WORLD
(2012) by A. Razor.
HALF-CENTURY STATUS (2013) by A. Razor.
DAYS OF XMAS POEMS (2014) by A. Razor

THE DAUGHTERS OF BASTARDS (2012) by Iris Berry
ALL THAT SHINES UNDER THE HOLLYWOOD SIGN
(2019) by Iris Berry

IMPRESS (2012) by C.V. Auchterlonie

TOMORROW, YVONNE - POETRY & PROSE FOR SUICIDAL
EGOISTS (2012) by Yvonne De la Vega

MIRACLES OF THE BLOG: A SERIES
(2012) by Carolyn Srygley-Moore

8TH & AGONY (2012) by Rich Ferguson

UNTAMED (2013) by Jack Grisham
CODE BLUE: A LOVE STORY (2014) by Jack Grisham

MOTH WING TEA (2013) by Dennis Cruz
THE BEAST IS WE (2018) By Dennis Cruz

SHOWGIRL CONFIDENTIAL (2013) by Pleasant Gehman

BLOOD MUSIC (2013) by Frank Reardon.

273

MORE PUNK HOSTAGE PRESS BOOKS

YEAH, WELL... (2014) by Joel Landmine

STEALING THE MIDNIGHT FROM A HANDFUL OF DAYS
(2014) by Michele McDannold

HISTORY OF BROKEN LOVE THINGS (2014) by SB Stokes

DREAMS GONE MAD WITH HOPE (2014) by S.A. Griffin

HOW TO TAKE A BULLET AND OTHER SURVIVAL POEMS
(2014) by Hollie Hardy

DEAD LIONS (2014) by A.D. Winans

SCARS (2014) by Nadia Bruce-Rawlings

WHEN I WAS A DYNAMITER, Or, how a Nice Catholic Boy
Became a Merry Prankster, a Pornographer, and a Bridegroom Seven
Times (2014) by Lee Quarnstrom

I WILL ALWAYS BE YOUR WHORE/LOVE SONGS FOR
BILLY CORGAN (2014) by Alexandra Naughton
YOU COULD NEVER OBJECTIFY ME MORE THAN I'VE
ALREADY OBJECTIFIED MYSELF (2015)
by Alexandra Naughton

NO PARACHUTES TO CARRY ME HOME
(2015) by Maisha Z Johnson

INTROVERT/EXTROVERT (2015) by Russell Jaffe

#1 SON AND OTHER STORIES (2017) by Michael Marcus

LOOKING FOR JOHNNY, The Legend of Johnny Thunders (2018)
By Danny Garcia